# Does God Have a Future?

## A Debate on Divine Providence

Christopher A. Hall
and John Sanders

Baker Academic

A Division of Baker Book House Co
Grand Rapids, Michigan 49516

© 2003 by Christopher A. Hall and John Sanders

Published by Baker Academic
a division of Baker Book House Company
P.O. Box 6287, Grand Rapids, MI 49516-6287
www.bakeracademic.com

Printed in the United States of America

Library of Congress Cataloging-in-Publication Data
Hall, Christopher A. (Christopher Alan), 1950–
    Does God have a future? : a debate on divine providence / Christopher A. Hall and John Sanders.
         p.    cm.
    Includes bibliographical references.
    ISBN 0-8010-2604-0 (pbk.)
    1. Providence and government of God.  2. Free will and determinism—Religious aspects—Christianity. I. Sanders, John, 1956–  II. Title
BT135.H25  2003
31—dc21                                        2002043715

# Contents

# Chris and John: What This Book Is—and What It Is Not

We have been friends for a number of years, ever since John was offered a position at Eastern University. Through the intricate process of interviews and visits involved in hiring a new professor, we couldn't help but start talking theology. At that time Chris was largely uninformed about openness theology, and John was more than adept at both explaining his ideas and critiquing the more traditional position Chris espoused! After the faculty search ended we remained friends and continued to correspond occasionally, both by phone and by e-mail. Family issues and concerns, particularly regarding children, were frequently the centerpiece of our conversations, but it should surprise no one that two theologians invariably found themselves discussing theology.

What was encouraging to both of us was that our strong theological disagreements never threatened our friendship, nor did we ever feel that friendship precluded vigorous argument and debate. In fact, we believe that our friendship has actually facilitated our ability to really listen to one another. Knowing that for each of us our strongest desire in doing theology was to help others improve their relationship with God, we did not see our conversation as a debate to be "won" but as an opportunity to learn from one another. At the end of this phase in our extended e-mail debate we still remain friends, although we admit to sometimes feeling bruised and occasionally misunderstood! Perhaps what has facilitated our discussion and enabled a frank exchange to be carried on over such an extended period of time was the trust we felt and continue to feel toward one another. For instance, though Chris

7

fundamentally disagrees with the openness model, I know that Chris would never intentionally misrepresent or caricature my ideas. Likewise, though my ideas sometimes drive John crazy, I know that John carefully listens to what I have to say.

Indeed, if we were to offer a model to the broader church that we both can agree on, it would be that of generous, empathetic listening, a type of listening and responding that is grounded in specific dialogical virtues that we are attempting to cultivate in our relationship and also in our debate. That is, as we discussed and debated, both of us worked hard to think the best of the other's position. We strongly attempted to avoid caricature, name-calling, and premature rejection of the other's point of view. On our best days it was only when we felt that we truly understood the other's ideas that we put on the gloves and boxed.

In offering our exchange to a broader public we are simply inviting others into the discussion. The impetus for these letters began when the editors of *Christianity Today* magazine wanted to do an article on open theism. Chris, who is an editor at large for the magazine, suggested that the two of us should do the article as a series of letters. Letters 1–9 in this book originally appeared in May and June 2001. Many people liked the format, and since we did not come close to saying all we wanted to say, we decided to continue the exchange over the next year.

We have left the letters in the order in which we wrote them rather than grouping them together topically. Though we knew that others would be reading our letters, we purposely stayed with the e-mail format, convinced that in this informal approach to theological engagement we might incorporate insights, clarity, concerns, and even humor that a more formal approach might stifle. For example, both of us felt the freedom to simply think out loud, at times spinning off a quick response, at other times chewing on each other's ideas like a cow chews its cud. Our letters occasionally betray a fleeting sense of frustration or irritation, and they contain, like most informal exchanges, some repetitions, dead ends, and unresolved questions. (We have added two sections at the end that may help the reader fully participate in our discussion: some informal notes and a brief glossary to clarify the sense in which we both use certain terms.) What we offer, then, is an informal, spirited, and hopefully interesting correspondence between two friends and theologians—no more and no less.

Readers will quickly see that certain issues keep coming up: questions about how to interpret Scripture, the role of tradition in theological reflection and biblical exegesis, the problem of evil, the nature of freedom, God's relationship to time, and the extent of God's knowledge of the future. These are important and sometimes complex issues, and we do not pretend that these matters are easily settled. Those who think they can merely cite a few biblical texts to settle this debate will learn that it is not so simple—for either side.

How have we changed our basic positions as a result of our extended discussion? On the broad issues, we are pretty much in the same place as when we first began exchanging letters. John thinks the openness model offers the best interpretation of the Bible's presentation of God, God's relationship to humanity, and God's saving acts on our behalf. Chris continues to think he's wrong. Though we remain in disagreement on many issues, John has spurred Chris to think through more carefully his understanding of the nature of freedom and Chris has determined to do so. Chris has helped John rethink aspects of his Christology as well as see times when he has stated things in uncharitable ways.

Hopefully, our exchange of letters will encourage readers to investigate the issues surrounding the openness model fairly and thoroughly. Our correspondence is a small part of the testing and sifting process any theological model must undergo if it is to be wisely and safely offered to the church. So, to pirate a popular line, "You've got mail!"

# 1  **John:** How I Came to the Open View

Dear Chris,

When I was in high school one of my brothers was killed in a motorcycle accident. For the first time I began to think about God's role in human affairs—was God responsible for my brother's death? A few years later, while in Bible college, I read what my theology textbooks said about the nature of God. According to these books God could not change in any way, could not be affected by us in any respect, and never responded to us. I was shocked! The piety that I had learned from other evangelical Christians was directly opposed to such beliefs. For instance, I was taught that our prayers of petition could influence what God decided to do—not that God *has* to do what we ask, but that God has decided that some of his decisions will be in response to what we ask or don't ask. Such problems put me into a state of questioning—either the piety I had been taught was wrong, or the theology I was reading was wrong, or both my piety and the theology had to be modified in some way. I continued to wrestle with these issues while in seminary, and it took me more than twenty years to formulate the views I now have. My conclusion is that the evangelical piety I was taught as a young Christian was biblically correct, and that therefore we need to modify our theology at certain points (not every point!) so that our theology corresponds, rather than conflicts, with our biblically grounded piety.

11

Let me summarize the perspective I now hold—the so-called openness of God theology. According to openness theology, the *triune* God of love has, in *almighty* power, created all that is and is *sovereign* over all. In *freedom* God decided to create beings capable of experiencing his love. God loves us and desires for us to enter into a reciprocal relationship of love with himself as well as with our fellow creatures. The divine intention in creating us was that we would come to experience the triune love and respond to it with love of our own and would freely come to collaborate with God toward the achievement of his goals. God has granted us the freedom necessary for a truly personal relationship of love to develop. Despite the fact that we have abused our freedom by turning away from the divine love, God remains *faithful* to his intentions for creation.

Second, God has, in *sovereign freedom*, decided to make some of his actions contingent on our requests and actions. God elicits our free collaboration in his plans. Hence, God can be influenced by what we do and pray for, and God truly responds to what we do. God genuinely interacts and enters into a dynamic give-and-take relationship with us.

Third, the only *wise* God has chosen to exercise general providence (God has overarching control) rather than meticulous providence (God tightly controls every detail), allowing space for us to operate and for God to be creative and resourceful in working with us. God has chosen not to control every detail of what happens in our lives. Moreover, God has flexible strategies. Though the divine nature does not change, God reacts to contingencies, even adjusting his plans if necessary, to take into account the decisions of his free creatures. God is endlessly resourceful and wise in working toward the fulfillment of his ultimate goals. Sometimes God alone decides how to accomplish these goals. Usually, however, God elicits human cooperation in such a way that it is both God and humanity who decide what the future shall be. God's plan is not a detailed script or blueprint, but a broad intention that allows for a variety of options as to precisely how his goals may be reached. What God and people do in history matters. If the Hebrew midwives had feared Pharaoh rather than God and killed the baby boys, then God would have responded accordingly and a different story would have emerged. Moses' refusal to return to Egypt prompted God to resort to plan B, allowing Aaron to do the public speaking instead of Moses. What people do and whether they come to trust God makes a difference in what God does—human history is not a scripted play in which human choices and decisions are simply what God wanted to happen.

Finally, the *omniscient* God knows all that is logically possible to know. God knows the past and present with exhaustive, definite knowledge and knows the future as partly definite (closed) and partly indefinite (open). God's knowledge of the future contains knowledge of what God has decided to bring about unilaterally (that which is definite), knowledge of possibilities (that which is indefinite), and knowledge of those events that are determined to occur (e.g., an asteroid hitting a planet). Hence, the future is partly open (or indefinite) and partly closed (or definite). It is not the case that just anything may happen, for God has acted in history to bring about events in order to achieve his unchanging purpose. Graciously, however, God invites us to collaborate with him to bring the as yet open part of the future into being.

Your fellow servant in Jesus,
John

# 2 **Chris:** My Pilgrimage

Dear John,

Like you, I think it's quite helpful to reflect on what has shaped each of us and how this no doubt influences how we do theology and the conclusions we reach. My questions and struggles have surely shaped me. Probably the greatest question I've faced over the years, theologically, spiritually, and emotionally, has been the problem of evil. And lurking behind this question, especially during my early days as a Christian, was the question of God. More particularly, is God good? Can God be trusted?

The divorce of my parents when I was a very young believer, for example, caused me great anguish, especially when it appeared as if God had remained deaf to my fervent prayers that my parents' marriage be preserved. At that time it seemed to me that my petitions had bounced back into my face, ricocheting off the shut gates of an inaccessible heaven.

During the same period I worked as a driver and handyman for one of California's largest mortuaries, and thus I daily faced the question of evil and suffering. Is God in control of human history? Does God genuinely realize how many people are dying in Los Angeles, often alone, in despair, and in horrific circumstances? Does God care?

Then, during my later college years, I began traveling internationally, and I quickly learned that the tragedies I had encountered in my family and behind the wheel of a hearse are multiplied worldwide. Indeed, the

14

level of suffering I observed in countries such as Indonesia and India surpassed anything I had experienced in the States. I specifically recall visiting a refugee camp in Calcutta as war broke out between East and West Pakistan in the early seventies. As I witnessed children dying from starvation and disease I again wondered, "Where is God in all this? Is God in control of human history? Does God know the end from the beginning? Is God sovereign over time itself? Is God's knowledge of the future perfect and complete? Is God ever caught off guard or surprised by what occurs as history unfolds? Is God good? Is God loving? Can God be trusted? Are there certain decisions, events, and accidents that God could not have prevented, either because he did not know they were going to occur or because he did not want to violate human freedom? Did God possess the power and knowledge to protect me from my own folly, sin, and error? What could I expect from the God portrayed in the Scripture?"

How have I gone about finding answers? Two key sources come to mind.

First, there is the Bible. I, like you, affirm the absolute authority of the Scriptures over my life and thought. This affirmation is not a guarantee that I'll read and interpret it well or correctly, but Scripture and its inherent authority are an indispensable starting point for theological reflection. Hence, if you can convince me that the Bible affirms and supports the openness position, I'd have to make serious adjustments in my own thinking and practice as a Christian.

Second, the church's history of exegesis or "exegetical tradition" deeply influences the interpretive choices I make as I read the Bible. Tom Oden has particularly helped me to see that the church's exegesis, particularly in its earliest years, must never be overlooked as we work exegetically and theologically in the modern context. Thus a key question is, "Has the church, Orthodox, Roman Catholic, or in its many Protestant communities, ever taught that God's knowledge of the future is limited, or that God is surprised or caught off guard by what occurs as time progresses?" Stan Grenz ponders the same question in his comments on your work in his recent book *Renewing the Center*. "What is perhaps even more disquieting about Sanders's proposal," Grenz writes, "is that it seems to require the rejection of such a broad swath of the Christian theological tradition. He intimates that on something as fundamental as our basic conception of God nearly everyone from the fifth century to the present has deviated far from the true understanding of biblical texts."

I acknowledge that there have been figures in the church's history who have argued that God's foreknowledge is limited, but they are minor figures at best, and the church as a community has never validated their conclusions. While the interpretive tradition of the church is not infallible, extremely convincing exegesis will need to be forthcoming if the two hallmarks of openness theology are to be accepted, namely that (a) God's knowledge of the future is limited, and (b) God's knowledge grows as time proceeds.

Finally, James Packer taught me that while biblical revelation is absolutely infallible, it presently contains certain irresolvable tensions, largely because God has chosen to keep certain things to himself, at least for the present. Thus, while God always speaks truthfully, God might well choose to remain silent or incomplete in his communication. Indeed, Moses taught Israel that the "secret things belong to the LORD" (Deut. 29:29). Packer has warned me, both as his student in Vancouver and in many of his writings, to beware of draining the mystery out of the Scriptures in a misplaced desire for rational consistency. In Packer's words, we can frequently trace theological confusion and error to "the intruding of rationalistic speculations, the passion for systematic consistency, a reluctance to recognize the existence of mystery and . . . a consequent subjecting of Scripture to the supposed demands of human logic." Hence I have learned to live with incompleteness, paradox, incomprehensibility, and deep mystery in my relationship with God and in my theological thinking.

Simultaneously, though, the Bible makes certain things quite clear. For instance, while evil in its essence may remain inexplicable to me, God has clearly spoken against evil and sin, most clearly in Jesus Christ. While I may not understand why God has allowed certain events to take place, or why he has seen fit to remain seemingly silent in answer to certain of my prayers, I *can* know that God loves me and his world infinitely because God has demonstrated this love and goodness in the incarnation, ministry, crucifixion, and resurrection of Jesus Christ. While God allows evil to occur and, indeed, uses it to further his own purposes, God has spoken and acted against that very same evil, as seen in the earliest sections of the biblical narrative (cf. Gen. 3). In Christ we have God's definitive statement against sin, evil, and suffering. God's last word will always be a redemptive one.

I find Tom Oden's comments in *The Living God* to be helpful, both concerning the nature and extent of God's knowledge and concerning God's relationship to time itself. In a manner of speaking, Oden is simply summing up the ecumenical consensus reached on these issues in the early centuries of the church's history. God's knowledge is "without limitation or qualification." It is, as the psalmist writes, "beyond all telling" (Ps. 147:5). What about God's knowledge of the future? "God's incomparable way of knowing knows the end of things even from the beginning: 'I reveal the end from the beginning, from ancient times I reveal what is to be; I say, "My purpose shall take effect, I will accomplish all that I please"'" (Isa.

46:9). God knows "past, present, and future . . . external events and inward motivations." Unlike human knowledge, God's knowledge is not partial or fragmentary, most importantly because God's knowledge does not occur "from a particular nexus of time." Rather, God "knows exhaustively, in eternal simultaneity." In short, God's knowledge is "incomparable." Surely this is what we should expect if we're dealing with God.

A further word or two regarding God's relationship to time might be appropriate, particularly in light of the openness model's contention that there are aspects of the future God does not know. I contend that this is incorrect, largely because God's relationship to time forecloses the possibility that God does not know all aspects of the future. Here Oden is again helpful. The argument runs along the following lines:

1. God's knowledge of the world is infinite. Hence, God in relationship to time "must be aware of duration and succession, even though not bound by them. If God did not understand duration and succession, God would understand even less about time than we do."
2. Even though God understands time, God is not trapped within it. God remains eternal. Thus, God "views all times as eternal now," while simultaneously understanding "the process of temporal succession." Here is a key distinction between divine and human knowledge. "We do not know next year until next year, but God knows next year already. We learn only successively through experiencing, but God does not have to learn something God already knows. We know things in part and by pieces, but God knows things fully, all at once," while still understanding duration and succession.
3. Thus, future events are not future for God "but simply present." This seems to me to be a critical distinction that clearly sets off the classical model from that held by openness theologians.

Let me know what you think.

---

**With warm greetings,**
**Chris**

# 3  **John:** Practical Problems for Classical Theism

**Dear Chris,**

Thank you for your thoughtful and challenging remarks. Theology is, and always has been, produced in dialogue and I'm delighted to be in conversation with you. In response, let me say that I agree that Jesus is God's definitive response to our evil, demonstrating the divine love toward us. This is no small agreement! I agree that God "allows" evil to occur and that God has "acted against that very same evil." However, you as a classical theist and I as an open theist disagree on the role of evil in God's plans. Since you believe that God cannot change in any respect, cannot be affected by us in any way, and that God meticulously controls everything that happens, you have to say that every evil that occurs is part of God's plan and that each and every evil is for the good. Given this, I wonder how you can claim that God acted "against" the very evil he ordained in the first place. Do you have a schizophrenic God? According to your view, nothing happens except what God specifically wants to happen, so God never takes risks and his will is never thwarted in the least detail. Hence, you are forced to deny that God genuinely grieves over our sin (Gen. 6:6), since it makes no sense to say that God grieves over what he wanted to occur!

Moreover, if God never responds to us, you must affirm the doctrines of irresistible grace (we cannot reject God's will) and unconditional elec-

18

tion (God chooses those who are saved without responding to anything the saved do). Of course, you may simply appeal to "mystery" and say that we cannot understand God's ways. To that I say, "A contradiction by any other name is still plain nonsense." You claim that I subject Scripture to the demands of human logic. Actually, we all use human reasoning when reading the Bible—which is why you and I understand at least parts of it. Moreover, your view is not so "mysterious" as you suggest. To claim that divine sovereignty and human freedom are contradictory, one must give the terms precisely opposite meanings. However, you do not, since you believe that God micromanages everything in such a way that his will is never thwarted and humans are "free" to act on their desires but do not have the freedom to do other than what they do. That is, you affirm "compatibilistic freedom" (determinism and human responsibility are compatible). In your view all God has to do is ensure that we have the desires he wants us to have and then we will "freely" do what God has ordained. There is nothing contradictory or logically mysterious about that! However, we, along with the Arminian tradition, believe that God does not tightly control everything and that humans have "libertarian freedom." We have the freedom to do otherwise than we did (e.g., a murderer could have refrained from murdering) and we can thwart some of God's will.

Moving on, we believe that God's knowledge of the future is partly fixed and partly left open for three main reasons. First and foremost, we believe that the Scriptures teach this (e.g., God grieves, changes his mind). Second, though we agree with Arminian theology on all but two points (divine timelessness and exhaustive definite foreknowledge), we believe that complete foreknowledge of our future decisions implies the loss of our free will. Third, the "future" does not yet exist, so there is nothing "there" to be known. Hence, we do not believe that "God's knowledge of the future is limited." We believe that God knows all that can be known, and thus we cannot say that it is a limitation for God not to know "nothing."

Finally, you beat on us with the club of church tradition. Nearly everyone has said that God possesses complete knowledge of what humans will do in the future, so how can we even think of going against such a cloud of witnesses? To begin with, theologians have debated the nature and content of God's omniscience for millennia. There are several traditions regarding exactly what God knows. Second, we do respect theological traditions: to disagree with the great theologians of the past is serious business. Nonetheless, like Luther we feel compelled to affirm our view because of Scripture and sound reason. You sound like John Eck, the Catholic inquisitor of Luther, who claimed it to be unimaginable that so many theologians could have been wrong on so central a teaching as salvation. I would have thought that someone such as yourself, teaching at a Baptist college, would have more empathy for those who challenge certain traditions. The Lutherans, Reformed, and Catholics killed the Anabaptists for espousing beliefs that most evangelicals today take for granted. Clearly, Protestants believe that traditions sometimes need changing. After all, it was not until the eighteenth century that the virtually unquestioned tradition was challenged that all unbaptized children (or those born of non-Christian parents) who die are damned to hell! However, proponents of openness do not reject the entire tradition. We affirm the ecumenical creeds, the main teachings of the Reformation, the authority of Scripture and the importance of prayer and community. It is a gross overstatement to claim we reject the entire tradition.

Blessings on your ministry trips overseas and I look forward to hearing from you.

---

John

# 4 **Chris:** Abraham and the Sacrifice of Isaac

Dear John, _____

Since for both of us the Bible remains the ultimate authority, it's probably best to compare notes concerning key exegetical issues. The key question for me is this: does the exegetical work that is being produced by openness scholars possess the exegetical strength to overturn the heart of the church's interpretive teaching regarding God's knowledge of the future and God's relationship to time? What if we focus on two key texts: God's testing of Abraham in Genesis 22, and Judas's betrayal and Peter's denial of Jesus?

You once asked me, "What do you do with all the Old Testament references to God grieving, changing, delighting, and repenting? Does not God say to Abraham, 'Now I know you fear God' in response to Abraham's willingness to sacrifice Isaac? Does this not indicate that God's knowledge of Abraham has grown in response to Abraham's act of great faith?"

Good question. You're right in seeing that we both will need to make sense of God's words in Genesis 22:12, "Do not stretch out your hand against the lad, and do nothing to him; for now I know that you fear God, since you have not withheld your son, your only son, from Me" (NASB). Brueggemann, whom you quote in *The God Who Risks*, writes that "God genuinely does not know. . . . The flow of the narrative accomplishes

21

something in the awareness of God. He did not know. Now he knows." What did God need to know that he did not yet understand? Why the test to elicit the needed information? You write: "The answer is to be found in God's desire to bless all the nations of the earth (Gen. 12:3). God needs to know if Abraham is the sort of person on whom God can count for collaboration toward the fulfillment of the divine project. Will he be faithful? Or must God find someone else through whom to achieve his purpose? God has been faithful; will Abraham be faithful? Will God have to modify his plans with Abraham?"

The straightforward, literal meaning of Genesis 22 is that God *now* learned that Abraham would be faithful. Even an opponent of openness theology such as Bruce Ware admits that unless compelling reasons can be found for not accepting the straightforward meaning of the text, this meaning should be accepted. Ware, though, lists at least three fundamental problems with accepting the "literal" meaning, objections that appear quite reasonable to me.

First, if God must test Abraham to find out what is in his heart, this surely calls into question God's *present knowledge* of Abraham's inner spiritual, psychological, mental, and emotional state." Yet other biblical texts teach that God does know the inner thoughts of human beings. Indeed, one of the characteristics that sets God apart from humans, a trait that demonstrates the glory of God, is God's ability to do this very thing. The chronicler writes that "the LORD searches all hearts, and understands every intent of the thoughts" (1 Chron. 28:9). In 1 Samuel 16:7 we read, "the LORD does not see as mortals see; they look on the outward appearance, but the LORD looks on the heart." David writes, "O LORD, you have searched me and you know me. You know when I sit and when I rise; you perceive my thoughts from afar. You discern my going out and my lying down; you are familiar with all my ways. Before a word is on my tongue, you know it completely, O LORD" (Ps. 139:1–2).

It escapes me how God could possibly know David's thoughts before he expresses them, if God cannot know fully his unexpressed inner life. In fact, it is God's wondrous ability to far surpass humans in his knowledge that elicits David's praise: "Such knowledge is too wonderful for me, too lofty for me to attain" (v. 6). Of course it is. David is not God. Surely texts such as these can provide a lens through which I interpret what is going on between God and Abraham. If I can't use them to interpret the Abraham narrative, then one must conclude that there are at least some of Abraham's thoughts—indeed, his most important ones—that are beyond the ability of God to discern until Abraham actually acts. Thus God's foreknowledge is not only limited as to the future, but also in the present.

Second, as a result of the test, God now knows that Abraham fears God. Ware rightly asks if God did not know this already. Is this lack of knowledge plausible? Had not Abraham's actions, from his response of faith to God's promises in Genesis 12 to his willingness to continue to live a life of faith in Genesis 15, shown that he deeply feared God? Is it then plausible to believe that God did not know that Abraham feared him until the very moment when Abraham raised his knife above the child of the promise? If so, Abraham seems to have understood God better than God understood Abraham, for Abraham realized that God possessed the power to raise Isaac from the dead (Heb. 11:19). Did God not perceive that Abraham understood that God possessed this power? Abraham understood this before he ever attempted to sacrifice Isaac. And yet God couldn't perceive this tremendous faith in Abraham?

Think, too, of Abraham's instructions to his servant in Genesis 22:5. He instructs the servant to wait for both him and Isaac. Why? Abraham fully expected that both would return, even if a resurrection were required for the return trip to take place. Such a perspective seems to be demanded if the logic of Hebrews is included in the interpretive grid of Genesis 22. If so, how can your interpretation be correct? A "literal" interpretation of Genesis 22 appears to run into insuperable difficulties.

Ware points, I think rightly, to Paul's words in Romans 4:18–22 as evidence of Abraham's long track record of faithfulness and reverence, well before the command to sacrifice Isaac. "Against all hope," Paul writes, "Abraham in hope believed and so became the father of many nations. . . . Without weakening in his faith, he faced the fact that his body was as good as dead . . . yet he did not waver through unbelief regarding the promise of God." Abraham's demonstration of faith and reverence, a faith credited to him by God as righteousness, is already established by the time we reach Genesis 22. Is that same God suddenly second-guessing himself by asking Abraham to sacrifice Isaac? Was God not convinced by the long history of faithfulness that had already occurred between Abraham and him?

Third, Ware asks how God can possibly know, at least from an openness perspective, that Abraham will remain faithful in the future? In Ware's words, "What open theists claim God gained from this was, on openness grounds, either already known to God (so he did not learn something new in this test) or at best was a transient and passing truth (which could give no real assurance of how Abraham would act in the future). The straightforward meaning open theists commend simply cannot be the intended meaning of the text."

But if the text does not concern the extent of God's knowledge, what does it concern? When we find New Testament writers such as James or the author of Hebrews commenting on this text, they focus on Abraham's willingness to sacrifice Isaac as a sign of faith manifesting itself in good works, and on Abraham's faith in God's power to raise the dead. Even if Isaac dies at Abraham's hand, Abraham believes God can bring him back to life (cf. Heb. 11:17–19; James 2:21). No New Testament writer uses this text to develop ideas concerning the nature or extent of God's knowledge. Hence, if I'm to find the heart of the text's meaning, I need to hear the text as apostolic witnesses are hearing it.

This reading of the text, one that focuses on Abraham's faith in God's power to raise the dead, is also emphasized by early patristic commentators on this narrative. Origen does mention briefly that some opponents (probably non-Christian critics of the gospel) have "thrown out against us that God says that *now* he had learned that Abraham fears God as though he were such as not to have known previously" (emphasis added). Origen dismisses this possibility out of hand, as do almost all patristic commentators on Genesis 22. Why? He—and they—constantly compared Scripture with Scripture.

The interpretation that Origen offers, along with other early Christian commentators such as Ambrose, Chrysostom, and Caesarius of Arles, is multilayered. For example, the fathers frequently understood Isaac to be a type of Christ; so was the ram caught in the bush. Caesarius understands Abraham to be a type of God the Father, who later is to willingly offer his Son as a sacrifice for the sin of the world. Indeed, Caesarius notes that in the liturgical rhythm of the year, Genesis 22 was read at Easter, "when the true Isaac, whose type the son of Abraham showed, is fastened to the gibbet of the cross for the human race." I find this multilayered reading of the text to be exegetically fruitful and theologically profound. Perhaps more to the point with respect to the openness position, the comments of the New Testament writers as well as of the patristic commentators insist that the heart of Genesis 22 is Abraham's faith, not God's knowledge. If the openness interpretation of Genesis 22 is valid, why do neither canonical nor patristic writers advocate it?

---

**With warm greetings,**
**Chris**

# 5 **John:** Abraham and the Sacrifice of Isaac

Dear Chris,

You raise the issue of the divine testing of Abraham. Let me begin by pointing out that God puts a great many people to the test in order to find out what they really value and believe. God repeatedly tested the people of Israel to see whether they would trust and follow him or not (Exod. 16:4; 20:20; Judg. 2:22) and God tested people such as King Hezekiah so that God would "know what was in his heart" (2 Chron. 32:31). Why all this testing if God already knew the outcomes? Yes, God knows our hearts, but he seems to obtain this knowledge by testing.

The openness interpretation does not call into question God's "present knowledge" of Abraham's character. Rather, the point would be that Abraham's character is *not fully formed* in crucial respects until he has faced this ultimate test. What God knows about Abraham is different after the test because Abraham himself has become something different than he was previously. Abraham's decision and actions are part of the character-forming process and the question for God is whether Abraham will trust him in this seeming reversal of the divine promise. Moreover, though God may have had a very good idea of what Abraham would do, Abraham's free decision was not enacted until that point. You and I have different views about human freedom. You believe in a form of "soft determinism": Abraham could not have done otherwise so there is no uncertainty as to what Abraham will do and so God's test is not a test at all. However, I believe that Abraham could, even at the last moment, have refused to obey God and so the test is genuine.

You claim that Abraham's faith is already established by the time we reach Genesis 22. Contrary to what you suggest in your last letter, I do not believe that God is "suddenly second-guessing himself." Rather, in Genesis 15:6 God indicates that Abraham is in the right sort of relationship with God. Abraham is making progress in trusting God and God informs him that Abe is on the right track. However, the relationship is not static. True, Abraham has a history of faithfulness, but it is mixed with a history of not trusting God as well. He twice passes Sarah off as his sister because he fears man rather than God, has a son through Hagar, and complains to God that God has not fulfilled what he has promised. That is, Abraham, like all of us, is a mixed bag. All through his life Abraham is worried about protecting his own life and is anxiety ridden about passing on his inheritance to his "real" son. All this is to say that Abraham is not a finished person, or the kind of person God believes he can count on, until he passes this test.

You chide me for finding something in an Old Testament text that neither the canonical nor the patristic writers advocate. This is a dubious principle of interpretation if left unqualified. If we can only repeat what the New Testament writers said about Old Testament passages, then we shall not have much to say. Though the interpretations of the canonical writers are correct, they do not say everything that needs to be said regarding the Old Testament. Just because Paul highlights certain parts of the narrative that suit his purpose does not mean that there are no other points to the narrative. Following your principle, the patristic writers you cite were wrong to see Isaac as a type of Christ since none of the canonical writers do so. How can you let the fathers get something out of the text that is not in the apostolic witness?

You ask why the fathers do not interpret the "now I know" in Genesis 22:12 the same way I do. Elsewhere I have documented that though the fathers were correct to engage and make use of Greek philosophy, they accepted certain philosophical notions that prevented them from reading some (not all) biblical texts in the correct way. We all have our presuppositions, and theirs led many of them to conclude that God cannot actually grieve or change his mind or be affected by our prayers. I find this quite unscriptural. Let me give some examples. God does grieve over our sinful rebellion (Gen. 6:6; Eph. 4:30). Though God originally planned to have Saul and his lineage be kings over Israel, God changed his mind due to Saul's sin and selected David instead (1 Sam. 13:13; 15:11). The prophet Isaiah says to King Hezekiah, "Thus says the Lord," you will die and not recover from this illness. Hezekiah prays to God asking him to change his mind. God does and sends Isaiah back to announce, "Thus says the LORD," you will recover from this illness (2 Kings 20:1–6). Our prayers can have an effect on God's plans. It makes no sense to say that God grieves, changes his mind, and is influenced by our prayers and also claim that God tightly controls everything so that everything that occurs is what God desired to happen! Furthermore, on several occasions God expected Israel to repent but they did not do what God expected (e.g., Isa. 5:2; Jer. 3:6–7, 19–20). Also, God uses words such as "might," "if," and "perhaps," indicating that some of the future is open (e.g., Exod. 4:8–9; Jer. 26:3; Ezek. 12:3); but such words make no sense in your view—in fact, God seems less than genuine to offer forgiveness when he already knows they will not repent.

There are two types of texts concerning divine omniscience in Scripture: those that portray God as knowing precisely what will happen (e.g., Jer. 5) and those that portray God as not knowing precisely what will happen (the texts I've just cited). We believe that the best way of holding on to both sorts of texts is to see the future as partly definite and partly indefinite, even for God. The typical strategy is to claim that the texts portraying God as knowing exactly what will happen are literally true while those that depict God as grieving or not knowing do not tell us the literal truth about God. You accuse us of "subjecting Scripture to human logic," but that is exactly what you are doing here! We uphold both types of texts rather than subsume one under the other, so we believe that openness is the perspective that is more true to the biblical data.

---

**Your fellow servant,**
**John**

# 6 **Chris:** Judas's Betrayal and Peter's Denial

Dear John,

How about your interpretation of Judas's betrayal of Jesus? I would argue that this narrative clearly demonstrates God's perfect and complete knowledge of the future. Jesus is not caught off guard by Judas's action. Rather, Jesus demonstrates a full awareness of what Judas is soon to do (Matt. 26:23–25). Perhaps even more telling, however, is the comment of Matthew that the purchase of the potter's field with Judas's blood money and its subsequent naming as the "Field of Blood" fulfilled a prophecy of Jeremiah made hundreds of years before the event (Matt. 27:5–10).

I find your interpretation of the Judas narrative in *The God Who Risks* to be both selective and strained. First, you appear to base your explanation of Judas's actions on the highly idiosyncratic *interpretation* of William Klassen, a study you argue "demonstrates that Judas was not 'betraying' Jesus." Is Judas, as Klassen and you seem to believe, acting to bring the high priest and Jesus together so that they "could resolve their differences and bring about needed reforms"? When Jesus tells Judas "Do quickly what you are going to do," does this instruction truly violate "a fundamental rule of Judaism" by telling Judas "to go out and deliberately commit a sin"? You appear convinced by Klassen, writing that "in this light it is clear that Judas is not betraying Jesus and that Jesus is not issuing any prediction of such activity." I remain unconvinced, especially because of the role Jesus assigns to Satan in Judas's activities.

28

Second, you argue that *"paradidomi* does not mean 'betray'" to the temple authorities. Why not? Liddell and Scott provide clear instances in secular Greek sources where *paradidomi* does mean "betray." If so, why can't it mean betray here?

Third, you write that "because Judas has come to symbolize villainy, we tend to think Jesus' words are clear and that everything is working out according to some foreordained plan." I don't agree. Judas is almost invariably considered a villain in the history of interpretation because that is precisely how Matthew, Mark, Luke, and John portray him. John, for example, gives us a glimpse into Judas's character when he explains the motive behind Judas's objection to Jesus' anointing at Bethany. "He did not say this because he cared about the poor but because he was a thief; as keeper of the money bag, he used to help himself to what was put into it." If such was Judas's character, then it seems plausible to me to view his betrayal of Jesus as an opportunity for Judas to make a quick buck that goes terribly awry; I don't think Judas realized that his shortsighted action would lead to Jesus' death.

While you don't see the Judas narrative linked "to some foreordained plan," Matthew clearly makes such a connection through his reference to Jeremiah's prophecy (Matt. 27:9–10). Peter also distinctly connects Judas's actions and fate to a prophecy spoken "through the mouth of David" (Acts 1:16). Neither Matthew's nor Peter's comments make sense if this predictive/prophetic element is drained out of the Judas narrative.

As I mentioned earlier, strikingly absent from your discussion of Judas is any mention of the role of Satan in the whole affair, while Matthew insists that "Satan entered Judas" the evening of the Last Supper, indicating that demonic motivation or inspiration lay behind Judas's thoughts and actions (cf. Matt. 22:3). Not only so, but John had previously informed his reader of the shady character of Judas. Jesus, it seems to me, clearly predicts Judas's betrayal in John 13, just as he predicted the exact number of times Peter would betray Jesus.

How, by the way, could Jesus possibly know that Peter would choose to deny him three times if God cannot know beforehand the choices of free individuals, a position held by many openness theologians? Was Peter not free? Did God force him to deny Jesus? Was he simply a puppet? If so, why would Jesus consider him morally responsible for his actions and call him to repentance and renewal in John 21?

Blessings,
Chris

# 7  **John:** Judas's Betrayal and Peter's Denial

**Dear Chris,**

Regarding my interpretation of Judas's sin and Peter's denial, please realize that not all proponents of openness agree with my particular understanding. Not all Calvinists agree on how to interpret each passage either. In my book I do say that it is not necessary to agree with Klassen's interpretation, so I go on to give other possible readings compatible with openness. L. D. McCabe, a nineteenth century Methodist proponent of openness, believes that God removed the free will of Judas and Peter in these particular circumstances in order to accomplish his purposes. Thus, they were not morally responsible for their actions. But then, you ask, if Peter is not morally responsible, why does Christ rebuke him for his actions in John 21? McCabe's answer needs some modification, in my opinion. If I were to go in this direction I would highlight Jesus' statement in Luke 22:31 that Satan is after Peter, which is why Jesus tries three times to get the disciples to pray with and for him in Gethsemane. They needed to be spiritually prepared for the events ahead. They let him down and were not properly prepared. Peter was to have a special role in God's forthcoming work, so God works especially with him. At this point I would modify McCabe and say that Peter was free to acknowledge his relationship with Jesus but was spiritually unprepared. Jesus knew this well and makes the prediction. All that need be determined by

30

God in this case would be to have someone question Peter three times and have a rooster crow.

As for Judas, all three Synoptic Gospels say that Judas first made his agreement with the authorities *before* Jesus announces that one of the disciples will hand him over. Jesus' statement is not "out of the blue." It is likely that Jesus and Judas have been discussing the issue. You cite Matthew 27:9 to claim that this happened to "fulfill" prophecy, arguing that it was part of God's foreordained plan. However, if you examine the texts Matthew cites (Zech. 11:12; Jer. 32:6–9) you will discover that these are not predictions about future events at all! Matthew does the same thing in 2:15 when he claims that Hosea 11:1 has been "fulfilled." However, Hosea 11:1 is not a prediction but a statement of historical fact. Does Matthew not know how to read Scripture? The problem is not with Matthew, but with us, since we are the ones who see the word "fulfilled" and jump to the conclusion that these Old Testament texts must have been predictions of future events. Not at all. Rather, Matthew is using the word "fulfilled" here to say that what happened in the past is happening again. He is appropriating these Old Testament texts for events in the life of Jesus. To borrow an idea from one of the early fathers we could say that these Old Testament passages are "recapitulated" in the life of Jesus and so are "fulfilled." We really do need to grasp how Matthew used the term. Again, I do not believe that these are the only possible interpretations available to openness. We shall have to see if others arise.

By the way, though you address Genesis 22:12 you have not answered how you interpret the wide array of biblical texts that, in my view, teach that God grieves, responds to us, changes his mind, and the others I've written about. You have not given me one *biblical* reason why I should believe God is not affected by us.

Looking forward to your next letter,
John

# 8 **Chris:** Implications of Open Theism

**Dear John,**

What are the implications of the openness position for our understanding of God, of God's knowledge of and relationship to the future, and of God's relationship to time itself? I'm focusing on the issue of the extent of God's foreknowledge and God's relationship to time because it is at these two specific junctures that openness theology clearly moves beyond classical Arminianism and, indeed, classical theism. In addition, I think it's fair to say that if the theological implications of a given model prove untenable, it is best to rethink and reconstruct the model. Finally, I'd argue that the implications of openness theology are still only bubbling to the surface of the church's consciousness, for good or for ill. The openness model, as Nicholas Wolterstorff has commented, is acting much like a strong tug on a thread dangling from a sweater. When one pulls on the thread, how far will the fabric of classical Christian orthodoxy unravel? If we posit that God's foreknowledge is limited, for instance, what other doctrines will require significant revision? Let me mention a few very troubling implications of the openness model.

The openness model surely allows—indeed, describes—situations where God, on the basis of acquiring knowledge that God did not possess in the past, can and does reassess his own past actions. I find this position to be deeply flawed, largely because it well-nigh necessitates

32

that God will make mistakes, however unintentionally. How can God help but err if God acts on the basis of what he thinks humans may do, yet can't be entirely sure of how they will act or respond in a given situation? The result is a God who is constantly learning, who is sometimes taken by surprise, and who occasionally acts in a mistaken fashion on the basis of a misdiagnosis of the future.

The plausibility of openness exegesis must be tested by the implications it produces. While conservative openness theologians affirm the authority of Scripture and treat it with great seriousness, we are faced with the irony that openness exegesis leads to a devaluated view of God. We are presented with a God who fumbles along like the rest of us, trying to do what seems best, but often ruing what he has done in the light of how things actually turn out. Yes, God responds to his creation, but these responses might well turn out to be wrong, at least when viewed from the fuller knowledge God will possess in the future. How often might God prove to be wrong? And in what circumstances? Isaiah contends that what sets Yahweh apart from all false gods is Yahweh's wondrous ability to know the future. This characteristic is part of the great glory of Yahweh that sets him apart from the false idols Israel is continually tempted to worship (Isa. 41:21–24). Sadly, it is this very glory that fades dramatically in the openness model.

---

**With warm greetings,**
**Chris**

# 9 **John:** Implications of Open Theism

Dear Chris,

No theological position, including my own, is free of difficulties. Sometimes it comes down to deciding which problems we are willing to live with. However, I don't believe my problems are as severe as you suggest, and your view has some rather unsavory implications that I shall mention.

To begin with, you claim that according to Isaiah 41:21–24, what sets God apart from false gods is Yahweh's ability to know the future. Please read the text carefully along with Isaiah 46:9–10 and 48:3–5. The glory of Yahweh is not that he simply knows what is going to happen. Rather, it is that he can declare what will happen and bring it about that it does, in fact, occur. Isaiah is not touting foreknowledge, but contrasting Yahweh's power with the impotence of the other gods.

Next, you are correct that openness modifies traditional Arminian theology with regard to divine foreknowledge and timelessness. Nonetheless, we agree with the freewill tradition in Christian theology against those who, like you, deny both that God can be affected by us and that humans have genuine free will. These are the watershed issues in our debate! Here we are solidly on the "Arminian" side of the fence. However, we do have some "family squabbles" with our fellow freewill theists

34

and only time will tell whether Arminians and open theists can resolve their differences.

You claim that if God does not tightly control all that we do and if God does not know with absolute certainty what we shall do in the future, then God just "fumbles along like the rest of us." This is hardly the case. God knows all the past and all the present completely, and he has the wisdom and power necessary to work with us, and often in spite of us, in order to achieve his purposes. Do we sometimes fail to do what God wants us to do? According to classical theism, no. But according to openness and Arminianism, yes, we can sometimes thwart God's will. The only way to guarantee that God's will is never thwarted is for God to micromanage everything and this is the position of classical theism. Arminianism and openness, however, believe that God grants us free will and so it is possible that we can go against God's will. The key issue is not whether God foreknows what we will do—Arminians believe that God foreknows our evil actions but does not control them. Rather, the crucial point is whether God tightly controls each and every thing we do. As an aside, I'm astounded that our critics fail to realize that many of their criticisms (e.g., that we are "Pelagian," God is not in control, etc.) apply just as much to traditional Arminianism.

Since you believe that nothing happens except what God specifically ordains to occur, you logically imply that God wants each and every rape, act of incest, and other atrocities to occur. So God wants little girls abused? And you think *our* view diminishes God's glory! John Wesley was correct to describe classical theism's understanding of God's love as "a love that makes the blood run cold."

Here are some of the implications of openness theology. God does not want women to be abused or children tortured. God is implacably opposed to sin, but because God does not tightly control us, we can do horrible things to one another that grieve God. God does not arbitrarily select some humans for salvation by giving them irresistible grace. Rather, God gives us enabling grace by which we may accept, but can also reject, the divine love. The Scriptures clearly teach that God is open to being influenced by our prayers. In fact, God makes some of his decisions contingent on our intercession for one another, so prayer really does make a difference. The open view places more value on intercessory and petitionary prayer than any other view. The open view exalts God's gracious working with us and his entering into genuine give-and-take relations with us. The open view exalts the true glory of God—the way we see God working with us in Scripture.

Having listed several of our differences, I would be remiss if I failed to observe that, as brothers in Christ, we share much in common. For instance, we both affirm that Jesus is the incarnate Son of God who lived, died, and rose again on behalf of sinners. We both agree on the authority of Scripture, even though we do not interpret every text the same. Moreover, as evangelicals we share belief in the importance of prayer, an active discipleship under the leading of the Holy Spirit, and the need for an ongoing personal relationship with God. Of course, we share more than these in common but the point is that we share a common core of Christian beliefs and values that make us Christian as opposed to, say, Hindu, and our theological differences must not overshadow our shared Christian faith.

**Your fellow follower of Jesus,**
**John**

# 10 **Chris:** Openness and the Problem of Good and Evil

Dear John,

I'm sitting at my desk, thinking of the problem of evil, and listening to a CD of *Schindler's List*. Quite a combination! I'm also thinking back to the debate we had at Huntington last November. I remember the last session we had together in the gym, and the terrible and moving story you told of the young girl who had been kidnapped, mutilated, and I believe eventually murdered. Surely here was evil present and active at its worst. Of course, the problem of divine foreknowledge immediately raises its head.

It's at this juncture that I have some difficulty in understanding how the openness position helps us to deal with this kind of evil. If I understand you correctly, God has perfect knowledge of the past, the present, and those aspects of the future that God has ordained will come to pass. Thankfully, God does not commit evil, and yet surely he permits it. How does the openness position move us beyond the divine-permission model toward the construction of a more helpful, coherent model, both theologically and pastorally?

I realize that openness theologians such as you are to a certain extent comforted or encouraged by presentism—God's perfect knowledge of present events—but I don't understand how presentism significantly

37

improves on the traditional model (divine permission within God's overarching sovereign will), at least as I presently understand matters.

Think, for instance, of the awful account of this young girl's murder. How does the openness position make this horror more comprehensible, acceptable, or tolerable? Even if God, in this particular instance, possesses only present knowledge, surely he is or was aware of what was occurring as the child was being tortured. This must have been present knowledge to God. And surely God possessed the power to intervene in these circumstances to rescue the child. That is, as David Hunt has argued, if God possesses "perfect knowledge of what is going on *now*," surely God could choose to intervene to prevent this murder.

Almost all theologians would agree that God could choose to do so, but for reasons almost always unknown to us, he elects to allow some horrific events to run their course. God permits the evil action to occur, but rarely if ever do we understand why. Classical theists generally argue that God's reasons include his overarching, sovereign plan for human history. From what I can understand, this response drives openness theologians crazy. And yet I don't understand how the openness model alleviates the problem. Can you help me here?

I suppose one might answer that God does not intervene because to do so would violate the exercise of human freedom. After all, the murderer has freely chosen to act in this horrific manner. To intervene would surely violate his freedom, preventing him from carrying out his warped intentions. And yet, don't we pray that God would act in such a manner all the time? For example, I try to pray regularly for you, your wife, and your children. I ask that God protect and keep the Sanders clan safe from all harm: emotional harm, physical harm, or spiritual harm. Indeed, my prayers for protection on your behalf would include the following: if for some reason one of your kids wandered—knowingly or unknowingly—into a situation of real danger, such as walking on a railroad track as a lark, I'd be praying strongly that God would intervene, whether your daughter liked it or not. The exercise of her freedom would be a nonissue for me at this point. Hence, I think there are clear instances, perhaps even the majority of cases, where we can and should pray that God intervene or overturn the free choices of human beings, for their sake and for the sake of others.

So I would pose two specific questions to you:

1. How does presentism and the overall openness position alleviate effectively the problems posed by the reality of evil? How is it a significant improvement on more traditional models of divine providence and omniscience? As I've argued, even present knowl-

edge would enable God to intervene quite effectively in the vast majority of instances of evil in the world today.

2. If human freedom is part of the answer to this question, don't we pray all the time that God overcome a person's freedom, particularly if the exercise of that freedom is harming others or that person him- or herself? This kind of prayer would appear to pertain to the prayers we offer for another person's conversion, but that will need to be a different letter. Looking forward to your response.

You're in my prayers,
Chris

# 11 **John:** Openness and the Problem of Good and Evil

Dear Chris,

We had a little snow today and brisk wind that puts the red in one's cheeks. The sun is out now, turning the snow brilliantly white. The purity of the snow contrasts sharply with the depravity of our world. You raise a question about the value of open theism in general and presentism in particular for explaining the problem of evil. (Presentism is the view that God knows all the past and present but only that part of the future that is definite and will occur.) In the past few years it has become clear to me that presentism itself does not contribute much by way of help in dealing with the question of evil. It seems to me now that early statements of openness overstated its value, for it is correct that, according to openness, God would "see" that something dreadful was going to happen and God has the power to prevent it, so why does God not prevent it?

Openness utilizes the traditional "freewill defense," which says that God grants humans genuine freedom to love, which also entails the ability to *not* love. Though God wants us to respond to the divine love by loving God and our fellow creatures, we may refuse and choose instead to hate and destroy. God cannot grant us freedom and guarantee that we will always use this freedom in loving ways. God cannot do what is logically contradictory, and it is logically contradictory to claim that God

40

grants us freedom *and* that God guarantees that everything we will do is good. God is responsible for creating the conditions by which evil could come about, but God is not responsible for creating evil itself.

So far, this is just the usual freewill defense used by Arminians and other freewill theists. Does openness have anything to add? I think so. First, let me distinguish two different issues.

The first is, what kind of sovereignty has God chosen to exercise: general or meticulous? Freewill theists affirm general providence, whereby God decides not to control tightly what humans will do. Meticulous providence (also called specific sovereignty) holds that God does tightly control everything that happens so that nothing happens except what God specifically intends to happen. This is the view of Augustinians and Calvinists.

The second issue is that those who affirm general sovereignty disagree as to whether God foreknew that humans would sin. Traditional Arminians hold that God knew prior to creation that humans would sin but that God decided not to rescind his gift of freedom. Though God knew the horrendous evils that would occur, he went ahead with his decision to create. As for presentism, it may be said that God did not know prior to creation that humans would commit all the evils we have. So God cannot be held responsible for creating a world knowing that horrendous evils would ensue.

However, does this really help, since God could have prevented each and every instance of human moral evil? Again, here the answer of openness is not any different from that of traditional Arminians. God could not prevent us from doing harm to one another without constantly violating the very conditions in which he created us to live. That is, God would habitually have to remove our freedom, rendering our lives a world of illusion. God has a role that is different from all others, for only God is responsible for upholding the very existence and structures of reality.

You suspect that you and I are in agreement here on the concept of divine permission. Though we do agree on some aspects there remains a huge difference between us, since you affirm meticulous providence and I, general providence. It is one thing to say that God, for reasons we don't fully understand, *allows* autonomous agents to do tragic and terrible things. It is quite another thing to say that God *deliberately plans and intends* for all these evil things to happen, so that *in no single respect would God want the world to be any different than it actually is*. Proponents of meticulous providence can go on saying that this difference makes no difference, but I think most people will see that it does make a difference. If you were consistent you would have to say that God does not grieve over the rape of a little girl for it is exactly what God wanted to happen. For me, God does not want such evils but he allows them and seeks to redeem them.

But, you ask, don't we pray that God would remove the free will of people? When we pray for the safety of our families, for instance, are we not asking God to override their freedom? Some Arminians may think this way, but those who reflect on it a bit will not. Removing our free will is not the only option available to God to answer such prayers. God may work to keep my wife safe by reminding her not to drive when she is sleepy. You say you would pray for God to intervene for one of my children if they were in danger on a railroad track. I have no problem with this, for God can intervene in a variety of ways without removing my child's free will by jerking her off the tracks. The difference here between freewill theists and proponents of meticulous providence is not whether God helps but the type of help God gives. For freewill theists, my child can resist the voice of the Spirit and continue walking into danger. For you, however, if my child continued walking into danger it would be because God specifically intended my child to do so because the harm brought to my child would help bring about the fulfillment of a greater good in God's plan.

Though we may disagree as to precisely what God does in answering our prayers, I want you to know, my friend, that I greatly appreciate your prayers.

Here is a question for you. Why is your God of meticulous providence not responsible for evil when he specifically intends for each and every evil to happen exactly as it does and does not want the world to be any different than it actually is?

---

Blessings,
John

# 12 **Chris:** Antinomies and Logic

Dear John,

I want to respond to some of your ideas in *The God Who Risks* regarding antinomy (the affirmation that two apparently contradictory truths are both true). For quite a while I've used antinomy as a methodological tool, following the coaching of one of my mentors, J. I. Packer. You have a fairly sharp, negative assessment of Packer's position in your book, so it will do me some good to see whether I can defend the possibility of using antinomy in theological reflection. What better person to discuss things with than someone who feels antinomy leads to a logical dead end?

I've talked to a colleague of mine, Phillip Cary, about the use of antinomy in philosophical and theological work, and I've found his ideas to be helpful. It will be interesting to see what you think of them. Cary mentioned various kinds of antinomies, ranging from superficial or apparent contradictions to those that are more profound. Phil commented that these apparent contradictions are not to be taken lightly. They always indicate that the reasoning process has been seriously disrupted. This disruption, however, may well be unavoidable and is not an infallible sign that we must immediately abandon our position. For example, we may simply not possess the information to resolve the contradiction. A world in which antinomy could not occur would seem to be a world of completely accessible information. Plug in the necessary information, think logically, and the antinomy must disappear. Or so it would seem.

Phil groups antinomies under four different headings.

1. In the first group are *merely verbal contradictions*. Included here would be statements biblical authors make that at first seem contradictory, but once the meaning of an author's terms or argument is clarified, the contradiction disappears. For example, Paul speaks of "Gentile 'sinners,'" at first glance seeming to place himself and other Jews in the class of nonsinners. Once Paul's meaning is clarified, "by putting the word 'sinner' in scare-quotes," the apparent contradiction disappears—there was no real contradiction in the first place. Irony rather than antinomy is the operative methodological category here. When we understand Paul's literary technique the contradiction is resolved without difficulty.

2. We sail into deeper water when we encounter *irresolvable antinomies that can be directly traced to a lack of knowledge and may well be irremediable*. For example, consider the wave-particle duality in physics. Phil comments that Einstein "always thought there must be some deeper theory that would eliminate the apparent contradiction." If so, such a theory still remains inaccessible to us. Einstein's opponents, physicists such as Nils Bohr and others, appear to have won the day, choosing to allow the antinomy of light as wave and light as particle to stand. In fact, by doing so, these physicists would argue, they have remained closer to the truth, though at present the truth appears incoherent. What is one to do? At times one must think of light as waves. At other times, as particles. In addition, one must restrict the implications of each pole of the antinomy so that we don't, as Phil puts it, end up generating contradictions all over the place. That is to say, an irresolvable antinomy needs to be contained in a specific conceptual area rather than allowed to spread like a virus.

3. It is striking to me that significant sectors of the scientific community employ the concept of antinomy in their scientific work, specifically because they have observed *empirical data that at first glance are (and often after many glances remain) contradictory and incoherent*. Light functioning or behaving both as waves and as particles represents just such an example. Conceptually, the empirical data are both observable and contradictory, at least within the boundaries of our present knowledge and models. Yet because the phenomena of light as both waves and particles have been observed, physicists affirm both sides of the antinomy and wait for further information to make sense of the observed phe-

nomena. In addition, physicists appear perfectly capable of speaking to one another about physics and even about the antinomies apparent in their science. The incoherence physicists must live with in certain areas of their discipline does not prevent them from effectively discussing the antinomies in question and possible ways in which they might be resolved.

4. When it comes to *theological antinomies*, many of them might well be resolved through further inquiry, through the construction of new theological models, and through further discoveries provided by linguistic, historical, and cultural research. At present, the openness model offers such a resolution.

The possibility does exist, however, that there are genuine antinomies in theology. If so, we would expect them to occur at precisely those junctures where our access to information or revelation is limited. Has God, for instance, purposely chosen to remain silent or "secret" concerning various matters we would like to know and investigate more thoroughly? The possibility of divine secrets actually seems probable to me. We have been told by Moses, for example, that "the secret things belong to the Lord" (Deut. 29:29).

If so, why should we be surprised if the purposely limited revelation given to us in Scripture leads to junctures where theological coherence seems to break down? Yes, like Einstein, we should do all in our power to resolve an apparent antinomy, working hard to distinguish between apparent and genuine antinomies. (William Lane Craig's work on middle knowledge may well provide a way past the use of antinomy in discussing foreknowledge and providence.) The possibility does exist, however, that there is a deeper level of divine wisdom to which we do not now have direct access. God, after all, has told us that there are certain secrets that remain his own. At this deeper secret level, antinomy would disappear.

Not only so, but Phil believes—I think rightly—that we should work hard to make sense of antinomies when we encounter them, making as much sense of them as we can. Simultaneously, though, we should attempt to limit or contain contradiction, containing or framing it within one conceptual context, lest we breed contradictions and incoherence on a vast scale. Still, at least for the time in which we live, the use of antinomy seems to be a viable and defensible tool. Its use, though, does require "discernment, astuteness, and honesty." It should not be a rabbit we pull out of the magician's hat whenever we feel intellectually lazy or can't resolve a difficult theological problem immediately. You are right, then, to challenge folks like Packer and me to defend the use of antinomy, particularly if there might be a resolution to the problem that is conceptually satisfying, coherent, and faithful to the biblical text. At least for the present, however, I'm convinced that the openness model creates more problems than it solves. And even though you may feel that the appeal to antinomy must inevitably lead to an inability to discuss theological matters publicly, I think you know exactly what I'm talking about! I'll sign off for now, but will add a thought or two on antinomy tomorrow. Know that you remain in my prayers.

---

**With warm greetings,**
**Chris**

# 13 **John:** Antinomies and Logic

Dear Chris,

Sorry for my tardiness in responding. As you know there are some people (including some in the denomination that owns my college) who are upset with some of my views. This outspoken group of people doesn't even come close to treating me the same way you do. The most vociferous among them do not even want to discuss matters. They know they are right, that I am therefore a "heretic," and that settles it. Some go so far as to claim I'm not even a Christian. What troubles me is not that people disagree with some (not all) of my views. Rather, it is their lack of Christian virtue in carrying out their crusade. The innuendo, gossip, hearsay evidence, and even outright distortion of my views, coupled with political power plays made to ensure their victory, leave me wondering whether there is any place for thoughtful people in evangelical theology. It appears to be much better in evangelicalism to be guilty of adultery than to be guilty of an errant belief, because evangelicals place much more emphasis on correct doctrinal beliefs than on correct living. So, having to respond to all these attacks has taken up a lot of my time lately, and that is why this is late.

Thank you for your comments on antinomy. Though I discussed this in *The God Who Risks*, it is helpful to make some clarifications. First, I want to point out that it is not merely proponents of openness who reject the use of antinomies. In his book *The Providence of God*, Paul Helm criticizes his fellow Calvinist J. I. Packer for putting forth this "solution" to the problem of divine sovereignty and human freedom. Helm and I share some of the same criticisms.

Precisely what *is* an antinomy? The word literally means "against law" (i.e., against the law of reason). Your colleague makes some helpful distinctions but does not go far enough. My colleague William Hasker holds that there are at least four different types of antinomy. First are the "merely verbal" or rhetorical type, such as the statement that unless a grain of wheat dies it cannot bring forth life. There really is no contradiction here. Next are those that are contradictions until a distinction is made. For instance, an unbeliever is a living dead person. In this case the words living and dead are not being used in the same sense—it means one is physically alive though spiritually dead. Third are those that are straightforward contradictions, when both sides of the contradiction are claimed to be literally true and neither must be given up. For example, God determines all things and God does not determine all things. These are both true and we must not try to resolve them. Finally, someone else may acknowledge that we have two contradictory statements but hold that we must try to resolve them even if we presently do not know how to resolve them. That is, there is no real contradiction but we don't know how to state the situation in such a way that the appearance of contradiction is removed.

Only in the third sense is there a genuine contradiction. Even Packer says that the antinomy of divine sovereignty and human responsibility is not a real contradiction—it is only an apparent one. What would be a genuine contradiction? The assertion "God's mind is eternally settled and God changes his mind as he relates to us in history" is contradictory. To say that a timeless being changes in any respect—for example, has changing emotions—would be contradictory for change involves time. The great classical theists such as Thomas Aquinas and John Calvin understood that this was a contradiction and so held that it is not true that God changes his mind or has changing emotions. A logical contradiction asserts that "A is non-A." Here are some examples of contradictions: "The universe exists and does not exist," or "This telephone is a bald eagle." They are gibberish, meaningless statements of which we can make no sense. So a logical contradiction is a very precise, narrow matter. It does not involve puns, riddles, and the like—only meaningless statements.

Packer seems to believe that God determines everything that happens, including human actions, and that humans are morally responsible for their actions. He says that believing both of these is contradictory. But actually there is no contradiction here whatsoever, since Packer defines "moral responsibility" as meaning that humans are responsible for their actions so long as they act on their desires. This is a "compatibilistic" account of human freedom because it holds that divine determinism and human freedom are compatible rather than contradictory. Hence, humans are morally responsible even though they are determined by God and could not have acted differently (since their desires are determined) because they act on their desires. Because he defines human freedom in this way there is no contradiction at all, so why bother to use the term *antinomy*? This is a standard Calvinist explanation and there is nothing antinomian or contradictory about it.

In order to have a contradiction we have to define moral responsibility to mean that humans are responsible for their actions only if they are not determined to act in that way (humans have "indeterministic" freedom). We would now be saying that God holds humans morally responsible for their determined actions and humans are not morally responsible for their determined actions. The gears in our brains grind to a halt here. One might as well say that I just saw a colorless blue car. This is literally nonsense. Are you claiming that humans are both indeterministically free (i.e., have libertarian freedom) and not indeterministically free? Do you hold that God determines everything and that humans are not completely determined? I don't think you do. But then, where is the contradiction and why bother to use the term *antinomy*? You say, "the use of antinomy seems to be a viable and defensible tool." Aside from the fact that you do not even have an antinomy, I fail to see how one could use something that is contradictory (a colorless blue car) as a tool. How do you work with meaningless statements?

Suppose we assert both that God determines all things and also that humans are not completely determined. Now we are faced with a choice: either both statements are simply true and genuinely contradictory, or they both *seem* to be true but we don't know how to resolve them right now. If we simply stop with the contradiction, we have abandoned logic and I for one don't find it worthwhile to discuss meaningless statements. If you wish to hold contradictory theological statements as "true" you can do so, but our conversation will be over. However, if we say that they only *seem* contradictory, then we are admitting that at least one of the statements is false. If one of the statements is false, then how can you object to my attempt to determine which one of them is false? You are welcome to disagree with my conclusion as to which one is false, but your attempt to short-circuit my attempted resolution is simply not fair. Let me be clear, I'm not against you saying that I have not solved the problem and you find it preferable to live with the problem rather than accepting any of the proposed solutions. But to say any attempt to resolve the problem is illegitimate is to reject the notion that one of the claims is false.

You uphold the wave-particle duality in physics as a scientific example of an antinomy. Scientists understand light both as waves and as particles—but do they see this as a contradiction? No, they do not. Physicists do not say that light *is* a wave and also *is* a particle. Rather, waves and particles are models, not literal descriptions. Each model is an attempt to explain some of the data. In different experimental situations light seems to operate differently. In some situations light has certain characteristics in common with waves and in other situations has characteristics in common with particles. Scientists are indeed puzzled by this, and no one has yet developed a single model that explains all the data satisfactorily—but it is not a contradiction. Consequently, your illustration fails.

You just had to bring up Deuteronomy 29:29, didn't you! Well, I have a few comments about this poor old, oft-abused little verse. The passage is about the nature of the covenant between God and the people of Israel. God says that faithfulness to the covenant will result in blessings, while faithlessness will result in curses. The future thus depends on the response of the Israelites. This might leave people wondering how they could be sure that they were faithful to God's covenant. The answer in the text is that God has revealed what they need to do—there is no mystery about it! God has revealed his will for them; it is not mysterious, unknown, or unfulfillable. God wants them to know that he has not made a secret of how he will relate to them. There is no reason for them to be uneasy about the future. This same theme carries on right into the next chapter, where it is said that what God expects is not too difficult for them (30:11). Though it is true that the people are not informed as to the way in which God will carry out the blessings and curses, they are to rest assured that they know how God will relate to them. So, in my view Deuteronomy 29:29 is not launching into some esoteric mystery but is giving hope to the people. This verse has been so incredibly abused in church practice that it is difficult for us now to see what the point of the text actually is.

Perhaps your underlying concern is that in our theology we need to leave room for the fact that none of us fully comprehends God and that there will always be areas of mystery. I affirm that this is the case. My concern about antinomy is rather narrow. I'm only claiming that logical contradictions (A = non-A) are not meaningful discourse and should be avoided. You may use the word *contradiction* in a broader sense, but I have this specific meaning in mind. If you speak to me in contradictions, I have no way of understanding what you mean. Although the doctrine of the Trinity is a mystery that cannot be fully grasped, I see no formal logical contradictions in it. So, I'm no rationalist—I just want intelligible conversation.

---

In the name of the Father, Son, and Holy Spirit,
John

# 14 **Chris:** Logic and Metaphor

Dear John,

I want to develop some of the ideas I mentioned in my last letter concerning antinomy and perhaps add a thought or two about metaphor. Here goes.

I've run across a set of essays by a group of Reformed theologians, none of whom is pleased with the openness project. The collection is entitled *Bound Only Once: The Failure of Open Theism*, edited by Douglas Wilson. It is Wilson's essay that has caught my eye, and I'm interested in how you might respond to aspects of his criticism of the openness model. I'm going to attempt to translate Wilson's language into my own, but if you run across an occasional statement surrounded by quotation marks, the words are Wilson's.

Wilson begins by noting "a fundamental tension" in *The God Who Risks* between your ideas on metaphor and your call for a theology based on logical consistency. Where does the tension lie? On the one hand you write that "many people will be shocked by the notion that God is a risk taker, for the metaphor goes against the grain of our accustomed thinking in regard to divine providence." And yet you rightly note that a good metaphor shakes people's conceptions, purposely rocking their conceptual boat. Those metaphors that speak of God risking, for instance, might well help us to see aspects of God's character we would too easily overlook because of the dominance of other key metaphors, such as God as king.

51

Where does the tension lie, and how is it related to the issue of antinomy and the demands of logical consistency? You write that "metaphors have the peculiar quality of saying that something both 'is' and 'is not.'" That is, a metaphor and anthropomorphic language are not designed to be logically consistent. Metaphors and anthropomorphisms inherently contain a yes and a no. Metaphors both affirm and deny. For instance, when we speak of Christ as a lamb we mean to affirm that in some sense Christ is a lamb and is not a lamb. What's the problem?

Wilson observes that a few pages later in the book you contend that all theological models should be judged on their "public" and "conceptual intelligibility." Entailed in intelligibility, you argue, is that "if a concept is contradictory, it fails a key test for public intelligibility, since what is contradictory is not meaningful. . . . If concepts integral to the model are mutually inconsistent, the coherence of the model is called into question." Does this stricture work well for metaphor? Wilson thinks not. Because metaphors inherently possess internal logical inconsistencies (e.g., Christ is a lamb and isn't a lamb), how do they manage to communicate coherently to us? If logical consistency is the standard for theological models, metaphor ends up meaningless, or else as a riddle that must be reduced to nonmetaphorical language, squeezed for its meaning like one squeezes an orange for juice.

What is the result? We end up reducing the metaphorical to the literal in our search for consistency. Truth, by definition, must be nonmetaphorical. Theology, by definition, must be reducible to publicly comprehensible logical statements. Though you have a strong allergic reaction to Hellenistic thought, Wilson argues that the preference for the literal over the metaphorical is rooted in the thought of Greek thinkers such as Aristotle, who argued that metaphor was "a deviation from and a mere ornament on the literal."

Can metaphors be squeezed like lemons to gain their inner truth, or is something essential lost in the squeezing? Can a metaphor be changed easily into a logical syllogism, publicly coherent and comprehensible? That, it seems, is the question. Of course, many thinkers have believed that the translation of metaphor into logical proposition is absolutely necessary if we are to attain genuine knowledge. David Kelley, for example, writes that when we reason "we are concerned with the logical relationship among propositions. . . . To know how a given proposition is logically related to others, we have to know exactly what the proposition does and doesn't say. If two people are using metaphorical terms in an argument, we won't know whether they are really talking about the same issue until we formulate their position in literal terms."

Metaphors in themselves tend to be murky, messy, and logically inconsistent. The real truth, then, lies underneath the metaphor. Mathematics and logic are able to communicate knowledge, then, in a manner that a metaphor cannot, a position Wilson identifies both with Hellenistic thinkers such as Aristotle and with Enlightenment thinkers such as Locke and Hobbes. Again, can metaphors be reduced to mathematical formulas or logical syllogisms? What is lost in this reduction—a reduction, it seems, based on the quest for logical consistency?

In Wilson's words, "Metaphor calls up many aspects of our being (emotional, moral, aesthetic, imaginative, bodily) that are central to knowledge but don't fit into neat mathematical boxes." Are there not "noncognitive depths" within metaphor that are lost when we employ too narrow a use of reason? This, at least, seems to be Wilson's argument, and I think it's worth chewing on. He's convinced that openness theologians such as yourself are trying to synthesize two worlds—the world of Enlightenment rationality and the world of metaphor, but the synthesis ends up drastically reducing the metaphorical.

Let's move on a bit. In your objection to antinomy, you write that those who employ antinomies seek "to escape the rules surrounding intelligibility." If we are going to do theology, you believe, "we simply have to 'play by the rules' of the game, and one of these rules is that our discourse must make sense." Fine, but then I begin to get a bit confused. On the one hand you state that your position "does not rule out paradox and mystery . . . or metaphors and riddles." On the other hand, the openness model "simply excludes discourse that lies outside the boundaries of consistency and coherence—that is, nonsense." A mystery or paradox, then, must be reducible to rational intelligibility.

I think this is precisely the problem. Your argument seems to be that all meaningful language must be literal, coherent, and capable of reduction to a logical syllogism. How is this stance significantly different from the logical positivism that seems to have run its course? To quote Wittgenstein: "The limits of my language means the limits of my world. Logic pervades the world: the limits of the world are also its limits. . . . The right method of philosophy would be this. To say nothing except what can be said." Or A. J. Ayer: "It is only if it is literally meaningful . . . that a statement can properly be said to be either true or false . . . [Otherwise] it would not be capable of being understood in the sense in which either scientific hypotheses or common-sense statements are habitually understood." Hence, the metaphorical must be reduced to the literal. At times, John, you sound a lot like these guys. But what's the problem?

Can the anthropomorphisms in the Bible be easily reduced to univocal terms? You readily acknowledge the broad number of anthropomorphisms in the Bible. Indeed, "the use of metaphors and anthropomorphic language (in the broad sense) when speaking of God is necessary."

Right. I agree when you write, "If God decides to disclose himself to us as a personal being who enters into relationship with us, who has purposes, emotions, and desires, and who suffers with us, then we ought to rejoice in this anthropomorphic portrait." I'm in agreement. All God's words are gifts and we should rejoice in all of them. I disagree, however, with the deduction you draw from the anthropomorphism. For you conclude that we should accept the anthropomorphic portrait as "disclosing to us the very nature of God." How so?

Here it seems you reduce the anthropomorphic to the literal. That is, the only interpretive option you seem to allow is the univocal understanding of terms such as desires, emotions, suffering, and so on. The both/and character of metaphor is reduced to the univocal, logical syllogism. This seems to me to be a serious weakness in the openness model. I'd better sign off for now.

---

You're in my prayers,
Chris

# 15 **John:** Metaphor and Interpretation

## Good morning, Chris,

It is a beautiful Saturday morning here and it was wonderful to see the ducks and geese swimming in the open water on the mostly ice-covered campus lake. In the distance I heard a dog barking and I thought of your letter on my understanding of metaphor. Woof! Woof! Can you hear it? That is the sound of a dog barking up the wrong tree. You followed Wilson down the path and continued to follow him when he left the path and now you have lost the trail and stand barking at a tree thinking you have treed the raccoon (me), but I'm not anywhere close to where you think I am. Since you have lost the scent so badly perhaps I should take some responsibility for not leaving enough on the trail for you to follow. So let me take this opportunity to get you back on my tail. Aren't these wonderful metaphors! Just for fun, in the rest of this letter I will boldface type for some of my metaphors so you see that I **relish** metaphors.

You say that Wilson **spots** a fundamental **tension** between my ideas on metaphor and my claim that our theological **discourse** must not be logically contradictory. He argues that metaphors, by their very **nature,** are self-contradictory. Since metaphors say that something both is and is not, there is a contradiction. For instance, Christ is both a **lamb** and not a lamb. We say that Jesus is the **lamb** of God who **takes away** the

55

sin of the world. But actually Jesus is a human and not a physical lamb at all so is this not a contradiction? No, it is not. In my last letter on antinomy I **defined** a logical contradiction as the claim that A = non-A. That is, **holding** that something both is and is not in exactly the same sense. For example, claiming that the walls of my office are completely white and completely purple at the same time. Is this the sort of thing we are doing when we say Jesus is a lamb and not a lamb? Not at all. Jesus is like a lamb in some senses and not like a lamb in other senses. If we said that Jesus is the sacrificial lamb whose blood **washes away** our sins and that Jesus is not the sacrificial lamb whose blood washes away our sins, *that* would be a contradiction. Metaphors are not inherently contradictory. Wilson is **out to lunch** on this.

You **go on** to claim that I reduce the metaphorical to the literal, since truth must, by definition, be nonmetaphorical. You think I'm saying "all meaningful language must be literal, coherent, and capable of reduction to a logical syllogism." You say that I'm **buying into** the preference of **placing** the literal **over** the metaphorical **rooted** in the thought of the Greek philosophers, **refined** by Enlightenment thinkers and that I **end up looking like** a "logical positivist." Ouch!!

Let me respond by saying that there has indeed been a strong prejudice against metaphor in Western philosophy. The **underlying** assumption has been that our **language pictures** reality in a **direct**, literal manner when we **exclude** metaphors. Metaphors have been considered **deviant** expressions that can be **translated** into literal words. Metaphors are simply **flowery** language for what can be said in **straightforward** words. This way of thinking **runs deep** in evangelical theological approaches to Scripture. It was what I was taught in the evangelical schools I attended and in the leading evangelical theology books. In fact, in a couple of unpublished papers, Charles White argues that one of the key problems in the debate between classical and open theists is the failure of the classical theists to **grasp** how open theists understand metaphor. White documents that evangelical Calvinist critics of open theism affirm the principle that the metaphorical language of Scripture is to be **reduced** to the literal and these same critics fault open theists for failing to practice this. However, now you say just the opposite. You accuse me of **operating** by the same rules accepted by my Calvinist critics. Well, do I or don't I affirm that the metaphorical must be reduced to the literal? Though I was taught this by my evangelical professors, I do not, in fact, accept it. I have **embraced** a "post-critical" approach to knowing and have rejected the "picture theory" of language.

So how do I **perceive** the use of metaphors? Though I have much more **reflection** to do on this subject, I will tell you that I have been **influenced** by the study of "cognitive linguistics." In *The God Who Risks*

I noted a number of studies on metaphor that have **shaped** my thinking. Among these is the work of George Lakoff and Mark Johnson. In their book *Metaphors We Live By*, they **show** how **basic** metaphor is to the way we **conceive** reality. The word "conceive" is what they call a "dead" metaphor in that we forget that it is a sexual metaphor and take it to be "literal." I hold that all of the biblical language about God is metaphorical. In *The God Who Risks* I wrote: "The metaphorical and anthropomorphic language of the Bible is taken seriously because it is through the idiom of Scripture and its various metaphors that we understand and relate to God. The language of Scripture is 'reality depicting' in that what we understand to be real is mediated through its metaphors and images. Metaphors help us make sense of things."

In these very few words I was trying to **sum up** a lot of discussion about metaphor. Lakoff and Johnson suggest that metaphors do not primarily "describe" one item in terms of another (a standard view of metaphor). Rather, they think of metaphors as **conceptual maps** by which we give meaning to our experiences. Conceptual metaphors are abstractions **drawn from** concrete objects or events by which we understand our experiences. One of their many illustrations of conceptual metaphor is "argument as war." Warfare is a very concrete, physical, event. Though not all cultures conceptualize verbal disputes in terms of warfare, we in the West do. That is, we make sense of our debates by **framing** them **in light of** war. For instance, we say:

1. Your claims are *indefensible*.
2. He *attacked* every *weak point* in my argument.
3. Her criticisms were *on target*.
4. I *destroyed* his argument.
5. I've never *won* an argument with her.
6. If you use that *strategy* he'll *wipe you out*.
7. She *shot down* all my ideas.

These expressions map our conception of war onto the activity of "argument." Other cultures do not understand argument in terms of war but we have **found** it useful to do so. We are not saying that argument actually *is* war. Rather, warfare is the **conduit** through which we **conceive** of argumentation. Conceptual metaphors are **vehicles** by which we understand our world. Hence, we can't do without them. However, conceptual metaphors map out reality only partially, and they **constrain** the ways in which we think. That is, thinking of argument as war may help us make sense of argumentation, but it also may **prevent** us from understanding argumentation in other ways. Conceptualizing God as an eagle carrying its young on its back to safety (Exod. 19:4) helps us make sense of God's relationship to Israel. Conceptualizing God as having protective wings over us (Ps. 17:8), as a husband (Hosea 2:2), or as stretching out his arm (Deut. 4:34) toward us "maps" the way the biblical writers understood who God is and the way God relates to us. God blew his nostrils and the waters parted (Exod. 15:8) is a delightful conceptualization of what God did for his people.

My evangelical Calvinist critics ask why open theists don't take the biblical language about God having arms and eyes or wings literally if we take the biblical language about God changing his mind, having emotions, and the like, literally. They say, "If you take one metaphor literally, you must take them all literally." Well, part of the answer is that the word *literal* is unhelpful here. For me, all of these are conceptual metaphors—I don't take them "literally" in the sense in which my critics employ the word *literal*. For them, *literal* means that the language is describing an object as it really is. They emphasize the descriptive function of language, while I emphasize the conceptual function of language. The biblical metaphors about God enable us to conceptualize (i.e., give meaning to) our experience of God in terms of very concrete events or objects.

Many of the critics of open theism take terms such as *immutable* (unchangeable), *impassible* (cannot be affected by another), and *sovereign* (has control over) as literal descriptions of God. But these terms are conceptual metaphors, not literal descriptors. However, we have long forgotten that *immutable* is a metaphor, and thus it has now become a dead metaphor that is taken literally. Many of my critics seem to take the dead metaphors for literal representations of God.

Let me move on to your last criticism: that I only allow for a "univocal understanding of terms such as desires, emotions, suffering, and so on" when speaking of God. I trust by now that you see this is not so. Nevertheless, there is one statement in chapter two of *The God Who Risks* where I slip up in this regard or at least need to explain myself. I did speak of a "hard literal core" or a "univocal core" to our talk about God. Thus far, David Williams, in an unpublished paper, is the only one who has called me out on this. I see now that my choice of words there could lead one to think that I agree with Carl Henry, Norman Geisler, and other evangelical theologians in disparaging the use of metaphors in favor of "literal" language for God.

If I don't agree with this line of thinking, then what do I believe? As already stated, I believe that we are using conceptual metaphors to think about the nature of God and God's relationship with us. This is the way things are, and it is good. Our conceptual metaphors are the means by which we give meaning to our experience of God. The position against which I was arguing in this section in my book is the view that, since

God is ontologically different from creatures, we cannot speak about or know anything about God. That is, I was arguing against the long-standing tradition of viewing the biblical language about God as "baby talk" and not the proper way to think of God. Many have held that there is a "God behind" or "beyond" the God of the Bible. For them, human language, including the biblical language about God, does not disclose any truth [any significant truth?] about who God is. With Luther and Barth I affirm that God genuinely discloses himself to us in the biblical revelation and most fully in Jesus (Heb. 1:3), such that there is no "God behind God." Rather, human language is adequate, though not perfect, for understanding the God who comes to us, especially in Jesus. I stand opposed to those who deny that the biblical portrayal of God, in all its manifold conceptual metaphors, is "reality depicting." We need the multitude of metaphors for God, since they paint different parts of the mosaic. But I hold that these metaphors are not necessarily contradictory just because they are metaphors.

Is all this clear as mud? It is well past time for lunch and I must get home. Let me admit that I've been rather **playful** with you in this letter and I hope you take it in the spirit I send it. When we are together we know how to tease one another even while we are doing "serious" theology. It is my hope that what I've said will put you onto my scent so that you will be able to find the right tree in which this raccoon is sitting.

Your fellow servant,
John

# 16 **Chris:** Impassibility, Immutability, and the Incarnation

Dear John,

I'm sitting at my desk, looking out the window lazily, and wishing I were outside hitting golf balls rather than inside trying to fathom God's providence, nature, relationship to time, the problem of evil, and why so many people seem to be angry with you! It's enough to give one a headache. I was musing, for instance, on a line of yours I mentioned in a previous letter. In part it reads, "If God decides to disclose himself to us as a personal being . . . who has purposes, emotions, and desires, and who suffers with us, then we ought to rejoice in this anthropomorphic portrait." Indeed, you write, it discloses "to us the very nature of God." Remember those lines? Well, they've got me thinking, and today I'm pondering the idea of God suffering.

Why am I both attracted to the idea of God suffering and confused by it? Why has the church insisted century after century that God is impassible (incapable of suffering or being affected by someone else)? Is this a doctrine that I should continue to defend? If so, why? If not, why not? Does God experience suffering or passion? Without a doubt, as you point out, some biblical texts portray God as suffering. One only has to think of Paul's words in Ephesians 4:30, "And do not grieve the Holy Spirit of God, with which you were marked with a seal for the day of redemption." If the Holy Spirit can be grieved, surely God can suffer.

60

Or so it would seem. Yet the church fathers, medieval theologians such as Anselm and Thomas Aquinas, and reformers such as Calvin affirmed divine impassibility. It's enough to make one want to grab a three wood and head for the first hole!

I can understand and to an extent appreciate openness theologians' insistence on divine passibility. It is deeply comforting to know that God is near to us, understands our suffering and fears, and loves us deeply. And if God is genuinely open to us in the manner you describe, surely God can be disappointed, wounded, saddened, grieved, and so on. If God experiences these reactions within "the very nature of God," God can and must actually change.

Furthermore, it certainly seems that a robust understanding of divine passibility goes hand in hand with the reality of God changing in response to situations or influences outside of God. If I can grieve God by my attitudes or behaviors in the same manner that I can grieve my wife, then my actions in time can move God from a state of happiness or joy to a state of grief or sadness, at least with respect to the relationship between God and me. Hence, God would surely be vulnerable: I, as an external cause, could cause suffering and its attendant changes in God.

I don't seem to be the only theologian struggling with impassibility. Many folks have jettisoned the doctrine because they have felt that it is simply indefensible. Clark Pinnock comes to mind. Clark writes, for example, that "impassibility is the most dubious of the divine attributes discussed in classical theism, because it suggests that God does not experience sorrow, sadness or pain. It appears to deny that God is touched by the feelings of our infirmities, despite what the Bible says about his love and his sorrow." Impassibility does seem to separate God from some of the most significant aspects of human life. And yet I'm still unwilling to let it go. Why?

Well, one reason is that there seems to be quite a bit in Scripture that affirms God's impassibility, that is, God's wondrous self-sufficiency. Part of the wonder of God is that he does not need anything outside himself to complete or satisfy himself (Job 22:2–3; 35:6–7; Ps. 50:10–12). God as Father, Son, and Holy Spirit has always enjoyed an ineffable relationship of exquisite love. No aspect of the divine nature is insufficient or wanting. In a manner of speaking, God does not need us but freely invites us into the family—for our sakes, not his.

Second, Scripture does seem to teach that God is not obligated to us. When God responds to Abraham's request to spare Sodom, for example, he does so out of mercy, not obligation.

Third, I still find it difficult to understand how God can possibly learn anything from us that would surprise God, catch him off guard, or elicit an emotional movement of grief in God as God. I do think this is possible for God incarnate, but I would limit this movement to the humanity the Word has assumed for our sake.

We probably need to discuss biblical texts in more detail regarding the nature of God's response to human beings. I realize that there are biblical texts that speak of God being surprised or grieved at the behavior of Israel. You've been reminding me of this for months! The question for me is how we are to interpret these texts. For instance, is God somehow accommodating himself to us in these texts or should they be interpreted univocally? That issue will have to be set aside, at least momentarily. I would contend, though, that texts such as Romans 11:33–36 indicate that God is neither obligated to any human being nor counseled or instructed by any human being. He doesn't need our advice and is not surprised by what we do. And yes, I realize I will have to make sense out of the biblical texts that portray God as listening to Moses, being surprised by Israel's behavior, and so on.

Finally—and here's the big one for what we finally decide about impassibility—I don't believe God changes. Impassibility is inextricably linked to immutability. If suffering entails change, God cannot suffer. Numbers 23:19, for example, states "God is not a human being, that he should lie, or a mortal, that he should change his mind." Also 1 Samuel 15:29 and Malachi 3:6 come to mind. It was biblical considerations such as these that convinced the church fathers that God was both impassible and immutable. This does not mean, however, that I'm forbidden to affirm "God suffers." What is decisive is what I mean when I say this.

Cyril of Alexandria, for instance, argued for years with Nestorius over the phrase *theotokos* ("God-bearer" or "mother of God"). Should Mary be called the mother of God? Cyril said yes. Nestorius said no. At first glance, Nestorius's position seems both more biblical and more logical. After all, can God be born? This possibility seems a contradiction in terms. And yet, Cyril argued, Nestorius's reluctance to call Mary the mother of God demonstrated a failure to understand the wonder of the incarnation. Who was being born in Bethlehem? Who had joined himself to human nature in Mary's womb? Simply divinity? No. Rather, the second person of the blessed Trinity had joined himself to human nature and was born on Christmas day. Thus it was not only appropriate to call Mary the mother of God (*theotokos*), but to fail to do so would be to seriously undercut and weaken the gospel itself.

Cyril unapologetically defended the use of theological language that at first glance makes little sense: God has been born, God has died, God suffers. However (and this is the point where I think I differ from openness theologians), it is the incarnate Word who genuinely suffers in his humanity. Thus we affirm that God suffers. In Cyril's words, "The mystery of Christ runs the risk of being disbelieved precisely because it is so incredibly wonderful." How so? "For God was in humanity. He who was above all creation was in our human condition; the invisible one was made visible in the flesh; he who is from the heavens and from on high was in the likeness of earthly things; the immaterial one could be touched; he who is free in his own nature came in the form of a slave; he who blesses all creation became accursed; he who is all righteousness was numbered among transgressors; life itself came in the appearance of death." God is born, suffers, and dies because God the Word has joined himself to human nature, and in that nature the Word experiences birth, suffering, and death.

In a sense I've come full circle in this letter and understand more clearly where we differ. You understand the portrait of God painted by biblical authors as "disclosing to us the very nature of God." What I might describe as accommodation you see as univocal communication. I would argue, then, that the incarnation is the clearest instance of God's accommodation to us. In the incarnation the Word enters our world, accommodating his divinity to our humanity, and indeed suffers and dies with us. This is possible because of the hypostatic union—the Word has genuinely joined his nature to ours. In that nature he suffers with us. As for the "very nature of God," however, God remains wondrously and ineffably impassible and immutable. This thought needs further development, but I'd better sign off for now.

---

You're in my prayers,
Chris

# 17 **John:** Impassibility, Immutability, and the Incarnation

Dear Chris,

Some pastors in the denomination that owns my college are upset with my publications on open theism and inclusivism (my hope that God will provide a means of salvation for those who have never heard the gospel). One of the regular committees has decided to look into the matter. Yesterday I met with the chair of the committee and found him to be gracious and thoughtful. Moreover, he is able to state my views correctly! That is something that many folks are either unable or unwilling to do. Some evangelicals make little or no effort to understand. Instead, they resort to hearsay, innuendo, and inflammatory rhetoric. Some evangelicals seem to believe that getting rid of someone who is teaching something they don't like allows them to use even unethical means to accomplish this end. Again, it seems that correct belief matters more to evangelicals than moral behavior. I'm amazed that even scholars are resorting to underhanded measures in order to discredit my views. Their acerbic tone and their, I believe sometimes intentional, misstating of my position shows that they do not want to have dialogue with me, they simply want to bury me. That is why the conversations between us are so refreshing. We disagree, but we are trying to learn the truth through the process. Moreover, we are both able to take our work seriously without taking ourselves too seriously. Of course, we

64

both seek to serve our Lord but neither of us believes that the kingdom of God stands or falls with us.

Now to your discussion of divine impassibility. The term *impassibility* has a range of meanings, and historical theologians debate its meaning when used, for example, in the Council of Chalcedon in A.D. 451. Generally, however, the term may be understood to mean that God is not affected by creatures. We do not influence God nor does God respond to us. What we do has no affect on what God decides to do or on what God experiences. For example, God cannot be made sorrowful. This seems to go against the clear teaching of Scripture. The biblical writers portray God as "grieving" over human sin (Gen. 6:6; Eph. 4:30), being disappointed in the failure of Saul (1 Sam. 15:11, 35), being provoked to anger in response to habitual faithlessness (Exod. 32:10; Isa. 5:25), and as being affected by the prayers (or lack of them) of his people (Exod. 32:14; 2 Kings 20). These are but a few of the sorts of texts we cite in our books as evidence that the notion that God is not responsive to us and is unaffected by us is simply wrongheaded.

You ask, "Why has the church for century after century insisted that God is impassible?" I have two responses to this.

First, it is correct that the majority voice in the Christian tradition was for impassibility. However, it is no longer the majority voice. For the past two centuries the doctrine of divine impassibility has been increasingly discarded by Christian thinkers. Today, it is a minority position, even within evangelicalism. Wayne Grudem, for instance, criticizes the Westminster Confession for accepting the "unbiblical" notion that God is "without passions." Millard Erickson surveys recent evangelical theologians and concludes that "the traditional doctrine of impassibility is not the current one" among contemporary evangelicals. So you are incorrect to say that "the church" has always affirmed this doctrine (unless you don't think that these modern thinkers belong to the church). Moreover, from the beginning there has been a tension in the writings of many theologians regarding divine impassibility. For instance, Justin Martyr discusses the issue but then blurts out, "But God is not a stone!" He is wrestling with the problem and does not know how to resolve it. In the ninth century John Scotus Erigena affirmed absolute impassibility but then admitted that the Bible "shouts on all sides" that this is false. In addition to this tension there has been a "protest" minority position. In the third century Gregory Thaumaturgus wrote a treatise on divine impassibility in which he argued that, unlike us, God cannot be forced to suffer but God can voluntarily choose to become vulnerable and open to suffering. It is God's free will to decide whether or not to be open to being affected by us. If God cannot choose to suffer, says Gregory, then God is subject to great suffering for then God is limited. My point is that the church has not been of one voice on this matter, and today you represent the minority view while I affirm the majority position. Can you see my chest all puffed out with pride about this?

Second, great Christian thinkers did read their Bibles and yet still affirmed impassibility. Why? They had powerful arguments that shaped the way they interpreted Scripture. One of these arguments is that God is perfect and a perfect being could never change, for any change would only be a change for the worse. If God suffered because of us or was affected by us in any way, that would be a change in God and thus God would not be perfect. Another argument that goes along with this is that as creator God must be absolutely independent of us—he cannot rely on us for anything. Also, God must be timeless, and a timeless being cannot experience any change (because change involves time). Since suffering involves a change, a timeless being cannot suffer. All of these arguments center around the notion that change is contrary to perfection. The desire for something that is unchangeable seems to have been an influential value in Greek thought. Today we no longer hold that all change is imperfection. In fact, to be in relationship and not change seems less than perfect. But in the centuries after the apostles, the Christian writers swam in the waters of the predisposition that all change is bad for divinity. This notion was taken for granted and few challenged it. Instead, the route taken by most Christian writers was to uphold the assumption of impassibility and yet try to say in some way that God cares for us. In my opinion it would have been better if Gregory Thaumaturgus's view had won the day—that God could voluntarily choose to suffer. However, the influence of this Greek philosophical notion (any change is bad for God) proved, in the end, too strong for most Christians to overcome.

This led many Christians to the very conclusions you now affirm: God, as God, cannot suffer. You are not saying that God chooses not to suffer. Rather, you are asserting that there is something that *God cannot do* even if he wanted to. Hence, when it comes to Jesus, you follow their lead and say that only the humanity of Jesus suffered because his divinity is incapable of suffering. The "God side" of Jesus "knows" about the suffering of the human side of Jesus, but the God side never experiences suffering. I think the reason the Council of Chalcedon anathematizes anyone who says the divinity of Jesus suffered is because the Council members held the assumption that God, as God, cannot suffer, so you cannot allow the divine nature of Jesus to experience any suffering. But what if we did not accept this assumption and went instead with Gregory's idea that God cannot be forced to suffer but that God can voluntarily choose to suffer? I believe this opens up a much better way to go and avoids several significant problems.

One of the problems is your incorrect conclusion that if God can suffer, God is not self-sufficient. This simply does not follow. Nobody is saying that God had to create a world and that if God decides to create one, he has to suffer or depend on us. However, we are saying that God can choose to create a world in which he freely decides to delegate responsibility for *some* things to us. God can choose to be, for some things, dependent on us (e.g., feeding the hungry). God is not obligated to operate this way. Nobody is making God run the world this way, it is simply the way God decided to do it. Do you want to say, with Paul Helm, that *God cannot* do it this way? The open view emphasizes the eternal love of the Holy Trinity. God did not have to create in order for the Father, Son, and Holy Spirit to eternally share love. There is no "lonely God" needing to create. The loving Trinity freely created a world and wants to share the eternal divine love with creatures. But love cannot be forced, and so God freely took the "risk of love" in that it was possible that we would not respond to God's love by loving him back and loving our fellow creatures. Clearly, humanity has spurned God's gracious love and this has led to God's experiencing grief. Yes, God as God can suffer because God opens himself in his love to us to allow us to affect him. The self-sufficient God opens himself to include others even to the point of being, for some things, vulnerable to disappointment when we fail to love.

The next problem this approach avoids is summed up in the following question: Does Jesus reveal what God is really like? One of my Calvinist critics said at a conference: "You cannot use Jesus to establish what God is like because Jesus is also human." I about fell off my chair. This person was, however, identifying a problem in the tradition: affirming that Jesus is fully God and yet holding that what we actually see in Jesus is only his human nature. What then are we to make of statements such as "He who has seen me has seen the Father" (John 14:9); "Jesus discloses to us the very nature of God" (Heb. 1:3); and "in [Jesus] the fullness of deity dwelled in bodily form" (Col. 2:9)? You say that "the incarnation is the clearest instance of God's accommodation to us." I prefer to say that the incarnation is the clearest instance of God's self-disclosure to us. The things that Jesus said and did are what God is like. Unless, that is, you have some presumed concept of God that you use to filter the revelation of God. Do you have a presupposed notion of what God must be like (*dignum Deo*) that you then impose on the biblical text and on Jesus so that you know that the sufferings of Jesus are merely human, not divine sufferings? You say that you agree with Cyril that in Jesus "God has died, God suffers" and you go on to say that "it is the incarnate Word who genuinely suffers in his humanity." "Genuinely suffers?" How so if the divine Son cannot suffer? I affirm what you and Cyril want to get to: God suffered in Jesus. However, I think you folks took a wrong turn and cannot actually get to where you want to go unless you turn around.

The approach that says that God as God cannot suffer and cannot limit himself in any respect has led to all sorts of confusion regarding the claim in Philippians 2:7 that the divine Son "emptied himself" in becoming incarnate. Emptied himself of what? Some have said that the Son gave up certain divine attributes such as omniscience (Matt. 24:36). But then, was he really God? *God in Christ* saved us so the humanity of the Son cannot involve a surrender of divinity. Perhaps if we began with Jesus as the disclosure of what God is like it would lead us to modify our preconceived notions of what is fitting for God to be. Thus, self-limitation need not involve giving up deity. Perhaps self-giving, self-sacrifice, and self-limitation is part of what the loving Trinity is like. For me, what Jesus is like discloses what God is like. William Placher puts it well: "So the God who becomes a particular, limited human being is acting out just what it means to be a God of love." I agree with Luther: the cross discloses the very heart of God. If we allow Jesus to teach us what God is like, then we can say that God, as God, can suffer in his love for us and we need not go through the mental gymnastics to ensure that only the human nature of Jesus suffered.

Finally, I believe this approach overcomes the problem of accommodation. The issue is not, as you say, that I believe the biblical language to be a univocal (one-to-one) communication from God while you think it is an accommodating communication. I already said that they are conceptual metaphors. The real issue here is, from where do we get our most basic information about what God is like? In one sense I can agree with you that God has to speak our lingo if he wants to communicate with us. But you go on to say that God is speaking a sort of "baby talk" to us in most of Scripture. To know that someone is speaking baby talk you also have to know "adult talk." In the case of God, you also have to know God's grown-up talk in order to know that God is speaking baby talk to us. You believe I'm taking the baby talk of Scripture way too seriously. Well, please teach me God's grown-up talk. But how are you privileged to know God's grown-up talk? How did you come to know what God is really like so that you could read the Bible and pick out God's baby talk from God's grown-up talk? Again, is Jesus simply God's baby talk to us? I think not.

I say you see "most of Scripture" as baby talk because you do lift up some verses as describing what God is really like. You say that the Bible teaches divine impassibility because to suffer involves change and the Bible says that God does not change (Num. 23:19; 1 Sam. 15:29; Mal. 3:6). This sounds like you have, heaven forbid, some sort of "univocal" understanding in mind. Ha! Do these verses teach that God cannot change in any respect? These verses have been favorite proof texts for theologians throughout the centuries. The reason I say "proof texts" is because they already had preconceived notions about what God must be like (the philosophical arguments I mentioned above) and used these verses to support their claims of absolute immutability (unchangeability).

However, most biblical scholars today do not believe these verses teach this. The two texts that say that God will not change his mind refer to specific situations in which God refuses to reverse a particular decision. In one case God refuses to allow Balaam to change the divine mind and curse Israel (Num. 23:19), while in the other God rejects Saul's pleas to keep the kingship in his family (1 Sam. 15:29). The first Samuel passage is especially instructive. God informs Samuel that he "regrets" that he made Saul king (15:11) to which Samuel responded by praying all night for God to change his mind back and allow Saul to remain king. But God refused Samuel's intercession. Subsequently, Saul begs that the divine decision be rescinded. In response Samuel says that God will not change his mind back to his original plan (15:29). The story concludes by reiterating that God changed his mind about making Saul king (15:35). And sandwiched between two declarations of God changing his mind (15:11, 35) is the remark that God will not change his mind (15:29). This chapter says both that God changes his mind and will not change his mind. In its context the teaching is clear: God reserves the right to alter his plans in response to human initiative and it is also the divine right not to alter an alteration. God had originally planned on establishing Saul's household for a perpetual kingship in Israel (1 Sam. 13:13–14) but has changed his mind about this due to Saul's disobedience. Despite Samuel's intercession, God proclaims that he will not change his mind about this change of mind he has had. If one reads these "I will not change my mind" texts in their literary and historical contexts it becomes clear that they are not abstract propositions about divine immutability. Rather, they speak of God's steadfastness in certain concrete situations to reject the human petition.

Texts such as "I the LORD do not change, therefore you, O sons of Jacob, are not consumed" (Mal. 3:6) and "Jesus Christ is the same yesterday, today and forever" (Heb. 13:8) are also not about absolute immutability. After all, if the divine Son is interceding for us, that is a change. These texts are referring to God's steadfast love. God's love for Israel does not fail, thus they are not destroyed says Malachi. Open theists hold that the divine *nature* does not change (God's love, power, wisdom, and faithfulness) but that God can and does change in his emotions, thoughts, will, and actions. So I agree with you that something about

God is immutable. But I think you go too far in saying that everything about God is immutable. The divine Son was not always incarnate—that sure seems like a change to me!

Thanks much for prodding me to think through these issues.

_____

Blessings,
John

# 18 **Chris:** Impassibility and Prayer

Dear John,

It's Friday, the sun is out, and it's around fifty degrees outside. Too good to be true! Once again I hear the golf course beckoning. Before I succumb to temptation, though, I think I'll write a quick note to you. In my last letter I was beginning to comment on a few biblical texts. Why not continue to investigate biblical texts in this letter?

I've just re-read sections from your excursus on divine repentance in *The God Who Risks*. You mention more than once the account of King Hezekiah. You ask, "What do such texts intend to teach us if they do not mean what they say? If God knew all along, for instance, that King Hezekiah was not going to die, then what was God doing when he announced that Hezekiah would die shortly? Was God lying?" You then add that to claim that "biblical texts asserting that God 'changed his mind' are merely anthropomorphisms does not tell us what they mean. If, in fact, it is impossible for God to change his mind, then the biblical text is quite misleading."

I don't agree. The text concerning Hezekiah would only be misleading if God lied to Hezekiah by instructing him to put his affairs in order because Hezekiah's death was imminent. Are there other viable alternatives? I can see you rolling your eyes at me. "Why," you might say, "can't we simply take the text at face value? Why do we have to turn it into a 'mere anthropomorphism'?" Well, I don't believe in "mere" anthropomorphisms. Anthropomorphisms can teach us all kinds of things about God and about ourselves. Even more importantly, though, if we take

71

the text at face value, then we're going to run into significant problems concerning divine omniscience and will be forced to develop, as you presently are doing, a new theological model of what omniscience means. For instance, almost all models of omniscience that I'm aware of describe God's omniscience as encompassing past, present, and future. The openness model significantly modifies the traditional model. God knows fully the past and present, and those aspects of the future God has ordained to occur. God does not know beforehand, however, the free choices of human beings. If God knew these decisions, the future would already be decided and freedom lost. Or so I understand the openness position. I want to debate these particular issues further with you, but not in this letter. Back to Hezekiah.

You argue that God learns something from Hezekiah's prayer that he did not know previously. What might this be? Perhaps God did not realize adequately how the news of Hezekiah's forthcoming death would trouble Hezekiah. Perhaps God didn't understand how fervently Hezekiah desired to live for a few more years. Maybe God didn't realize that Hezekiah was going to pray so fervently. If God had understood the content and fervency of Hezekiah's prayer, God would not have predicted Hezekiah's death.

None of these possible interpretations make much sense to me. When I attempt to make sense of the account at face value as an openness theologian would, I don't seem to get anywhere. Is God actually this dim in his understanding? God's limited knowledge of Hezekiah's response to Isaiah's first prophecy—a response that could have been predicted by most people—has now necessitated a turn in midstream. "No. You won't die. If I had known how you would respond to the prediction of your death I never would have made it in the first place. My mistake." Divine ignorance births divine error. I find this interpretation fairly jarring.

If I reject a face-value reading of the text, though, what does the text mean? As you rightfully comment, "It has to mean something. Just what is the anthropomorphic expression an expression of?" You then comment, "Thus classical theists are left with the problem of misleading biblical texts, or, at best, meaningless metaphors regarding the nature of God." I think you're moving too fast in your criticism. That is, I don't think the text is misleading, nor do I think the metaphor is meaningless.

What other exegetical possibilities present themselves that preserve a robust understanding of divine omniscience and capture the meaning of the metaphor well? Your interpretation demands that God in some way be in time, responding in time, rather than outside of time. How might the Hezekiah narrative make sense if God is outside of time? Let me toss out a possible interpretation, one that I think is plausible and makes coherent sense of the text. It comes from Paul Helm and hence is based on the eternalist perspective, i.e., God is outside of time. While

I'm finding the idea of middle knowledge increasingly interesting, I still find Helm's ideas thought-provoking and enlightening.

The case of Hezekiah is indeed intriguing. Does God genuinely change his mind? For an eternalist such as Helm, the idea of God changing his mind makes little sense. Why would God change his mind? What could possibly lead him to do so? Only the acquisition of new knowledge, it seems, a knowledge gained as time passes and new knowledge becomes available. God's immutability, steadfastness, and omniscience all appear threatened. In Helm's words, "Can this [God changing his mind] be made consistent with what the Bible says elsewhere about God's immutability and steadfastness? If God is steadfast, how could God's first utterance—that Hezekiah will not recover—be sincere?"

Must Hezekiah believe that God may change his mind for Hezekiah's fervent prayer to make sense? Helm says no, for Hezekiah could believe that God's eternal, timeless decree could be either that Hezekiah will die shortly, or that Hezekiah will live a number of years longer, if Hezekiah prays to the Lord and changes his ways. Hezekiah doesn't know which of these alternatives is true, and thus prays accordingly, asking that he might live longer. What Hezekiah must believe, Helm argues, is that "what God says on one occasion is not necessarily a *full* account of what God has decreed." God might well be disclosing only part of what is to take place, perhaps to elicit a certain response from Hezekiah. That is, maybe God is testing Hezekiah, after the pattern of other biblical characters. If so, God as a being who exists timelessly must act within time to test Hezekiah's character and elicit Hezekiah's prayer. How must God act to produce such change in Hezekiah's life? Isaiah's first prophecy and God's later modification of the initial prediction suffice perfectly to carry out God's purposes. How so?

Helm argues as follows:

1. Suppose that at $T_1$ God announces A (Hezekiah will die), which X (Hezekiah) notices at $T_1$.
2. At $T_2$ God announces not-A, which X (Hezekiah) notices at $T_2$. From the point of view of Hezekiah, there is a change "in precisely the same sense in which a human person may be said to have changed her mind if she sincerely declares she believes A at $T_1$ and then sincerely declares that she believes that not-A at $T_2$." That is, "over the period of time in question God is perceived to have willed what, had this been a human action, would make it reasonable to say that the person in question has changed her mind." God, however, is not time-bound. Thus, though there may be a formal contradiction between A at $T_1$ and not-A at $T_2$, the succession in time from $T_1$ to $T_2$ does "not require a real change in the will of

God." All along God's design had been to elicit the fervent prayer of Hezekiah. The initial prophecy has served just this purpose.

3. What God has actually decreed outside of time is not the recovery of Hezekiah but the recovery of Hezekiah "upon request." God's announcement of Hezekiah's death at $T_1$ was specifically designed to elicit the prayer request of Hezekiah.

4. Now comes a very important juncture in Helm's argument. Because God is not time-bound, God must use "accommodated language . . . to be able to interact with his creatures in temporal sequence." Accommodation, then, is absolutely necessary, precisely because God is not time-bound in the manner that human beings are. God has no choice but to accommodate his timeless perspective to the time-bound understanding of Hezekiah. "It is a logically necessary condition of dialogue between people, or between God and humankind, that the partners in the dialogue should appear to act and react in time." God accommodates himself to the demands of a time-framed dialogue. Humans have no choice in the matter.

5. God must accommodate himself to us, precisely because his nature and perspective are timeless and we are time-bound. Hence, if God is timelessly eternal (I realize this is a disputed point), creates creatures in time, and desires to teach them by testing them, "he must represent himself to them in such a way that it is natural for them to think of him as changing even though (strictly speaking) he does not change and even though those who are in time can see, on reflection, that he does not change."

6. A key question then raises its head: Is God deceiving or lying to us as he uses the language of accommodation? Helm argues that from an eternalist perspective, God is not deceiving Hezekiah. "The king would be being deceived only if he believed that God's announcement that he would die was unconditional. But why need Hezekiah believe this?"

I'm not sure I'm entirely convinced by Helm's argument, but I believe it is plausible and coherent. If God is not time-bound, God must constantly accommodate himself to his creatures' situation in time. Hence, in the Hezekiah narrative, God is neither lying nor deceiving Hezekiah. Rather, God is accomplishing his purposes within time by graciously accommodating himself to the needs and perceptions of his creature. Of course, if one holds that God is time-bound, Helm's argument may fail to convince.

Let me know what you think.

---

**Chris**

# 19 **John:** Impassibility and Prayer

**Dear Chris,**

Sorry for my delay in getting back to you. On Monday I met with the denominational commission looking into my views on open theism and inclusivism. I felt the meeting went very well. One of the members of the commission who is sharply critical of my views on inclusivism, an Arminian himself, seemed surprised to learn that all the people who are writing books attacking open theism are strong Calvinists or theological determinists. I hope to comment more on this in another letter.

In your last letter you examine the interchange between God and King Hezekiah in 2 Kings 20 to see if you can come up with a "plausible and coherent" interpretation of the text that is an alternative to the open theist interpretation. Let me complement you on your good work. I do not claim that anyone who disagrees with our reading of such texts is stupid or disingenuous. I deeply appreciate your attempt to explain what the text means rather than simply saying that it is an anthropomorphic expression and giving me a "What is wrong with you?" look. There are several issues on which I want to comment. The first one concerns your remark that "the openness model significantly modifies the traditional model." This is a very important charge and I will address it in a future letter.

You don't like the idea that God "learns something" from Hezekiah's prayer. You list a number of options as to what God might have learned, find them all unappetizing, and wonder whether this means that God

75

thinks something like, "Darn. If I'd known you were going to pray, Hezekiah, I would not have uttered the threat in the first place!" "Is God actually this dim?" I do not agree with your way of stating things so let me see if I can do better.

First, let's take a look at the context. In chapter nineteen Hezekiah has decided not to pay his annual "tribute" (taxes) to the king of Assyria. In response the Assyrian army marches on Jerusalem and demands an amount of gold and silver that could not possibly be met. The Assyrians boast that no gods have been able to stand before them, so the people of Jerusalem should not trust that Yahweh the God of Israel will be able to help them. In response Hezekiah sends one of his men to Isaiah the prophet, and Isaiah predicts that the Assyrians will go away. Note that Hezekiah does *not pray* here and, as it turns out, the prophetic word of Isaiah is only partially fulfilled. The Assyrians return with renewed threats and insults. Hezekiah takes their letter and goes to the temple and prays before Yahweh, describing the situation and giving Yahweh a reason why Yahweh should do what the king requests—so that the earth may know that Yahweh alone is God (19:19). In response Isaiah says, "Thus says Yahweh, the God of Israel, 'Because you have prayed to me about Sennacherib King of Assyria, I have heard you'" (19:20).

In fact, Isaiah gives a lengthy statement about what will happen to the Assyrians, gives a sign that these things will indeed take place—and then God acts quickly in answer to his prayer. It is interesting that when Hezekiah failed to pray, things did not go exactly as God wanted, but when he did pray, things happened. God even gives a reason why he will do what he is about to do: *because* Hezekiah prayed! Prayer or lack of it is an important part of this narrative.

Sometime later Hezekiah becomes ill and Isaiah is sent to the king to announce that he will not recover from this illness, but will die shortly. This is stated in no uncertain terms, for Isaiah uses the "Thus says the LORD" formula and puts it unconditionally (20:1). God does not say, "You will die unless you pray." The threat is given in stark unconditional terms. When we read the formula "Thus says the LORD," we typically think that there is no possibility for such a word to turn out differently. Yet Hezekiah does not accept this word! He again prays and gives God reasons why God should heal him and let him live. The king does not acquiesce in the presence of the prophetic word but challenges it. This is something that Abraham, Moses, Samuel, and others did. In response to the king's prayer, God sends Isaiah back to the king to announce: "Thus says the LORD . . . I have heard your prayer and seen your tears, behold I will heal you." The same unconditional prophetic formula "Thus says the LORD" occurs, but this time with the exact opposite content. Note that there is no repentance on the part of Hezekiah, for he has done nothing wrong. He simply prays. That is the crucial change in the situation. This certainly seems to be a case where the prayer of a righteous person accomplished much (James 5:16).

You ask why God would change his mind in a situation such as this. As I see it, God has chosen to relate with us in such a way that part of God's decision-making processes for certain situations involves what we do or do not do. God has chosen to be responsive to us as we develop in relationship with him. God has sovereignly decided that, for some situations, what God decides to do will be influenced (not determined) by whether we pray or not. With Hezekiah God is putting forth what will be unless something in the situation changes. Though God states the threat unconditionally, Hezekiah does not take this word of God to be the final word. It may yet be changed. This is so simply because God wants it to be this way. God does not have to be open to our input.

What new knowledge did God receive? The knowledge of what Hezekiah specifically wanted and why he wanted it. Though God knew all the possibilities of what Hezekiah might do in response to God's announcement, he now knows precisely which of those possibilities Hezekiah chose to enact. It is not that Hezekiah's response surprised God in the sense that he did something God did not know was possible. What God previously knew as possible God now knows as actual.

I see this same sort of relationship going on between Moses and God in Exodus 32, where God tells Moses to leave the divine presence because God is going to destroy the people and start the nation over again with Moses. Moses, however, does not take this word of God as God's final word and so he prays, giving God three reasons why God should not take this route. In response, God decides to go the way Moses wants to go, not because God has to go that way but because God values what Moses wants. Moses does not provide God with new information that God had failed to consider. What Moses provides God with is the route Moses prefers to go. God does not have to go that route, but he so values his friendship with Moses that God is willing to go down that path if that is what Moses wants to do.

Some people flinch at this, wondering if we then can ever trust God's word. If God says thus and such is going to happen, can we believe it? Well, God had told Eli in apparently unconditional terms that his sons and their sons would be priests forever in Israel. However, because they were so wicked God responded by removing Eli's line from the priesthood (1 Sam. 2:30). God said that his original plan was to go with Saul's line as a perpetual kingship in Israel (1 Sam. 13:13). However, due to Saul's disobedience God gave the kingship to David's line. In each of these situations God's seemingly unconditional word does not turn out to be the final word. At other times, however, God's word is the final word, as Samuel found out when he prayed all night long for God to allow Saul to remain king but God turned down Samuel's prayers (1 Sam. 15:11). We don't know when God has finally made up his mind. God simply invites us to make our requests known, even to argue with God.

The motif of God changing his mind (divine repentance) is a major one in the Old Testament (e.g., Gen. 6:6; Exod. 32:14; 1 Sam. 15:11, 35; Jer. 15; Joel 2:13). Some people tend to dismiss this theme, but it is an important one. God may change his mind because the people repent, because someone prays, or simply because the divine compassion elects to forgive (Hosea 11:8–9). In fact, Jonah runs the other way instead of delivering God's message of judgment because Jonah wants God to destroy Nineveh. When God does not destroy the Assyrians, Jonah is furious with God. When God asks why he is so mad, Jonah responds, "because I knew you were a God who changes his mind" (4:2). Jonah knew that the unconditional word of the Lord may not actually be unconditional.

Some critics respond by citing the three verses that declare that God does not change as proof that God does not really change his mind. "I the Lord do not change therefore you [Israel] are not destroyed" (Mal. 3:6). I find it interesting that theology books typically only quote the first half of the verse and ignore the context. "I the Lord do not change" is lifted out as an ultimate truth about the divine nature: it is impossible for God to change in any respect. The verse does not say this, however. What it says is that God is faithful to his covenant people and he refuses to allow them to be destroyed. Malachi is not stating an abstract philosophical principle—although that is the way many theology books treat it, out of context. The same is true of Numbers 23:19 and 1 Samuel 15:29 (which is a quote of Num. 23:19). God refuses in these two situations to change his mind. These texts do not say that it is impossible for God to change, only that in these specific situations God will not change his mind no matter what the human response is. You believe that my view threatens "God's immutability, steadfastness, and omniscience." Not in the least. God's *nature* does not change, but God can change in his thoughts, will, and emotions. God is not wishy-washy, but neither is God a stone. God is steadfast to his covenant, but the exact way in which he carries out its fulfillment is not set in concrete. Christianity does not require an absolutely immutable God, one who cannot change in any respect—it only requires a faithful God.

You explain the Hezekiah case (and I presume these others) as God "testing" the king. In your view God always knew he was going to heal him and that he would not die shortly. You say this because you don't want God to look insincere or deceitful. Though I believe the "testing" interpretation is a valid one, I don't believe it is the best interpretation. You follow Paul Helm's explanation, so let me comment on it. First, Helm is a theological determinist, meaning that nothing happens except what God specifically wants to happen. God is in meticulous control of everything that happens. So, for Helm, Hezekiah cannot respond differently than God had eternally decreed Hezekiah would respond. If God had not wanted the king to pray, then the king would not have prayed. Hezekiah simply cannot respond differently than God has determined. True, Hezekiah does not know what God has eternally decreed, but so what? Whichever way Hezekiah responds—whether he prays or not—will be precisely what God ordained he would do. Hezekiah could not fail to pray in this situation. That does not seem like a personal relationship to me.

Moreover, when it comes to God's part in this situation you make it sound as though God was timelessly responding to Hezekiah's prayer. The notion of a "timeless response" is, in my opinion, a contradiction in terms. You have one event following another and that involves time. You seem to be saying that a timeless being experiences time. If so, it makes no sense. Also, to hold that God is responding to something outside of himself is to give up divine impassibility, since you are then saying that God is affected by creatures. To compound matters, it calls into question your affirmation of immutability, for a response is a change. If you affirm that God is impassible, immutable in all respects, and timeless, then it is inconsistent to also say that God responds to our prayers. Since many, many Christians believe that God does respond to our prayers, I think you will find this a tough sell.

Helm makes it clear that he rejects any "real change in the will of God." Actually, he rejects all change of any kind in God. That is why he says that the dialogue between God and humans "should appear to act and react in time." God is not reacting at all because, as Helm argues, God is immutable in all respects, is not affected by us (impassible), and is timeless, so God has no "reaction." Besides, everything that happens is precisely what God wanted to happen in the first place so what would there be to react to?

I think your "testing" interpretation runs into problems elsewhere as well. You say that this is why God has to use "accommodated language" with us. Hmm. Could not God have simply stated the truth to Hezekiah: "You will die *unless* you pray?" Could not God have said, "I am not really grieved about human sin (Gen. 6:6), it is just that you are experiencing my judgment on sin?" Were the biblical writers just intellectual dunces that could not understand the way God really was? Thank goodness someone has figured out that all this biblical language about God's grieving, being angry, changing his mind, and using words such as "if," "perhaps," and "maybe" do not depict reality but are only accommodations for us "duller folk." It is wonderful that at least someone knows the truth behind the accommodated language of Scripture. However, I see *no biblical basis* for affirming impassibility or absolute immutability.

In Exodus 3:16 God tells Moses to "go" back to Egypt, implying that their conversation is over. In 3:18 God says that the elders of Israel will believe that God has sent Moses. However, Moses replies, "What if they don't believe you have sent me?" (4:1). In response God gives Moses a sign but then says that in case the elders don't believe that sign, here is a second one, and if they don't believe the first two signs, here is a third sign. According to your view, God eternally knew that the elders would not believe without the signs. Hence, God needed to have Moses ask his question in order for God to provide the signs. If so, then it seems that God did not really mean for Moses to go in 3:16, since he needed Moses to stay there and ask his question. Moreover, the use of "if" by God in this passage must, on your account, be purely hypothetical, since God eternally knew precisely how many signs it would take for the elders to believe. Also, you have the problem of God asserting that the elders would believe, while knowing that they would believe only after Moses questioned God. God seems less than aboveboard in this view. You can escape this problem if you say that God knew the elders would believe without the signs, but God gives them to Moses as a concession to Moses' doubts. But then you have to explain why God keeps saying, "If the elders don't believe this sign, then here is another one." It seems the signs were for the benefit of the elders, not Moses.

A little later in this passage Moses says that he is not a good speaker and God seems to switch to "Plan B" by allowing Aaron to do the speaking. Again, one could interpret this text as another example of God "testing" Moses. In this case God would not be changing to "Plan B" because God had always planned to have Aaron do the speaking. I see a problem with this explanation, however. Why does God get angry with Moses (4:14) if God always foreknew that Aaron would do the speaking? Even worse, why does God get angry with Moses if it was always part of God's plan that Moses would *not* do the speaking? If everything is working out exactly according to God's plan, then why is God getting angry? Is God angry with himself? If God is impassible as you say, then God does not really get angry, for that would mean that God was affected by a creature. So again this text does not mean what it seems to mean. If God is impassible then it makes no sense to say that God gets angry, for the only being God could be angry with is himself. In your view, God suffers from some significant psychological problems.

A similar problem arises if we return to the promises God made to Eli and Saul. If God never intended to make the priesthood run through the house of Eli and the kingship through the house of Saul, then why did God make those promises? Was God deceitful? According to your view God is making promises to these people knowing that he will never keep his word because God has immutably and impassibly willed that the priesthood and kingship will pass to other families. That seems unethical on God's part. On your view, how could we trust what God says? So, even though interpreting these texts as God "testing" the people is a valid interpretation, I think it has serious problems. It is no "test" when God has decreed exactly what will take place. I think your view ultimately calls the integrity of God into question.

I have to get ready for a class. I hope what I've said is understandable.

---

Your friend,
John

# 20 **Chris:** Impassibility and Ontology

Dear John,

I want to return to our discussion of God's impassibility, both to extend the previous conversation and to respond to your recent letter. Do you recall a comment you made during our debate on openness at Huntington? I don't want to quote you incorrectly, but I believe the gist of your comment concerned the static nature of an impassible God. I have read Clark Pinnock saying much the same thing.

Clark, for example, in *Most Moved Mover*, compares the Greek view of God with the biblical one. Clark understands the Greek view to picture God as "absolute," "timeless," "unchangeable," "unconditioned," "unchanging," "impassible," and "totally in control." By way of contrast, the biblical God is "dynamic," "vulnerable," "sympathetic," "accessible," and "committed to relationships." Hence the openness model is designed to reflect more effectively the deeply personal nature of the biblical God, a wonder that Clark feels has been deeply obscured by Hellenic philosophy and the theology built on it. Clark hopes the "openness model will help us communicate belief in God more intelligibly to people at large and liberate believers to love God more passionately."

Does impassibility serve only to blur the biblical picture of God? Both you and Clark conclude that if God is impassible, God cannot genuinely respond to us. Words such as inert, static, unresponsive, lifelessly monolithic, impersonal, passionless, and lifeless come to mind as appropriate descriptors of the impassible Greek God. I can understand

82

how impassibility might be interpreted along these lines, but I believe that such an interpretation is a misunderstanding.

What if God's impassibility and immutability actually facilitate his ability to love with intense, infinite passion? Though Clark feels that Thomism's emphasis on immutability "must be criticized for threatening real relationships," perhaps Thomas's ideas might actually enhance our understanding of God's passionate nature. Creatures change because they further actualize their potential for good, thus moving closer toward perfection, or further actualize their potential for evil, thus becoming less perfect (an idea and phrasing I have borrowed from Weinandy's *First Things* article). God, however, cannot be further actualized because God, as Thomas argues, is "pure act." He cannot become more perfect. Weinandy believes two points immediately follow from the reality of God's perfect actualization.

First, God performs acts that are grounded in his perfect and complete actualization. Only God can perform these acts. The act of creation would be such an act. Hence, God as perfect act creates a world separate from himself, a creative act "that assures creation's immediate, intimate, dynamic, and enduring relationship with God as God truly is in all His transcendent otherness."

Second, as pure act, "all that pertains to God's nature is in pure act." Huh? Weinandy suggests thinking of divine impassibility this way: while both God and a rock may be impassible, "they are so for polar opposite reasons." A rock is impassible because it is an inert, impersonal object and lacks the characteristics that "pertain to love." God is impassible "because His love is perfectly in act ('God is love') and no further self-constituting act could make Him more loving." Impassibility does not extinguish or eliminate the possibility of passion within God. Why should it? In Weinandy's words, "God is absolutely impassible because He is absolutely passionate in His love." Human beings, as creations of God, are the immediate objects of God's passionate, intimate, impassible love.

Weinandy argues that this same impassible, passionate love characterizes Trinitarian relationships. The persons of the Trinity are impassible, not because their love is static, lifeless, inert, or unresponsive, but "because they are entirely constituted as who they are in their passionate and dynamic, fully actualized relationship of love." Impassibility within the divine nature, rather than quenching passion and reciprocity, actually describes divine love's infinite fulfillment as the Father eternally begets the Son and breathes forth (spirates) the Spirit. As Weinandy puts it, "human beings can actually abide within the very trinitarian relationships by being conformed by the Holy Spirit into the likeness of the Son and so becoming children of the loving Father."

Can such a God suffer? Indeed, would we desire for him to suffer if we realized what must be sacrificed for suffering to occur within the divine nature? While God is related to all creation as its creator, God exists, in Weinandy's words, "in His own distinct ontological order as the Creator." This is not something we should lament. Rather, God's ontological distinctness ensures that the evil and sin that mar the present created order cannot overcome or defeat God or contaminate God's goodness. Suffering within the divine nature would necessitate a blending or mixing of ontological orders that must remain separate. I think Weinandy's right. In fact, it is the suffering God who ends up more closely resembling the gods of the Greek pantheon, gods who are surely related to their creation but also subject to its evil and sin.

Does the model of divine passibility actually provide all it seems to promise? For instance, exactly what do we mean when we speak of God suffering with us? Does God grieve as we grieve? Suffer pain as we suffer pain? Experience sequentially sensations or emotions such as pain, suffering, happiness, and love? I can make some sense of pain and suffering on a human level. I experience pain, for example, as the nerve endings of my central nervous system communicate information to my spinal gate. I experience emotions of sadness or anger because I live in the midst of a fallen world and am subject to the evil that is present there. I am also subject to the evil present within me. I experience life sequentially, one moment at a time, from one situation to another. At this moment I'm happy. At another moment I grieve. My responses are related to the situation in which I find myself; or related to past, remembered events; or to future, envisioned situations. In addition, my grief and happiness are often related to, and sometimes grounded in, my limited knowledge. I know and recognize very little of the complexity that surrounds my own actions, the actions of others, and God's overall providential activity.

Can we describe God's relationship to the world and the characteristics of this relationship in the same way in which I analyze and describe my own physical and emotional responses to life? I don't know how to speak of this relationship apart from the use of metaphors such as the biblical authors employ. If God has emotional reactions of sadness and grief, joy and happiness, which are exactly like mine and subject to the same elations and descents I experience emotionally in response to my changing circumstances, how can we make coherent sense of these ups and downs within God? Imagine the millions of contrary emotions God would be experiencing. As Weinandy puts it, "If God did need to adapt and re-adapt and re-adapt Himself again to every personal situation in every momentary instance, He would be perpetually entangled in an unending internal emotional whirligig."

What do the different biblical metaphors mean to teach us, then, concerning God's differing responses to us? They communicate to us God's impassible love manifested in concrete situations. God is not changing from anger to sadness to joy. Because God's love "is perfectly existent, all aspects that pertain to that love are fully existent." The appropriate aspect of the divine love manifests itself to us situationally. Exactly what do I mean?

To use Weinandy's metaphor, "God is always in 'go position.'" That is, "when a person repents of sin, God need not change the manner of His love within Himself from that of an admonishing love to that of a forgiving love." From our perspective, however, the manifestation of God's fully actualized love does change according to our situation. When I sin I experience God's love as "rebuke and admonishment." When I repent I "experience God's love as compassion and forgiveness." God's impassible love burns unchangeably like a column of fire. Its manifestation within my experience changes as my situation changes.

I would likely embrace divine passibility if the model of a passible, suffering God was the only viable alternative available. It seems, though, that the gospel provides me with an even better model, for in Christ I encounter the transcendent, incarnate God. In this model, key ontological boundaries are maintained, while simultaneously God draws near to us in the incarnate Word. As I have maintained in earlier correspondence, the incarnation allows, even commands me, to affirm that "God suffers"—the very affirmation modern theologians long to proclaim. The incarnation, though, also prevents me from blurring ontological categories that must remain distinct, as I have mentioned earlier in this letter.

If we fail to preserve these absolute ontological differences, key divine attributes may well end up falling by the wayside. In your response to my previous letter on impassibility you argue that texts such as "I the LORD do not change, therefore you, O sons of Jacob, are not consumed" (Mal. 3:6) and "Jesus Christ is the same yesterday, today and forever" (Heb. 13:8) "are not about absolute immutability. . . . These texts are referring to God's steadfast love. God's love for Israel does not fail, thus they are [not] destroyed, says Malachi. Open theists hold that the divine nature does not change (God's love, power, wisdom, and faithfulness) but God can and does change in his emotions, thoughts, will, and actions."

My response? God's steadfast love is immutable precisely because it is ontologically grounded in the divine being itself. In short, the moral attributes you praise in God must have a sufficient ontological basis. It is this wondrous ontological grounding that establishes, or ontically supports, the moral qualities you rightly applaud. I contend with Weinandy that "for God to be ethically immutable, unchangeably loving and good," God must be "ontologically immutable—that is, ontologically unchanging in His perfect love and goodness."

In fact, it is only by maintaining God's transcendence, with accompanying characteristics such as immutability and impassibility, that we coherently express and worship the Trinity's wondrous ability to save us from sin. The transcendence/incarnation model assures me that God draws near to me in my suffering and sin, but is not overcome by them. All the benefits of the openness model without its defects!

"Hold on," you might say. Indeed, in your last letter you asked a number of important questions. One that keeps coming back to me concerns Jesus. "Does Jesus reveal what God is really like?" That's a great question and deserves a careful response. But this letter has already run on too long. I'll be writing soon.

_____

**With warm greetings,**
**Chris**

# 21 **John:** Thomism

Dear Chris,

So now you are a Thomist! You do present a "moving target," since you switch around from one position to another. In this discussion of impassibility you draw on the work of Weinandy, a Roman Catholic theologian who utilizes the philosophy of Thomas Aquinas (Thomism) to argue that God is impassible but not static. Aquinas drew on the metaphysics of the Greek philosopher Aristotle. The work of Weinandy is intriguing, although I find his arguments weak—especially the ones he supposedly draws from Scripture. Aquinas, of course, is one of the luminaries of Christian thought for whom I have great respect. However, I'm not attracted to Thomism as a solution to the debate between us. To explain why, I must begin with Aristotle.

Aristotle's interest lies in the "problem of change"—explaining how and why there is change or motion in the universe. In searching for an explanation for change he arrives at a God who is essentially a metaphysical principle needed only to explain motion. Aristotle argued that there must be an "unmoved mover" as the first cause of all motion. Though the universe is eternal, it must be eternally dependent on something. But the unmoved mover must move the universe without itself moving or changing in any way. For if it itself moved, then it would no longer be perfect, for "any change would be change for the worse." The way the unmoved mover moves the universe is by "final causation," not "efficient causation." That is, if God actually pushed or fashioned the world in any way, that would mean a change in God. Instead, God is the final cause or goal (*telos*) of the universe. God starts motion not because he acts as an agent but rather by simply being so beautiful and perfect that the universe desires (*eros*) to be like him, and so it moves toward God—but God does not move toward the world.

God must be absolutely independent of all others. God cannot even choose to enter into relationships with others, for if God enters into any sort of relationship with the world, God would then in some sense be dependent on the world. In any relationship, one party depends on another party for the relationship to exist. For example, a master is dependent on the slave in order to be master. Consequently, God has no real relationship with us.

This unmoved mover is pure actuality and possesses no potentiality (possibility of change). To have potential is to be susceptible to change, so God must have only actuality. This God is absolutely immutable. It also follows that this God cannot be affected by any other being—he is impassible, since he has no room for change. Then what does this completely actual being do? It thinks! Of what does it think? "It must be of itself that the divine thought thinks," since to think of anything else would be less than perfect. If God knows about us, God cannot be perfect. Moreover, for God to "receive" anything would imply dependency and deficiency. God cannot even receive our worship, let alone hear our prayers. Aristotle's God is unaware of the existence of the world and certainly cannot enter into relations with others. "Since he is in need of nothing, God cannot have need of friends, nor will he have any." God is literally apathetic toward the world as he has no concern for or feelings toward it. God does not interact with the world nor enter into covenantal relations with humans—God only "contemplates." God is neither providential nor righteous with regard to the world: "God is not an imperative ruler." For Aristotle, the unmoved mover is a metaphysical necessity needed to explain motion in his philosophical system. Though this God may not be religiously satisfying, several aspects of Aristotle's unmoved mover found their way into the Christian tradition.

Thomas Aquinas, the apex of medieval theology, sought to harmonize biblical statements about God with the classical synthesis and especially with the works of Aristotle. Clearly, Thomas, as a Christian, could not accept all that Aristotle said about God, since the Christian God most certainly knows that we exist and has come to redeem us in Jesus. Though there is nothing wrong with making use of philosophical resources in seeking to elucidate the Christian faith, I do not believe Aquinas successfully modified Aristotle's apathetic God enough.

Thomas believes that God is pure actuality containing no potentiality. That is, there can be no "becoming" (change of any kind) for God, since he is eternally actualized. When this idea is applied to divine election of individuals to salvation, it is clear that election does not depend on God's foreknowledge of how individual humans will respond, since that would make God dependent on creatures. Instead, God simply chooses those he will save. The "Arminian" view of salvation must be completely rejected, for humans have no "say" in their election whatsoever. If God's knowledge of what would happen in history depended on the creature, then God would be dependent and passive. But God is completely independent, immutable, and impassible. One of the things that Aquinas wants to protect in this discussion is the notion that the being of God is not altered by creation, since God would be God even without a creation. This is an important point and I agree with it. However, one can uphold that God is the independent creator without defending it by this particular philosophy. The problem with going with Aristotle here is that it makes it difficult, if not impossible, to think of God's "relationship" with us in personal terms. For Aquinas, the creatures' relationship with God is "real," while God's relationship to the creation is only "logical." God is like a stone column, he says, around which we move. Our relation to the column changes as we move, but the column never changes in relation to us. There is no give-and-take relationship with God.

Although this metaphor expresses God's steadfastness, I think it utterly fails when it comes to expressing the biblical portrait of God's relationship with us. The Thomistic understanding of God may be appealing to those who want a spirituality that emphasizes contemplation of the divine metaphysical principle, but it cancels out the give-and-take spirituality found, for instance, in the relationships between God and Abraham and God and Moses. Since God cannot receive anything, God simply cannot have the types of relationships with humans that God is depicted as having in the Bible. For Aquinas, our prayers can never affect God. Rather, God has ordained our prayers as a means of bringing about whatever the divine will has decreed. This cancels out the view of prayer held by many Christians. If that is what you want to do, okay, but please be up front about it.

Philosophical systems such as Aristotle's have been used by Christians to try to answer specific problems. That is legitimate. However, I think that the problems raised by many of these systems are worse than the problems they solve. A doctor prescribed an antibiotic for my father-in-law that caused a reaction that almost killed him. Of course, the doctor was well intentioned, but the medicine wound up causing more serious problems than the original illness. I think this is what has happened in Christian theology with respect to some aspects of the doctrine of God. As the zenith of medieval thought, Aquinas epitomizes the tensions of the biblical-classical synthesis in attempting to reconcile the God of historical action depicted in the Bible with the understanding of God as metaphysical principle needed to explain the cosmos.

Aquinas said the best name for God is "He who is," for God is the only being whose essence it is to exist. For me, the New Testament name for God is Father, Son, and Holy Spirit, and we know this God through the activities of the Trinitarian persons in salvation. If you desire to preserve the God of salvation history, then do not go this route. Begin with the God who comes to us in history and especially in Jesus, rather than beginning with a metaphysical principle used to explain why the world exists. After all, I know you approve of Athanasius, who argued from salvation in Jesus to the deity of Jesus against Arius. I think I'm defending precisely that sort of move here.

You say that God cannot become more perfect. Following Plato and Aristotle you assume that "perfect" means without change of any kind. However, I prefer to think of "perfect" in dynamic terms: relational perfection. God is always in perfect relationship with us, and as the relationship changes so God changes. It would be less than perfect *not* to change in a changing relationship. Ulysses had to be tied to his ship's mast in order to resist the Siren's call. Unless we tie ourselves to the mast of the God revealed in Jesus, we will end up following Plato's call to theological shipwreck.

You suggest that your approach will protect God from resembling the gods of the Greek pantheon. It has been a common complaint for two millennia that the biblical portrait of God is overly anthropomorphic, and even today critics of biblical personalism refer to this view of God as a "spook." In my opinion, the biblical writers present a view of God that falls between the fickle and capricious gods of Olympus on the one hand and the rationally understandable God of philosophical theology on the other. It is ironic that you chided me a few letters back for being overly concerned with rationality—now you are the one putting forward a fully logical and rational explanation of God that smoothes out all the problems of the biblical God who is too much like us.

You don't want God to suffer, for then God would be "subject" to evil and sin. We experience, you say, negative emotions of sadness and anger because we live in a fallen world. God does not live in a fallen world and is not subject to evil so God does not experience sadness and anger. I have two points to make in response. First, what about positive emotions? Does God experience them? If the Holy Trinity eternally experiences love among the three persons, then why not say that God experiences joy and satisfaction? If God loves us, is it then not possible that God experiences joy when we respond appropriately to God's love? You will reject this, because for you God cannot receive anything from us, including our love. If God could receive anything, then God would be less than perfect. So it seems to me that the God of pure actuality is locked into his own self-love and cannot be open to others. Weinandy argues that the Son of God cannot suffer in his divinity because "suffering is caused by the loss of some good." Since God does not "lose" anything, God does not suffer. But it seems to me that God does indeed "lose" something: he loses humanity in sin and works to restore us to himself. Did not God lose the love relationship with us due to our rebellion? The God whose heart breaks in Hosea 11 and who wanted to gather Israel under his wings (Matt. 23:27) is a God who does lose something he cherishes. To put it simply, one may read the biblical story as a romance: boy loses girl, boy gets girl back.

This leads to my second point. If God does not experience sadness and grief because God is not involved in this fallen world, then where is the God who redeems humanity? If God cannot become deeply involved in and affected by this world, then I think you have sacrificed the God of Jesus Christ to a metaphysical principle that protects God from all change, since a God who would get into the nitty-gritty of our sin would be less than perfect. This is not the God I see in Jesus.

You think that if God was affected by this fallen world, then God would be subject to experiencing "millions of contrary emotions." Though I believe that God suffers, I think that God suffers in a way proper to God. I don't claim that God suffers exactly in the same way we do, for God is the creator and I'm a creature. I do not profess to even begin to grasp how God could experience millions of different emotions due to the millions of different relationships God experiences at each moment, any more than I claim to understand how God hears millions of prayers each moment.

Let me return for a moment to the notion that God cannot receive anything. In his book *The Triune Identity*, Robert Jenson observes that Arius, along with many others, held God to be a "simple" being, one who has no differentiation. But the Nicene Creed affirmed that the Son is "out of the being of the Father," for the Son is "true God of true God, begotten not created." This differentiates the Son from the Father so that the godhead has internal relations. In Jenson's words: *"To be God is to be related.* With that the fathers contradicted the main principle of Hellenic theology." He goes on to comment on the statement that the Son is "begotten of the Father." "To be God is not only to give being, it is also to receive being. And there went the rest of Plato." This is a profound insight by Jenson: the writers of the Nicene Creed affirmed that God, as God, could be relational and that God was capable of receiving and not merely giving. Though Christian theologians have not consistently followed through on this insight (see Catherine LaCugna's *God For Us: The Trinity and Christian Life*), it is right there in the creed. Hence I feel in good company in maintaining, against you, that God, as God, can be open to the creation and receive prayers, worship, love (which includes the possibility of the pain of rejection).

You attempt to have your cake and eat it too when you say that "the incarnation allows, even commands me to affirm that 'God suffers.'" I am quite baffled now because you have been arguing up to this point that suffering is bad so God does not suffer, but now you reverse yourself and say that divine suffering is a good thing. Well, which is it, good or bad? You claim that via the incarnation "God draws near to me in my suffering and sin." I agree wholeheartedly but I wonder what you really mean. How does God, as God, "draw near" to our sin if God cannot experience this fallen world? You use gospel language here, but your view does not really allow God to experience this. I think you want to hold onto the gospel's view that God's suffering for us is a good thing, but you are torn by your commitment to Hellenic theology in which suffering is bad.

What is it that you want to protect that you believe I'm giving up? Following Weinandy you suggest that I'm sacrificing the "absolute ontological differences" between God and us. Am I giving up the important distinction between creator and creatures? No. I affirm that the triune God would exist even without any creation. God does not need a creation in order for God to exist. God has being even apart from us. However, if you push too hard on the word "absolute" in "absolute ontological difference," you end up making God absolutely different from us—having nothing in common. The problem with this is that you and I cannot know that which is completely, one hundred percent, different from ourselves. If we have nothing in common with God, not personhood, thoughts, love, relationality—absolutely nothing, then we cannot know anything about God nor can we have any sort of personal relationship with God. We could say that "God loves us" but it would have no meaning whatsoever. I don't see you wanting to go that route. I suggest we say that God created us different from himself but no more different than God intended us to be. We are creatures made in the "image of God" and so have some sort of similarity to God. We are different but not absolutely different. You suggest that God must be ontologically immutable in all respects in order to have steadfast love toward us. Again, I think this is overkill. God's nature is immutable: the divine love, power, wisdom, and faithfulness never fail. But God can change in some respects and can receive from us.

It is no problem in my view for God to "draw near" to us in the incarnation and suffer with us and for us, since this is what God is like in the triune identity. You want to use philosophical principles to "correct" the biblical portrait of God. We do use philosophy and science to "correct" biblical teaching from time to time. For instance, we no longer believe the earth sits on a foundation, nor do we believe that the earth is the center of the solar system as did the biblical writers. So, although it is legitimate in principle to use philosophical principles to "override" what biblical authors taught God was like, we should be up front about what we are doing. The Hellenic principles you utilize in reading Scripture do more harm than good. Also, I want to point out again that you have *never* given me a single *biblical* reason to affirm divine impassibility.

Whew! This is too long. I need to get to a basketball game—our college team is in the second round of the playoffs. My prayers are with you as you prepare to go to Thailand.

John

# 22 **Chris:** The Revelation of God in Jesus

Dear John,

In this letter I want to respond to the interesting question you posed in an earlier letter (letter 17) concerning impassibility: "Does Jesus reveal what God is really like?" I'm not sure whether I agree or disagree with the Calvinist critic who said, "You cannot use Jesus to establish what God is like because Jesus is also human." My agreement or disagreement would depend on what the Calvinist meant by "establish." If this critic meant to say that in the incarnation we can observe or perceive only the human nature of Christ, I would disagree.

I wasn't sure whether you meant to argue in your earlier letter that the tradition of the church affirms that all we see in Christ is his human nature. Am I misunderstanding you? If not, I don't believe you're correct. I'm also hesitant to accept the distinction you make between God's self-disclosure and what I understand as God's accommodation or condescension to us in the incarnation.

God does disclose himself to us in Christ. How? By condescending or accommodating himself to us in the wondrous and mysterious manner of the incarnation. Hence, many of the things Jesus said and did can teach us about God. Am I wrong, however, to draw a distinction between the humanity and divinity of Christ as I interpret the gospels? I don't think so, but your good questions do provide food for thought and are surely worth working through carefully.

Let's take a closer look at your argument. It appears to run something like this:

1. Does Jesus reveal what God is really like?
2. The "tradition" contains a "problem": it affirms that Jesus is fully God and yet holds that "what we actually see in Jesus is only his human nature."
3. Key texts indicate that "Jesus discloses to us the very nature of God" (cf. Heb. 1:3; John 14:9; Col. 2:9). If what we see in Jesus is only his human nature, what are we to make of these texts?
4. Jesus is the "clearest instance of God's self-disclosure to us. The things that Jesus said and did are what God is like."
5. This last point remains true unless I have "some presumed concept of God" that I use to "filter the revelation of God." As you ask, "Do you have a presupposed notion of what God must be like (*dignum Deo*) that you then impose on the biblical text and Jesus, so that you know that the sufferings of Jesus are merely human, not divine sufferings?"
6. If the divine Word "genuinely suffers in his humanity," how can this occur if "the divine Son cannot suffer"?
7. What did the Son empty himself of in becoming incarnate (Phil. 2:7)? The Son cannot give up "certain divine attributes such as omniscience" and still remain divine. The incarnation cannot involve "a surrender of divinity."
8. Hence, if Jesus is the disclosure of what God is like, we may need "to modify our preconceived notions of what is fitting for God to be. . . . Perhaps self-giving, self-sacrifice, and self-limitation is part of what the loving Trinity is like. For me, what Jesus is like discloses what God is like."
9. Does God change? "The divine Son was not always incarnate, that sure seems like a change to me!"

How to respond? What does the incarnation teach us about God? Perhaps we can ask the question in a different way. What is Jesus teaching us about God and about human beings? I think the second question is better. Why? Jesus was both God and human. Thus, in trying to make sense of the texts that speak of Christ's person and work, we need to keep three things in mind: Jesus is God, Jesus is human, and divinity and humanity have been joined together in a personal union in Christ. If we forget or confuse these three propositions, we will have difficulty making sense of the New Testament. Luther wrote, for instance, that the devil continually attacks the church's understanding of Christ as both God and human. "Now he does not want to allow that He is God, then, again, he does not want to allow that He is man."

What are the hermeneutical and theological principles the church has employed in interpreting texts concerning Christ? I like Athanasius's illustration of the skilled interpreter as an honest money changer. For instance, how do we determine whether a specific text about Jesus is intended to teach us about "what God is like" or what a human being "is like"? Can we simply argue, as you appear to do, that all texts concerning Jesus are designed to teach us what God is like? The possibility surely exists that some of these texts mean to teach us important truths about human beings. After all, Jesus was both divine and human. It would not be surprising, then, to find some texts focusing on Christ's deity and others on his humanity.

Athanasius argues that "expressions used about His [Christ's] Godhead and His becoming man are to be interpreted with discrimination and suitable to the particular context. . . . He who expounds concerning His Godhead is not ignorant of what belongs to His coming in the flesh; but discerning each as a skilled and 'approved money changer,' he will walk in the straight way of piety; when therefore he speaks of His weeping, he knows that the Lord, having become man, while He exhibits His human character in weeping, as God raises up Lazarus." The honest money changer would become a dishonest one by shortchanging either the divine or the human nature of Christ. Oden comments, "The honest money changer keeps the two currencies (divinity and humanity) in fitting congruence as one reads narrative after narrative." Thus, certain texts concerning Christ do teach me "what God is like," but others teach me what a human being "is like." In addition, some texts may simply be referring to Christ without carefully distinguishing between the two natures.

I often refer to Cyril of Alexandria concerning the issue of impassibility. It's interesting to note that as the Nestorian controversy finally began to settle, the Formula of Union between Cyril and the bishops of Antioch (A.D. 433) advised biblical interpreters to distinguish between gospel narratives that had primary reference to the one person of Christ or to one of the two natures. "As for the words of the gospels and of the apostles concerning the Lord, we know that theologians have considered some as *common* because they are said of the *one person (prosopon)*, while they have distinguished others as applying to the *two natures (physeis)*, reserving those which befit God to Christ in His *divinity*, while assigning those which are lowly to Christ in His *humanity*." The problem the interpreter faces, of course, concerns what the focus of a particular text is. Is the one person of Christ in view in a given passage, or one of the natures? This has been a continuing question for church exegetes over the centuries. John IV, for instance, wrote to Constantius in A.D. 641 that sometimes when a writer is "teaching about the supreme nature, he is completely silent about the human nature, but sometimes when treating of the human dispensation, he does not touch on the mystery of His divinity."

You are right in pointing me to texts such as Colossians 2:9, where Paul teaches that "in Christ all the fullness of the Deity lives in bodily form." I don't doubt this for a moment. When I look at Christ I do see God. The question, however, is whether every text concerning Christ is pointing to, or illustrating a truth about, his divinity. The church has, as far as I know, frequently used the model of *perichoresis* to make good sense of texts such as Colossians. That is, the divine nature in a wonderful, embracing movement ("proceeding around"; "walking around on all sides") "penetrates and perfects every aspect of the human," with the human "pervaded by the divine" (Oden's words). We don't have a mixture of the divine and the human in the incarnation. Rather, in Christ the divine pervades his humanity, much like iron being pervaded by heat. The iron remains iron while simultaneously penetrated by fire.

Of course, the analogy breaks down if too much weight is placed on it. Analogical language is just that—analogical. John of Damascus writes that "examples do not have to be absolutely and unfailingly exact, for, just because it is an example, one must find in it that which is like and that which is unlike. For likeness in everything would be identity and not an example, which is especially true with divine things. So, in the matter of theology and the Incarnation, it is impossible to find an absolutely perfect example."

My point so far is that yes, Jesus shows us what God is like, but this statement needs careful nuancing if we are to make good sense of the New Testament. Why? Christ is both divine and human. So I don't think we can immediately conclude that Jesus' suffering must mean that God suffers within the divine essence. Luther, for instance, drew a careful distinction concerning who suffered in the suffering of Christ. "If I believe that only the human nature has suffered for me, I have a Savior of little Worth. . . . It is the person that suffers and dies. Now the person is true God; therefore it is rightly said: 'The Son of God suffers.' For although the divinity does not suffer, yet the person which is God suffers in His humanity. . . . In His own nature, God cannot die; but now God and man are united in one person, so that the expression 'God's death' is correct, when the man dies who is one thing or one person with God." Luther's understanding seems quite similar to Cyril's.

Neither Luther nor Cyril seems to struggle, at least not in any detail, with the question you raise about the suffering of the Word. That is, as you put it, if the divine Word "genuinely suffers in his humanity," how can this occur if "the divine Son cannot suffer"? I suppose their answer would be that the Son suffers in the humanity the Word has assumed in the incarnation. How the Son suffers in such a manner remains incomprehensible and ineffable to me, but if we drain all incomprehensibility out of the incarnation I'm not sure we still have the wondrous reality we began with!

For the sake of thoroughness and perhaps overkill, let me go back to some earlier points I've made in this letter. You won't be surprised that Tom Oden has helped me to understand the church's reflection on Christ's attributes. At times Jesus did things that clearly manifested his divine nature. These things can teach us, as you put it, "what God is like." There were other things that Christ did, however, that teach us what genuine humanity is like. For instance, Jesus experienced physical suffering, emotional suffering, powerlessness, and physical death. He was able to experience these realities of human life precisely because he possesses a genuine human nature. The divine-human union in Christ enables, then, the second person of the Trinity to suffer pain in his humanity. As John of Damascus puts it, "It was in one nature that He worked miracles and in another that He endured suffering." Indeed, as I have argued, precisely because it is God the Word who has united himself with human nature, we can speak of God suffering. John of Damascus describes this wonder well: "Wherefore, the Lord of Glory is even said to have been crucified, although His divine nature did not suffer; and the Son of Man is confessed to have been in heaven before His passion, as the Lord Himself has said."

The economy of salvation enables me both to say "Jesus is what God is like" and to say "Jesus is what a human being is like." That is, Jesus as the second Adam demonstrates the glory of what a genuinely human person really is. If Jesus only shows me "what God is like," half the wondrous reality of the incarnation disappears. Gregory of Nazianzus captures both sides of the economy well:

He hungered—but He fed thousands . . .

He was wearied, but He is the Rest of them that are weary . . .

He was heavy with sleep, but He walked lightly over the sea . . .

He prays, but He hears prayer.

He weeps, but He causes tears to cease.

He asks where Lazarus was laid, for He was Man; but He raises Lazarus, for He was God.

> He is sold, and very cheap, for it is only thirty pieces of silver; but He redeems the world . . .
>
> He dies . . . but He gives life . . .

Gregory helps us avoid the very error I think you are committing, namely, overlooking the logic of the economy. When we fail to observe the inherent rhythms of the economy of incarnation and salvation, we inevitably end up blurring essential distinctions. We, for instance, can err by identifying human characteristics of Christ as predicates of his divine nature. I think you do so when you contend that Christ's sufferings teach us that God suffers within the divine nature itself.

The incarnate Word, by becoming what I am (genuinely human apart from sin), heals my wounds and restores my humanity while remaining what he has always been. He is able to do so, though, only because of the reality of both his natures, each with its own set of predicates or attributes. Leo, Bishop of Rome, explains: "As what is fitting to heal our wounds, one and the same 'mediator between God and men, the man Christ Jesus' (1 Tim. 2:5) could die in one nature and not in the other. The true God, therefore, was born with the complete and perfect nature of a true man; he is complete in his nature and complete in ours."

It is somewhat ironic that an early criticism of Christianity ran something like this: "If Christ is God, and Christ died, then God died," and "if God cannot die and Christ is said to have died, Christ cannot be God because God cannot be understood to have died." By failing to understand the economy of the incarnation, early Christian opponents couldn't make sense of the gospel. I like Novatian's response to this puzzling query. "What is God in Christ did not die, but what is Man in Him did die." Hilary says much the same thing. Ambrose writes that the Son "died according to the assumption of our nature, and did not die according to the substance of eternal life. . . . He himself, by a kind of new operation, though dead, opened the tombs of the dead, and indeed his body lay in the tomb, yet He himself was free among the dead." The Son, then, both suffers and does not suffer. In Athanasius's words, "He it was who suffered and yet suffered not. Suffered, because His own body suffered, and he was in it, which thus suffered; suffered not, because the Word, being by nature God, is impassible." Again, John of Damascus hits the nail on the head: "Christ, while being two natures, suffered in his passible nature and in it was crucified, for it was in the flesh that he hung on the cross, and not in the divinity. Should they say, while inquiring of us: Did two natures die? We shall reply: No, indeed. Therefore, two natures were not crucified either, but the Christ was begotten, that is to say, the Divine Word was incarnate and begotten in the flesh, and he was crucified in the flesh, suffered in the flesh, and died in the flesh, while his divinity remained unaffected."

Luther says pretty much the same thing hundreds of years later: "For God in his own nature cannot die; but now, since God and man are united in one person, the death of the man with whom God is one thing or person is justly called the death of God. . . . For though suffering, dying, rising are attributes of the human nature alone, yet since Christ is the Son both of God and of Mary in one indivisible person with two distinct natures, we correctly say of the entire person: God is crucified for us, God shed his blood for us; God died for us and rose from the dead, not God apart from manhood but the God who has united himself into one person with human nature."

I want to also respond to your question concerning Philippians 2:7 and the nature of the Son's self-emptying in the economy of salvation, but this letter is already too long. I'll be writing again soon. Bet you can't wait!

_____

**With warm greetings,**
**Chris**

# 23 **John:** How Do We Know What God Is Like?

Dear Chris,

Thank you for stating my objections so clearly and orderly in your letter. You spend most of your time arguing against my second objection: though the tradition affirms the full divinity of Jesus, it seems to suggest that what we actually see is only his human nature. You also touch on the sixth: how can the divine Word suffer in Jesus if the divine nature cannot suffer? You say that you will get back to number seven in a future letter. That will be fine, but I want to hold your feet to the fire on objections three and four and especially on five and eight (they are the same). I believe that you do have a preconceived notion of God through which you read the biblical texts, distinguishing texts that speak "appropriately" from those that speak "accommodatingly" about God. Unfortunately, you have yet to tell me precisely *what* this preconceived notion of God is and how you *know* this is the true God.

Let me begin with your response to my second objection, since most of your letter is given over to it. I do not maintain that all theologians have thought that *all* we see in Christ is his human nature. Of course they said that we see divinity in Jesus. But did the people you cite do an adequate job of this? I think not. Moreover, I have not affirmed that "every text concerning Christ is pointing to or illustrating a truth about his divinity." I do not believe that God bleeds or sheds tears as Jesus did.

101

Hence, I agree with you that not every biblical text about Jesus applies directly to his divinity. Also, I affirm that Jesus teaches us what it means to be truly human—to live the way God intended us to live. (In the near future I want to apply openness theology to social ethics.) So we have much in common here.

You do an excellent job of quoting several of the fathers, as well as Luther and Oden, to show that they spoke of the divine Son suffering and even dying in some sense of those terms. I do not doubt this. Hence I agree with most of what you say in the letter. However, for me the issue is whether what they say in this regard is coherent with other things they say. Again, I think not. You point out that people such as Cyril did not seem to struggle with the question I raise about the suffering of the Word. Well, so what? If you claim that a point in my theology is incoherent and I were to respond, "I really don't struggle with that, I simply affirm it all," would you think that a satisfactory answer? Just because I don't see a problem does not mean one is not there. The history of theology has seen many times where certain people saw no problem but later writers did. (For instance, that infants should be baptized, that all unbaptized children that die are damned, and that all Jews deserve persecution for killing Christ.) I suggested that there is a fundamental incoherency in saying that God, as God, cannot suffer and also saying that the divine Son suffered in the one person of Jesus.

Your answer to this is an appeal to incomprehensibility. You write, "How the Son suffers in such a manner remains incomprehensible and ineffable to me, but if we drain all incomprehensibility out of the incarnation I'm not sure we still have the wondrous reality we began with!" So I'm draining *all* incomprehensibility out of the mystery of the incarnation? Your remark is an ingenious rhetorical ploy—it sounds ever so pious—but it is not an argument against trying to get as clear as we can on the matter. Your accusation amounts to saying that if I disagree with your position on the suffering of the Son I'm doing a naughty thing. However, I don't believe I'm being naughty at all, for I'm not trying to rid the incarnation of mystery. Who can fathom it? I like what Charles Wesley wrote: "'Tis mystery all, the immortal dies. Who can explore its strange design? In vain the firstborn seraph tries to sound the depths of love divine." What I am trying to do is make sure we are not contradicting ourselves and hiding behind the cloak of incomprehensibility. This goes back to previous discussions, so I will say no more about it now.

I agree that God, as God, cannot suffer *physically* and cannot cease to exist. How do I know this? I would argue from Scripture and philosophy that God, as creator, cannot do these things because they are contrary to the divine nature. You say that "Jesus experienced physical suffering, emotional suffering, powerlessness, and physical death" and hold that God *cannot* experience any of these. Hence, only the human nature of Jesus experienced these. First, let me say that Jesus did not experience "powerlessness." Rather, he exercised the power of love and chose not to use other types of power available to him. It was not that he had no power. Rather, he chose to restrain the full use of his power. When I wrestle with my young children I can restrain the full use of my power, but that does not mean I'm suddenly powerless. Now this opens the question whether God, as God, can restrain the full use of his power. I believe that God can and has done so repeatedly in human history. Consequently, the fact that Jesus chose not to utilize powers that were available to him says nothing against his divinity. If we go this route there simply is no need to hold that this applies only to his human nature. The New Testament writers speak of the power of the cross and resurrection (Rom. 1:18), for the cross of Christ manifests God's power and wisdom (1 Cor. 1:22–25).

The same principle applies to your claim that God, as God, *cannot* experience emotional suffering. As I've pointed out in previous letters, the Scriptures have many passages depicting God as experiencing emotional suffering (e.g., Gen. 6:6; Hosea 11:8). You claim that such Scriptures are "accommodations" to us because we cannot really understand the way God is. Well, you understand the way God is enough to tell me that I'm being impious for taking such passages as disclosures of what God is like. You claim to know that God, as God, cannot have emotional suffering. My question to you is: *How does Chris Hall know this?* You do not give biblical support for your claim—in fact, you say that these biblical texts cannot mean what they say. I conclude that you have some as yet undisclosed philosophical conception of God whereby you filter the divine revelation. Like a stock boy in a grocery store you know how to sort the biblical texts into those that are appropriate to apply to God from those that are inappropriate. From where do *you* get such knowledge of proper sorting?

Following Athanasius you claim to "walk the straight way of piety," and from Cyril you claim to know which passages of Scripture truly "befit" divinity and which texts are "lowly" and should not be applied to God. That is wonderful. Can't you teach me how to do this? What criteria do you employ to know what God must be like (*dignum Deo*)? I do not want you to give me a fish, as you did in your letter—I want you to teach me how to fish! That is, don't just restate your conclusion over and over. Tell me how you got there.

The Old Testament writers depict God as suffering. The New Testament writers worship Jesus as God in the flesh and they speak of the suffering of the Son of God. In fact, they see the way of God (God's wisdom and power) as going through suffering rather than being impermeable to it. It seems to me that the New Testament writers believed that God was in Jesus and that Jesus suffered even as God. If this is correct, then it casts doubt on the church fathers you quote. It seems to me that the burden of proof is on you to demonstrate that you are interpreting the Bible correctly when it seems, on the surface, that Scripture is teaching that God, as God, can suffer.

It is correct that the majority of early Christian pastors who wrote theology held that God cannot suffer. So did Arius. It was an important argument for him. God cannot suffer, Jesus suffered, so Jesus cannot be fully God in the same sense as the Father. This conclusion was rightfully rejected at Nicea. However, nobody seemed to call into question the fundamental Greek philosophical assumption (that is where it came from, not Scripture) that God cannot suffer. Even the Gnostic Christians said that God cannot suffer! Their argument went like this: since God cannot suffer, the Son of God associated with Jesus cannot suffer. Hence, they came to two possible solutions. Either Jesus only appeared to be a human being (he was not really human), or the divine Son "adopted" the human Jesus such that the human Jesus suffered but not the divine Son. Again, people just took for granted that God cannot suffer; the differences lie in their solutions.

This notion that God cannot suffer seemed to be in the very air the early Christians breathed. However, some early Christian writers thought the air was polluted. They attempted to return to the biblical portrait of God without sacrificing what orthodox Christians took to be important in affirming impassibility. For instance, I mentioned in a previous letter that the third-century writer Gregory Thaumaturgus wrote a book on divine impassibility. He argued that if God cannot choose to suffer, then God's will is confined and hence God is subject to great suffering! A better solution, says Gregory, is to say that God's suffering is not identical to ours, though it is similar. It is not identical because we can be forced to suffer, but no one can force God to suffer. Gregory thinks that the purpose of the doctrine of impassibility is to keep God safe from being forced to do something. Consequently, he believes that it solves the problem the fathers you cite were wrestling with if we say that God voluntarily chooses to share in the sufferings of his creatures for the sake of human salvation. What is wrong with that?

Lactantius, a Latin writer, also criticized the supposed impassibility of God, producing a treatise on God's anger in which he defended the reality of divine emotions. He held that God's blessedness does not prohibit the experience of joy, benevolence, anger, or pity. If you remove these from God, he says, you remove any genuine religion and relationship with God. Amen! Preach it brother! Against those who claimed that God is perfectly impassible and at rest, Lactantius replied that to be perfectly at rest is to be dead.

Thus not all the early Christians agreed on this issue. I believe that Gregory and Lactantius were on the right track. In my opinion, if we say that God, as God, can suffer, then it removes a major incoherency in much of the tradition regarding the incarnation (even though it does not remove all mystery or imply that we fully comprehend all there is to know about it). Is human suffering fundamentally different in kind from what God can experience? The theologians you cite say yes. But if we allow that God, as God, can suffer or restrain the full use of his power (*kenosis*), then the suffering of the divine Son is not at odds with the divine nature. In fact, it discloses an aspect of the divine nature. So, again I repeat your citation of me in point eight of your letter: "We may need to modify our preconceived notions of what is fitting for God to be. . . . Perhaps self-giving, self-sacrifice, and self-limitation is part of what the loving Trinity is like. For me, what Jesus is like discloses what God is like."

You believe that God *cannot* suffer—God cannot even voluntarily choose to suffer. According to classical theism (which is what you seem to espouse) God does not have changing emotions. This forces you to go through the Bible sorting out which texts really apply to God and the divine nature of the Son and which texts do not because they are inappropriate for God. I believe my position is superior for a number of reasons. First, there is no contradiction in saying that the divine Son suffered. Second, we can learn much about God from Jesus. Do we learn everything there is to know? Of course not. But this does allow us to affirm, with the biblical writers, that the life, ministry, death, and resurrection of Jesus do disclose the nature of God to us.

In conclusion, I've noted in this letter that you and I have much in common on this issue. However, I point out again that you have never given me a single biblical reason to affirm divine impassibility. Moreover, you still have not disclosed the philosophical notions of God that you use to filter the Scriptures. These notions involve timelessness, immutability, impassibility, and used to involve simplicity (but few affirm that anymore!). There is nothing wrong with using philosophical arguments in this way, but we need to get them on the table so we can argue their merits.

Thanks for your friendship and efforts to teach me.

Have a meaningful Easter,
John

# 24 **Chris:** The Church Fathers on Impassibility

Dear John,

It was good to hear from you in your most recent letter on impassibility and I'm thankful for the opportunity to resume our discussion. I know you're eager to hear my understanding of the biblical arguments for impassibility, but before I get to biblical issues I want to respond to some of your specific ideas and inquiries as expressed in your most recent correspondence.

For instance, you've mentioned more than once that you believe that I have a preconceived notion of God by which I'm reading the biblical texts: my understanding of what is worthy of God (*dignum Deo*) is causing me to misread the Bible. That is, this preconceived notion serves as a filter I use to determine which texts speak "appropriately" of God and which speak "inappropriately" or "accommodatingly." You then comment in your most recent letter that I have yet to tell you "precisely what this preconceived notion of God is and how [*I*] know this is the true God."

Fair questions, I suppose, but I have to ask in response, Am I the only one of the two of us who has a preconceived notion of God? Do you mean to say that when you approach the text of Scripture you do so with your mind as a kind of *tabula rasa*? Do you somehow have a pristine, unmediated access to the biblical text? I've heard you speak of

106

yourself as a "Bible-thumper," tongue in cheek I think, but behind the rhetoric appears to be a specific hermeneutical stance: I, John Sanders, am starting with the Bible and am simply going to allow this text to speak directly to me. If I run across a text that appears to teach that God changes his mind, grieves, or suffers, I'm going to allow the text to shape my understanding, rather than straining out the meaning of the text through the application of foreign ideas or presuppositions.

Can any of us say we have no preconceptions when we come to the text? We all have been influenced and molded by our family circle, culture, teachers, churches, pastors, theologians, and key life experiences. As I read and interact with openness theologians I'm more than ever convinced that they, too, have their own set of lenses through which they read the Bible. So what is the lens through which *you* read the text? What are *your* preconceived notions? What or who has deeply influenced *your* perspective as you read the text of Scripture?

Back to the issue at hand. Who has deeply formed or shaped my approach to Scripture? As you already know, I attempt to read the Bible with and through the history of exegesis as practiced in the church over its history. I acknowledge that the history of exegesis is complicated and diverse. What I attempt to do is listen carefully to the voices of the past (and occasionally the present!) and hopefully discern through this the consensual heart of the church's reflection on a given biblical text or theme.

I don't believe that the exegesis of the fathers was always correct or that the fathers always agreed with one another. Alexandrian and Antiochian fathers sometimes strongly disagreed with each other. Neither do I believe, however, that we read Scripture well by attempting to interpret it individualistically rather than communally. This is one of the reasons why, by the way, I think it's important to listen to you and others such as Greg Boyd and Clark Pinnock. You're part of the community of faith and surely have insights that will aid me in reading the Scriptures more effectively. It does me good, for example, to attempt to defend a doctrine such as impassibility with other members of the church who seriously question it. Our debate forces me to rethink issues, to clarify my thinking on past formulations, and again to listen carefully to my community, past and present.

All of us, including yourself, have a theological and hermeneutical pedigree. As Harold O. J. Brown puts it, no biblical interpreter ever came to the Bible "cold, as it were, but each had been exposed to the Christian message and to forms of Christian life before being 'reformed' by the text of Scripture." In my own case my first Bible teachers were premillenial dispensationalists such as Hal Lindsey. Only later in my journey was I exposed to figures such as Chrysostom, Basil, Gregory,

Athanasius, Augustine, Cyril, Luther, and Calvin. So I agree with you that the notion of preconceived ideas is an important one. We all have been shaped and formed by others.

How have the fathers taught me to read the Bible? First, they insist that I read the Bible holistically. That is, a particular text must be read and interpreted in light of the overall narrative and thematic structure of the Bible. Key themes and words—God, Jesus, Israel, church—must be interpreted in light of the biblical narrative's overarching story line as presented by biblical authors.

Second, I try to listen to the fathers as they encourage me to read the Bible christologically. All the fathers, as far as I can tell, read the entire Bible through the prism or lens of Christ's incarnation, crucifixion, resurrection, and ascension. As Hilary puts it, "Every part of Holy Writ announces through words the coming of Our Lord Jesus Christ, reveals it through facts and establishes it through examples. . . . For it is our Lord who during all the present age, through true and manifest foreshadowings, generates, cleanses, sanctifies, chooses, separates, or redeems the Church in the Patriarchs, through Adam's slumber, Noah's flood, Melchizedek's blessing, Abraham's justification, Isaacs's birth, and Jacob's bondage."

Third, as I have already mentioned, I try to read the Bible communally within Christ's body, the church. In a word, biblical interpretation is an ecclesial affair. It takes place in the church for the church. As Jenson puts it, "It is the *church* that knows the plot and *dramatis personae* of the Scripture narrative, since the church is one continuous community with the story's actors and narrators, as with its tradents, authors, and assemblers." Thus, since you, Clark, and Greg are members of the church, I need to listen and test carefully what you are saying, both by the primary standard of Scripture and by the history of the church's reflection on that same text. It may well be that you are observing aspects of the text or are offering interpretations of the text that the church has overlooked or misinterpreted. Could be. On the other hand, it may also be true that you are offering a viewpoint that will ultimately have to be rejected. Time will tell.

One more illustration and then on to the specific issues you raise concerning coherency, impassibility, divine emotions, and so on. Ponder the following symphonic illustration. Imagine the first movement of the symphony as the Old Testament, the second movement as Jesus' birth, ministry, crucifixion, resurrection, and ascension, and the third movement as the apostolic interpretation of the first two movements. In addition to the symphony, though, we also have a postlude of sorts, the music the church has produced over the centuries in its exegesis and theological reflection. The question is whether the postlude is in harmony with the preceding symphony, or whether its harmonic structures are actually discordant. To extend the metaphor a bit, the music of the postlude seems to me to interpret the primary movements of the symphony well. And what is heresy? Interpretations of the symphony that are fundamentally discordant with its major themes and melodic variations.

Am I, then, as you contend, applying a preconceived notion of God to the biblical text? Perhaps. That is one of the issues under dispute. But the possibility does exist that rather than applying a foreign, discordant melodic line to the symphony, i.e., a preconceived notion of God that is foreign to the biblical narrative itself, I'm actually singing musical interpretations composed and played by musicians that knew the original score well and developed faithfully and skillfully the original symphony's rhythms and tonal qualities. The key question, at least for this letter, is whether impassibility is a discordant or harmonic interpretation of the original score. Where, for instance, can the idea of impassibility be found in the original symphony itself? In a word, is there biblical evidence that God *in se* does not experience passion or suffering?

Before we look at the biblical background for impassibility, though, I think it is important to note that fathers such as John Chrysostom did not understand impassibility to mean that God was a Stoic or Epicurean deity, divorced from his creation, a metaphysical, static, stone pillar of some sort. For instance, Chrysostom writes that divine providence is neither mechanistic nor distant. "For he does not simply watch over us, but also loves us; he ardently loves us with an inexplicable love, with an impassible yet fervent, vigorous, genuine, indissoluble love, a love that is impossible to extinguish."

Chrysostom, then, does not view impassibility and fervent love as mutually exclusive. G. L. Prestige, commenting on the fathers' understanding of impassibility, believes that impassibility guarantees the consistency of all God's attitudes and actions toward humanity. While the passions that plague fallen people cause their love to weaken or disappear as circumstances change, God's transcendent, impassible nature remains above "the forces and passions such as commonly hold sway in the creation and among mankind." Prestige writes, "It is clear that impassibility means not that God is inactive or uninterested, *not that* His will is determined from within instead of being swayed from without. It safeguards the truth that the impulse alike in providential order and in redemption and sanctification come from the will of God. If it were possible to admit that the impulse was wrung from Him either by the needs or by the claims of His creation, and that thus whether by pity or by justice His hand was forced, He would no longer be represented as absolute; He would be dependent on the created universe and thus at best only in possession of concurrent power."

I'm unconvinced that a defense of impassibility demands that we deny an emotional life in God. Hence, Chrysostom readily describes God's love as both impassible and fervent. God always acts toward us in consistent, unchanging, fervent love.

Impassibility *would* mean, however, that God experiences emotions in a manner different from the way humans experience emotions. In addition, God does not experience all the emotions humans experience (God does not experience the emotional remorse that normally accompanies sinful human actions), nor is God's emotional life characterized by the distorted passions that mark sinful human existence. Exactly what is a distorted passion?

Roberta Bondi describes the desert fathers' understanding of a passion along the following lines: a passion "has as its chief characteristics the perversion of vision and the destruction of love. A passion may very well be a strong emotion, but it need not be. A passion can also be a state of mind, or even a habitual action. Anger is usually a passion, but sometimes forgetfulness is called a passion. . . . Strong emotions which accompany love, lead to love, or even are an expression of love are not passions."

Thus, at least in the minds of many early Christians, to speak of God as being passionless or impassible would not necessarily mean that God was emotionless. Rather, it would mean that God did not possess either emotions or dispositions that crippled God's ability to love. By definition, the passions cripple the human capacity to love. As Bondi puts it, the "passions blind us so that we cannot love. They create for us interior lenses through which we see the world, lenses which we very often do not even know are there. When we are under the control of our passions, even when we think we are most objective, we cannot be—we are in the grip of emotions, states of mind, habits that distort everything we see."

Thankfully, God does not possess passions such as these. Hence, Chrysostom's words concerning both impassibility and fervent love are not incoherent. In Chrysostom's *Exhortation to Theodore After His Fall*, he highlights the pastoral implications of the distinction between changeable human passions and God's unchangeable tenderness. He writes, "For if the wrath of God were a passion, one might well despair as being unable to quench the flame which he had kindled by so many evil doings; but since the Divine nature is passionless, even if He punishes, even if He takes vengeance, he does this not with wrath, but with *tender care, and much lovingkindness* [my emphasis]; wherefore it behoves us to be of much good courage, and to trust in the power of repentance. . . . He acts with a view to our advantage, and to prevent our perverseness becoming worse by our making a practice of despising and neglecting Him."

Chrysostom employs the example of parental love in a later work to make a similar point. He knows that his readers, especially in the time of persecution they and he are presently experiencing, will be tempted to feel abandoned by God. Could this actually be the case? Chrysostom reminds his audience of Isaiah's words: "Can a woman forget her nursing child, or show no compassion for the child of her womb?" (Isa. 49:15). According to Chrysostom, the lesson to be learned from Isaiah is clear: "The prophet says this to make the point that just as a woman would not forget her own children, so neither would God forget humankind."

Chrysostom exhorts his readers, however, to meditate even more deeply on the wonder of God's love. The interface between the human comparison and the love of God is insufficient in itself to communicate the incomparable reality of the divine love. We must immediately exercise our reason to move beyond the boundaries of the metaphor. Thus he exhorts: "I have given these examples so that when I introduce other illustrations you wouldn't limit your thinking to the measure of what is spoken by the prophets, *but having this rule you should use your reason to go even further and see the unspeakable excess of the love of God*" (my emphasis).

Chrysostom continually prods his readers to move beyond human comparisons. "Do you see how the degree of God's love exceeds that of a mother? In order that you might see how God's love super abundantly transcends the warm affection of a mother and the love of a father for their children. . . . As great as is the difference between light and darkness, between evil and goodness, so great is the difference between the goodness and providence of God in comparison to the tender love of a father."

What of the issue of suffering? Impassibility does entail the idea that God does not experience suffering as the result of actions imposed on him by others. This affirmation, as I have already argued, does not mean that God is emotionless. Rather, in the relationship of creator and creature God remains and will always be ontologically distinct, the active partner in the dance, so to speak. That is, God as God and as creator does not need anything or anyone outside of himself to fulfill a need, lack, or desire. God as Father, Son, and Holy Spirit was dancing the rhythms of love before creation ever took place. In the act of creation God has invited us to join in the dance, but as creatures. The ontic distinction between God and humanity remains and will always remain. God does not need us to be absolutely fulfilled as God. Even Job's counselors seemed to get this right: "Can a mortal be of use to God? Can even the wisest be of service to him?" (Job 22:2–3). "If you have sinned, what do you accomplish against him? And if your transgressions are multiplied, what do you do to him?" (Job 35:5–6). Or compare the words of the Psalmist: "For every wild animal of the forest is mine, the cattle on a thousand hills. I know all the birds of the air, and all that moves in the field is mine. If I were hungry, I would not tell you, for the world and all that is in it is mine" (Ps. 50:10–12).

In addition, impassibility affirms that God, as God, is under no obligation to anyone outside himself. He is obligated to act justly toward his creation, not because anything in creation itself obligates God to act justly, but because justice itself is fully actualized in God's character. To put it somewhat crassly, God cannot help but act justly. It is ontologically impossible for God to act otherwise. He is the source of life and all its accompanying goodness to us, but he needs nothing from us and is obligated to no one. As Paul puts it in his evangelistic sermon in Athens, God is not "served by human hands, as though he needed anything, since he himself gives to all mortals life and breath and all things." If God ever stopped acting on our behalf, an acting that is enabled by the absolute ontic distinction between God as creator and us as creation, we would cease to exist, as would the universe. He does not need us, but we surely need him. "'Or who has given a gift to him, to receive a gift in return?' For from him and through him and to him are all things" (Rom. 11:35–36).

As you have already commented, impassibility is connected to a series of other important issues we need to discuss: God's immutability, omniscience, relationship to time, the problem of evil, and so on. Before we move on, however, I want to respond specifically to a few comments you made in your last letter. As I mentioned at the beginning of this letter, you chide me for having a preconceived notion of God by which I read the biblical texts, a notion or understanding I use to distinguish between texts that speak "appropriately" of God and those that "speak accommodatingly" or "inappropriately." I don't think you're correct or consistent in your criticism.

First, I will continue to argue that texts in which God accommodates himself to us are appropriate, not inappropriate. This is probably something we need to discuss more thoroughly. Perhaps more importantly at this juncture, you write that you "do not believe that God bleeds or sheds tears as Jesus did . . . I agree that God, as God, cannot suffer *physically* and cannot cease to exist. How do I know this? I would argue from Scripture and philosophy that as creator God cannot do these things because they are contrary to the divine nature."

Of course, I agree with you. But I'm not sure that you're being consistent with your own hermeneutic. What of the many texts in the Old

Testament that portray God as having a body? Moses, Aaron, Nadab, Abihu, and seventy elders of Israel see God on Mount Sinai. Under God's "feet" they see "something like a pavement of sapphire stone." Yet despite seeing God these men do not perish. God does "not lay his hand on the chief men of the people of Israel; also they beheld God, and they ate and drank" (Exod. 24:10–11). How do you know God does not have feet or hands? Only, it seems to me, by applying other texts and philosophical principles to texts such as these—the very error you lay at my doorstep. Are you practicing a consistent hermeneutic? Other texts speak of Moses speaking "face to face" with God, "as one speaks to a friend" (Exod. 33:11). Later in the same chapter Moses is described as being allowed to see God's "back" but not God's "face" (Exod. 33:23). Does God have a body or not? Is God corporeal or not?

It seems to me that Clark Pinnock is applying the openness hermeneutic more consistently than you. You're too much like me! In Clark's most recent book, *Most Moved Mover: A Theology of God's Openness*, he lists and comments on the texts from Exodus I've just mentioned. I'm interested in your response to his ideas, though of course you don't have to agree with Clark. Clark writes: "There is an issue that has not been raised yet in the discussion around the open view of God. If he is with us in the world, if we are to take biblical metaphors seriously, is God in some way embodied? Critics will be quick to say that, although there are expressions of this idea in the Bible, they are not to be taken literally. But I do not believe that the idea is as foreign to the Bible's view of God as we have assumed." How so? "Human beings are said to be embodied creatures created in the image of God. Is there perhaps something in God that corresponds with embodiment? Having a body is certainly not a negative thing because it makes it possible for us to be agents. Perhaps God's agency would be easier to envisage if he were in some way corporeal. Add to that the fact that in the theophanies of the Old Testament God encounters humans in the form of a man."

I began to get nervous as I followed Clark's argument, for it seemed to me that he was moving toward viewing the metaphors concerning God's hands, feet, and face as in some way pointing to some kind of a literal reality. Perhaps Clark was simply pondering the incarnation. And yet further in his argument Clark writes that "God loves to draw near to us through nature, theophany, and incarnation." Fine. But then Clark writes, "It is possible that God has a body in some way we cannot imagine and, therefore, that it is natural for God to seek out forms of embodiment. I do not feel obliged to assume that God is a purely spiritual being when his self-revelation does not suggest it."

Clark is clearly linking personhood and embodiment. I don't have a hard time with this coupling if we limit the connection between personhood and embodiment to human beings. Clark, though, appears to be taking a huge step in seeming to argue that even for God embodiment and personhood are linked. As Clark states matters, "The only persons we encounter are embodied persons and, if God is not embodied, it may prove difficult to understand how God is a person. What kind of actions could a disembodied God perform?"

The direction Clark is moving in his thinking and interpretation hits me as a consistent openness hermeneutic, and I'd like to know what you think of Clark's ideas. Is Clark reading the Exodus texts well or not? In addition, on the basis of an openness hermeneutic, how do you know that God doesn't bleed, shed tears, and experience physical pain? What preconceived notion of God are you applying to the text that prevents you from viewing God as embodied?

A few lines further Clark writes: "As human subjectivity expresses itself in, with, and through bodies, so the transcendent subjectivity of God is somehow immanent in the patterns, processes, and events of the world." Clark seems to be close to saying that the world and its various processes, patterns, and events might well be the embodiment of God. Clark's ideas are troubling to me and yet consistent with the application of the openness hermeneutic to the text of Scripture. What do you think?

To move on, in your letter you continue to argue that Cyril is speaking incoherently when he writes that the Word suffers in the humanity he has assumed for our sake. How can God the incarnate Word genuinely suffer and God not suffer *in se*, a suffering that both Father and Holy Spirit would experience? In your words, "there is a fundamental incoherency in saying that God, as God, cannot suffer and also saying that the divine Son suffered in the one person of Jesus." I don't know how the Word suffers in his assumed humanity. How God pulls this off is a mystery to me. But I believe that the stick you like to spank me with—the issue of incoherence—is just as applicable to you. How so?

While you don't like Cyril's model, you do "like what Charles Wesley wrote: 'Tis mystery all, the immortal dies.'" Sorry, but to speak of one who is immortal dying is a contradiction in terms. How is it coherent to speak of one who cannot die actually dying? This is indeed a "strange design," as Wesley writes. I resonate with his words, but I don't know why you would. After all, if coherency is a fundamental criterion for public discussion of theological issues, as you have contended, why would you agree with Wesley? Maybe I'm missing something here, but your support of Wesley seems surprisingly incoherent to me. Wesley's expression becomes more coherent when interpreted against the backdrop of the Cyrillian model, where the incarnate Word indeed dies as his human nature expires on the cross. But this is the position I've been arguing all along.

Finally, it's unclear to me why you would argue that Jesus did not experience "powerlessness." In my letter I grouped together four expressions: physical suffering, emotional suffering, powerlessness, and physical death. Perhaps my inclusion of powerlessness is less than wise, but it seems that Jesus surely underwent the human limitations that all human beings experience. Why? He was human as well as divine. At times Jesus manifested his divinity quite clearly. The incident of Jesus' walking on water comes to mind.

At other times, as you rightly point out, Jesus purposely chose in love "not to use other types of power available to him. It was not that he had no power. Rather, he chose to restrain the full use of his power." I also agree with you that God "can restrain the full use of his power." God does so all the time for any number of reasons. Sometimes, as you indicate, divine restraint is a manifestation of divine love. At other times divine restraint might well be a sign of divine judgment. Paul teaches in Romans 1, for example, that a sign of God's judgment against sin is his willingness to "give people up" to their sin (Rom. 1:24, 26, 28). This giving over is surely a divine refusal to act, a divine restraint of what God could do if God chose to do so.

If we refuse to ascribe "powerlessness" in any sense to Jesus, however, we can easily lapse into a kind of docetic error. For instance, if Jesus chose not to exercise his divine power, he would not as a human being inherently possess the capability to swim under water for long periods of time, breathing oxygen through gills like a fish. Why? Christ's body was a genuine human body, with all of a body's characteristics. If someone had attached weights to Jesus' ankles and tossed him into the sea he would have drowned, as far as I can tell, apart from his choosing to exercise divine power. Jesus was not a ghost. He possessed a human body, a body subject to the limits and, yes, powerlessness and vulnerability that all humans experience when placed in certain contexts. Having said all this, it remains unclear to me why the issue of Christ's powerlessness was such a red flag for you. I'm not sure how this relates to the openness position.

Finally, I think you need to move more slowly in some of the deductions you make. For example, you write "it seems to me that the New Testament writers believed that God was in Jesus and Jesus suffered even as God. If this is correct, then it casts doubt on the church fathers you quote. It seems the burden of proof is on you to demonstrate that you are interpreting the Bible correctly when it seems, on the surface, that Scripture is teaching that God, as God, can suffer." Maybe so. New Testament writers do insist that Jesus is God. That is not, however, the same thing as saying that God suffered as God when the divine Word suffered in his incarnate humanity. Your conclusion that "Jesus suffered even as God" is a theological deduction based on your exegesis of certain New Testament texts, none of which you mention in your letter.

You closed by noting that I have not yet broached the topics of timelessness, immutability, simplicity, and omniscience. You're right. Perhaps a discussion concerning omniscience is the next aspect of our debate we should develop. The validity and coherence of the openness position surely hangs on what we mean by omniscience. How much does God really know after all?

With warm greetings,
Chris

# 25 **John:** The Western Fathers and Impassibility

Dear Chris,

You raise about six different issues in your letter. I will not address all of them, and some of them I will barely touch on, but we can return to them.

Let me begin by saying that I do not claim to approach the biblical text empty-headed. We are all shaped by traditions that include sermons, Sunday school, and for me, academic studies. I've already written you previously that I'm a critical realist in my epistemology, not a commonsense realist. So I do not believe that I read the meaning of the biblical text without any interpretation. As I said before, I approach the text with assumptions and teachings absorbed from other Christians. These assumptions can be questioned. In fact, I was taught many of the same presuppositions you hold, but I've come to reject some of them. As a critical realist I have to be open to correction, for our learning is always an ongoing enterprise.

You ask who has deeply influenced my reading of Scripture. Fair enough. Abraham Joshua Heschel's *The Prophets* really challenged me as an undergraduate to understand some of the basic differences between Hebraic and Hellenistic thought. Though they are not completely different, there are some crucial distinctions. One of them that Heschel points out is the nature of God's love and suffering. Greek thought simply

117

could not allow for these conceptions and, unfortunately, many—though not all—Christians bought into the Greek philosophical approach to deity. Other influences included my professors: Walter Kaiser when I was majoring in Old Testament and then Donald Bloesch when I switched to theology. Bloesch taught a seminar on the doctrine of God in which we traced the development of the "biblical-classical synthesis" in church tradition. That is, the bringing together of the biblical portrait of God with Greek philosophical concepts. It is not that what the Greeks thought is automatically wrong, but the Hellenic concept of divinity created a number of problems for the Christian understanding of God. Also, the detailed studies on God and providence by Hebrew Bible scholar Terence Fretheim, as well as my doctoral supervisor, the Dutch Reformed theologian Adrio Konig, have influenced my reading of Scripture. Finally, let me say that the work of contemporary Christian philosophers has been very important to me. In the past three decades incredibly detailed work has been done on divine attributes such as impassibility, immutability, omniscience, and atemporality. Here I have in mind people such as Nicholas Wolterstorff, Vincent Brümmer, Alvin Plantinga, William Alston, and my colleague William Hasker. I will return to these in a moment.

What I asked you in my previous letter was to tell me why passages such as Genesis 6:6 and Hosea 11:8 do not mean what they seem to mean. The Scriptures portray God as suffering, so why must we interpret them to mean God does not suffer? I asked how Chris Hall knows how to correctly interpret these texts. Your response seems to be "because that is the consensus of the first eight centuries of the church." I have a number of problems with this response, but they will have to wait for a future letter. Suffice it to say that I wonder which "church" you mean. You seem to gravitate towards the Eastern fathers and don't bother with Western thinkers such as Augustine. The Western church came to the conclusion that unbaptized infants that die are damned (though they don't suffer pain). Very few Christians believe that today. Are we wrong?

Just a brief note on divine embodiment. I don't agree with everything that Pinnock wrote. Please recall our discussion of metaphors, as well as what I said previously as to why I don't take "God walked in the garden" to imply that God has physicality. The biblical writers claim that neither temples nor the heavens can contain God. "God is spirit" (John. 4:24), though I do not profess to understand what this means in any positive sense, for we cannot envision a formless being. Yet the elders of Israel "saw the God of Israel" (Exod. 24:11) and in the new heavens we will "see the face of God" (Rev. 22:4). I take these expressions to be about an experience with particular manifestations of God.

You say that I'm committing the "very error" of which I accuse you. I am not accusing you of error in having preconceived notions of God when reading Scripture. I just want to know your definitions of the divine attributes and from where you get these definitions.

I'm so glad we can agree on a good sense of the term "impassibility" (that God is not overwhelmed by emotions). However, this is not the usual definition. If it were, there would not have been a huge debate about it in the early church and again for the past two centuries. Why would Justin Martyr defend impassibility and then cry out "But our God is not a stone!" if he only meant what you say it means? Why did Gregory and Lactantius write what they did in opposition to others if your definition of impassibility is correct? In my historical surveys of the divine attributes in *The Openness of God* and *The God Who Risks* I detailed the debates about the definitions of God's attributes. Why all the scholarly studies on this issue? Why do contemporary evangelical theologians such as Wayne Grudem, Ronald Nash, and Gordon Lewis call impassibility into question? Why does the classical theist H. P. Owen, in his important historical survey of the divine attributes, say that "this is the most questionable aspect of classical theism" if impassibility only means that God is not overwhelmed by negative emotions?

You appeal to Chrysostom for your understanding, but his view is not the standard view, especially not in the Western church. If we turn to Augustine, Anselm, Aquinas, and Calvin we see the term used in its most accepted sense that has dominated Western theology, both Catholic and Protestant. Gordon Lewis gives the standard definition of impassibility: *"The doctrine that God is not capable of being acted upon or affected emotionally by anything in creation."* Although this became the "consensual" view for most of church history, an incredible number of biblical scholars, theologians, and philosophers today reject it both as being unbiblical and as having philosophical problems. Very few defend this doctrine in its classical sense.

So, I have two main problems with your argument for impassibility. First, your definition is not the one I'm criticizing. Second, the biblical support you give for it will not work. Let me comment on the biblical problem first. I've repeatedly asked you to give me biblical support for impassibility. You promise to do so at the beginning of your letter but it is not until you are two-thirds of the way through that you mention three texts. You give two texts from Job and one from the Psalms. However, none of these are about impassibility! These texts do not even address your weak definition of impassibility that God is not overwhelmed with negative emotions. So, I claim that you still have given me *no biblical support* for impassibility.

Now to the proper definition and what it is that open theists don't like about it. You say that God is not dependent on creatures—he does not need us. I agree that God would be God even without creation. However, that is a statement about God's self-sufficiency, not about the issue of impassibility—unless you add to this definition that God cannot even *will* to be dependent on creatures for some things. Self-sufficiency and impassibility are not identical but they can be related. Returning to what Gordon Lewis said, impassibility is the notion that God *cannot* be affected by us. God cannot respond to what we do. Nothing we do, including our prayers, ever influences what God decides to do. God's will is never affected by us. God may have bliss, but God never experiences anger, pity, joy, or grief. Following Augustine's discussion of impassibility we may say that God is blissfully aware of us, but our failings and the harm we do to one another never bring God pain. Nothing that happens in our lives changes God's blissful, unperturbed serenity.

Following Augustine, Saint Anselm says in his *Proslogium*, "But how art thou compassionate, and, at the same time, passionless? How, then, art thou compassionate and not compassionate, O Lord, unless because thou art compassionate in terms of our experience, and not compassionate in terms of thy being." That is, the biblical language about God's mercy, love, and compassion are "accommodations" to us. God cannot have such experiences. What then really is God's compassion? It is God's benevolence towards us that *we* interpret as compassion. God cannot experience anger either. Again, it is an accommodation to us. God is not really angry at sin, it is we who interpret divine judgments as God being angry.

Anselm did not invent these ideas; they are part of the tradition beginning early on in Christian thought. The Gnostics, Arius, Athanasius, and Augustine all agree that this is what God is like. Why did the ancients go this way? Wolterstorff proposes that they had two powerful arguments. The first, derived from Plato, is the argument from perfection (I've discussed this in a previous letter). A perfect being cannot experience changing emotions, say, from joy to grief, since this would destroy perfect bliss. After all, perfect bliss is what all of us desire, so God must have it unchangingly. The second argument is that God must be totally unconditioned by creatures, since the quality of God's life cannot be dependent in any way on us. In other words, if we affected God in such a way that God experienced something that he did not already have, then we are adding to God's life, and the thought of that is utterly alien to the notion of deity. This goes back to Aristotle's idea that for God to have a relationship with us would make God dependent on us for the relationship.

These are the hurdles that Gregory and Lactantius were trying to overcome when they argued that although we cannot force God to experience joy or grief, God can freely choose to enter into the kinds of relationships with us where such experiences are possible. That is, if God freely chooses to suffer because of us, then creatures are not forcing God to suffer. As I mentioned before, however, their ideas lay dormant for over a millennium.

Let me finish by pointing out some doctrines related to, and implications of, strong impassibility. Using the above arguments for impassibility also led the ancients to connect it with *immutability* (God cannot change in any way, for a change would only be a change for the worse), *timelessness* (God cannot experience time, since that would be change), *necessity* (God must exist), *omnipotence* (God must be all powerful, since he cannot lack any power), *omniscience* (nothing can be added to God's knowledge as that would imply deficiency), *omnipresence* (God cannot move), *aseity* (totally independent and unconditioned by anything else), and *simplicity* (God actually has none of the foregoing properties, since God is not distinct from God's essence—we really can't differentiate between the attributes of God). The doctrine of simplicity is difficult to understand, but the basic idea is that although we speak as though God has various characteristics (omnipotence, immutability), God actually has none of them, for God, unlike us, is not composed of parts. Rather, God's essence is an indivisible unity. Not many people today have even heard of the doctrine of simplicity, let alone believe it. Nonetheless, it was a key doctrine throughout the Middle Ages and an essential argument used by Aquinas to support his understanding of timelessness and impassibility. Get rid of divine simplicity and you seriously undermine Aquinas's concept of God.

This cluster of divine attributes came to be known as "classical theism." It is an exceedingly influential conception of God that was developed by a line of thinkers from Plato through Philo of Alexandria to Plotinus and on into Christian theology, picking up steam in Augustine and Anselm, and finding its apex in Thomas Aquinas. This is quite a prestigious pedigree and many critics of open theism claim to be classical theists. Are you a classical theist? It does not seem that you really affirm the definition of impassibility. However, the ancients put these attributes together for very strong reasons, and once you begin tinkering with one it is going to affect many of the others. Listen to Wolterstorff: "Once you pull on the thread of impassibility, a lot of other threads come along. Aseity for example—that is, unconditionedness. The biblical witness seems to me clearly to be that God allows himself to be affected by the doings of the creatures God has created. One also has to give up immutability (changelessness) and eternity [timelessness]. If God really *responds*, then God is not metaphysically immutable; and if not metaphysically immutable, then not eternal [timeless]."

Today, many people want to jettison impassibility and simplicity but retain strong immutability, timelessness, and unconditionedness. Perhaps I'll address this in a future letter.

What implications are there if we do affirm impassibility? If none of God's decisions are ever affected by what creatures do, then the doctrines of unconditional election, irresistible grace, and meticulous providence follow, as Augustine, Aquinas, and Calvin clearly saw. The view of many of the early fathers that God uses his foreknowledge to "look ahead" and see how we will respond to the grace of the Holy Spirit, and that he will elect us if he foresees us putting our faith in Christ, is absurd if God is strongly impassible. It cannot be that God's decision to elect is in any way dependent on a decision we make, for that would make God conditioned by and dependent on us for something. Everything that happens in our lives is then exactly the way God wanted it to be. God does not want *anything* different than it is. Our prayers of petition never influence what God decides to do. Rather, our prayers are the divinely ordained means of bringing about what God has already ordained to happen. In other words, God never responds to our prayers, we respond to God's will. *Do you believe these teachings?*

I want to elaborate more on classical theism and its implications, since this will take us into the key points of difference between open theism and other views.

Your friend,
John

## Chart: Classical and Open Theism Compared

| | Classical Theism | Open Theism |
|---|---|---|
| **Operative Root Metaphors** | God as creator, judge, and king. | God as savior, lover, and friend. |
| **Nature of God** | Emphasis on divine sovereignty. God is unchangeable and unaffected by creatures. | Emphasis on divine relationality. God is changeable in will and emotions and is affected by creatures. |
| **Type of Sovereignty** | God exercises unilateral power in creation, providence, and redemption. God takes no risks because he tightly controls every detail. | God exercises unilateral power in creation, but bilateral power with creatures in providence and redemption. God takes risks because he exercises general control. |
| **Creaturely Freedom** | Humans have compatibilistic freedom. | Humans have libertarian freedom. |
| **Relationship between God, Time, and Eternity** | God as eternal—i.e., timeless—even if the eternal divine decisions have temporal effects. | God as everlasting—i.e., enduring forever—and interacting genuinely in a give-and-take relationship with temporal creatures. |
| **The Nature of the Future** | The future is completely definite—it will turn out exactly as God decided it should turn out. | The future is partly definite and partly indefinite—God is working with us to bring about the future. |
| **Foreknowledge** | Eternally definite foreknowledge of all future events. God knows the future because he determines the future. | Presentism: God knows the past and present exhaustively and that part of the future that is determined. |
| **Problem of Evil** | All evil is planned by God to display the divine glory. | Evil is permitted but not wanted by God in order to make relations of love with creatures possible. |
| **Salvation** | Solely of God's choosing—we respond to God's choice. | God's choosing is based on our choice—we cooperate with God. |
| **Petitionary Prayer** | Never influences God; it is God's means of bringing about what God has ordained. | May influence God; God makes some of his decisions dependent on whether we pray or not. |
| **God's Will** | God has a blueprint for our lives regarding job, marriage, etc. | God does not have a blueprint for our lives regarding job, marriage, etc. Together with God we determine what our futures will be. |

# 26 **John:** Scripture on Immutability and Foreknowledge

Hey, Chris,

I want to try to tie some of the different topics we've discussed together: how to interpret Scripture, immutability, and foreknowledge. Most of us are well aware of some of the longstanding debates on important theological matters. For instance, did Jesus die for every single human being or only for the elect? Christians are reading the same Bible, but they do interpret some key passages differently. There is disagreement as to the "clear meaning" of the biblical texts. Arminians argue that John 3:16, 1 Timothy 2:4, and 2 Peter 3:9 are the clear passages, so we should conclude that Jesus died for everyone. Hence, they claim that texts on divine election such as Ephesians 1:11 and Romans 8:28–30 should be interpreted in light of the clear passages. On the other hand, certain Calvinists quite naturally disagree, claiming that Ephesians 1:11 is very clear, so we should conclude that the Bible teaches unconditional election to salvation. They reason that the Bible clearly teaches that God totally controls everything that happens. Hence, if God wanted everyone to be saved then everyone would be saved. Since the Bible clearly teaches that not everyone will be saved it is reasonable to conclude that texts such as John 3:16 and 1 Timothy 2:4 cannot mean what the Arminians claim they mean.

124

Is there a way to settle such disputes? Is there a neutral hermeneutical method on which all will agree and by which we can come to a foolproof, absolutely certain understanding of the biblical texts? That is, is there a way of determining the clear teachings of Scripture such that, once determined, one would be either irrational or sinful to disagree with these clear teachings? Many evangelicals have sought such a method, but none has achieved it. Personally I don't believe it is possible to find a foolproof method of reading Scripture. One reason is that we are finite or limited. None of us ever knows everything—there is always more to learn. Moreover, sin can even affect our reading of Scripture. We might overlook certain passages or dismiss someone else's interpretation because of sinful motives. For instance, are there aspects of Scripture that I, as a Western Christian, overlook that Christians in Brazil or Sudan might call to my attention? Due to our finitude and sin, our understanding of the biblical texts is not infallible or immune to correction. We cannot arrive at absolute certainty with regard to the interpretation of Scripture. Hence we need each other. You and I are in dialogue seeking to understand how the other is reading Scripture and formulating theological beliefs. This is helping me immensely.

Now I want to apply all this to some of the issues we've discussed in previous letters. Let me begin with divine immutability. There are passages that say that God does not change: "I the LORD do not change therefore you (Israel) are not destroyed" (Mal. 3:6); God is not human that he should change his mind (Num. 23:19; 1 Sam. 15:29). There are also passages that say that God does change: the Lord was grieved that he made humans because they continually sinned (Gen. 6:6); God changed his mind about what he said he would do (Exod. 32:14).

What are we to do with these seemingly contrary teachings? In his book *The Providence of God*, Paul Helm says that Scripture does not contradict itself, so we must do something with these apparent contradictions. According to Helm we have two options: (1) we can hold that the texts that say that God changes are the clear, strong, and correct texts and subordinate the passages about God not changing to them; or (2) we can reverse this and claim that the passages about God not changing are the clear, strong, and correct texts and subordinate the changing God texts to them. That is, we must resolve the problem by positing one set of texts as the clear passages and interpreting the other set of texts (the unclear ones) in their light. One set gives us the clear teaching about the nature of God while the others are "anthropomorphisms." But which set is the "clear" teaching?

If we subordinate set (2) to set (1) then, according to Helm, we can say that God can change his mind, that he is open to persuasion, that he is surprised by some things, and that some of his plans can be thwarted.

Moreover, we could attribute a "rich, ever-changing emotional life" to God. Many will find this appealing, but not Helm. The choice, he says, "seems obvious." We must subordinate set (1) to set (2). The texts about God not changing are the clear and correct teachings about God. If we did not say this, says Helm, then we will allow the "weaker" statements in Scripture to control the stronger, resulting in "theological reductionism in which God is distilled to human proportions." That is, we must use the clear, strong texts of Scripture that teach strong immutability and meticulous providence to interpret the unclear, weak texts that seem to teach that God changes and that God's will can be resisted. Otherwise, we make God into a very large human—we create God in the image of humans. Who wants to do that?

Helm's method for handling the problem is rather common, but there are a number of problems with it. First, we should notice that Helm has used a philosophical criterion to determine the correct interpretation of these biblical texts. This is legitimate, but we should be up front about what is going on—subordinating biblical texts to philosophical argument. Helm claims that it is improper to think of God as having human characteristics such as changes of mind and emotions. Why? Because we don't want to reduce God! Reduce God from what? From an exalted conception of divine transcendence and sovereignty. After all, any God worth his salt is strongly immutable, impassible, timeless, exercises total control over creation and never, ever, takes any risks that humans would do things God does not want done. But wait just a minute. If we are going to use philosophical arguments to tell us which texts of Scripture teach the truth about God and which texts are merely metaphorical, then we need to put those philosophical arguments on the table in order to debate them. Simply asserting that I'm "reducing God" or that I'm being impious are rhetorical devices intended to scare me off.

A second problem is that Helm begs the question. He says we must take the clear/strong texts and read the weaker ones in light of them. But hold on—that is precisely what is being debated. On what grounds does he decide which texts are the strong ones? Those texts that agree with his view of God! Isn't that interesting? The passages about God not changing and exercising meticulous providence are the clear teaching of Scripture because they agree with his understanding of the divine nature. Otherwise we don't really have a God at all. In other words, for Helm only the strong Calvinist view affirms a "real" God. However, this begs the question by assuming that his view of God is the correct one. Moreover, it can be argued that Helm's understanding of God is a reduction of God to human proportions. After all, for many the image of the ideal Western male is a do-it-alone individual, not relying on anyone's cooperation, who is never affected by what others do and whose will is always done. God is a real Marlboro man!

Helm's methodology here is replicated by most of the critics of open theism to characterize the open view as holding to a diminished deity. For Helm and others, any deity that does not exercise total control is deficient and diminished. Any God who takes risks is a lesser God than one who takes no risks. What many fail to notice is that this claim means that Arminians worship a lesser God, not the real God. This attack on open theists is also an attack on all Arminian theology as well as on the theology of many of the early church fathers.

Instead of taking the scriptural texts about God responding to what we do and subordinating them to the texts about God not changing, I propose a better solution. Do we have to subordinate either set to the other? We need to ask whether the two sets of texts are actually in conflict with one another. In order to have a conflict between these different texts we have to interpret, as Helm does, Malachi 3:6 to mean God cannot change in any respect. If God cannot change in *any* way, then clearly God does not grieve over human sin or respond to our prayers. But do the verses about God not changing say that God does not change in *any* way? No, they do not. What Malachi says is that God is faithful to his covenant people and refuses to allow them to be destroyed. Malachi is not stating an abstract philosophical principle about divine immutability! He is speaking of God's covenant faithfulness to his people. The same is true of Numbers 23:19 and 1 Samuel 15:29 (which is a quote of Num. 23:19). God refuses to change his mind in these two situations. These texts do not say that it is impossible for God to change, only that in these specific situations God will not change his mind no matter what the human response is.

In my view, we can affirm both sets of biblical texts rather than imposing one on the other. (You should like this both/and thinking instead of either/or.) There is no conflict between the texts if we hold that God's nature does not change but that God can change in some respects. The evangelical professor of Old Testament and president of Gordon-Conwell Seminary, Walter Kaiser, recently wrote on this issue and discussed these very texts. God does not, says Kaiser, change in his nature or his unconditional promises, but "God is not a frozen automaton who cannot respond to persons; he is a living person who can and does react to others." Open theists agree with this and, going a bit further, hold that God can change in his thoughts, will, and emotions. God is not wishy-washy but neither is God a stone. God is steadfast in keeping his covenant, but the exact way in which he carries out its fulfillment is not set in concrete. Christianity does not require an absolutely immutable

God, that is, one who cannot change in any respect—it only requires a faithful God.

Now I want to briefly apply this same line of reasoning to the issue of divine omniscience and the status of the future. There seem to be two types of texts in Scripture: (A) those where God is portrayed as learning (Gen. 22:12), changing his mind (Exod. 32:14), and being surprised (Jer. 3:7), and (B) those where God is portrayed as declaring that X will occur or knowing that X will occur (Isa. 42:9; 44:28). That is, sometimes God says something specific will happen and it does, but there are other times where God says something specific will happen and it does not come about. Bruce Ware, Paul Helm, and others say that we must subordinate one set of Scriptures to the other. To say that God changes his mind, switches to Plan B, or is surprised in some way is to diminish God. Instead, the "clear" teaching of Scripture is that God knows every detail of what will happen in the future—the future is completely definite for God. Again, there are good philosophical arguments to support this view of God. However, open theists (as well as others) find these arguments problematic.

Proponents of openness think that there is a better way of handling such scriptural texts. They claim that we do not have to place either set of texts, A or B, "over" the other. Set A above may be called the "motif of the open future" while set B is the "motif of the closed future." That is, some aspects of the future are definite or settled while others are indefinite or not determined. Helm and others believe that the motif of the closed future is the way God really is in relation to us, while the motif of the open future is the way God only "seems" to be in relation to us. Hence, one set of Scriptures is true while the other set represents God's "accommodation" to us (i.e., they do not depict God as he really is). But what if both sets are true? Helm and Ware believe that set B teaches that God has exhaustive definite foreknowledge such that the future is *completely* definite or determined. Consequently, they believe that only one set of Scriptures teaches the real truth. Proponents of openness reject this. Instead, they say, set B is about that *part* of the future that is definite or determined. Some aspects of the future are definite and God knows them as such, and so God can utter predictions about what will happen. Set A then is about that *part* of the future that is indefinite or open—yet to be determined—and God knows it as such. Hence, both sets of texts teach the real truth about God and neither has to be subordinated to the other. Thus there is no apparent contradiction in Scripture. God can declare the future regarding those events that are definite and be surprised, change his mind, etc., about those future events that are indefinite.

This approach allows us to maintain that God is open to our prayers and allows himself to sometimes be persuaded by them, that God has a rich emotional life, and that God enters into reciprocal relations of love with us, responds to us, and is faithful and steadfast. This model better handles the scriptural data Helm wants to explain, and it does so without sacrificing notions of God that many of us find important, such as divine relationality and divine faithfulness. Also, it does not subordinate one set of texts to the other but allows both sets to speak to us, since there is no contradiction at all. Hence this is a more excellent explanation (theology).

I look forward to your thoughts.

Your friend,
John

# 27 **Chris:** Omniscience and Foreknowledge

Dear John,

Just got your most recent letter on "two types of texts in Scripture," and I am eager to discuss these important issues with you. I have a few initial responses to the letter itself and then some general thoughts concerning divine omniscience.

1. I'm in full agreement with you that the search for a "foolproof method of reading Scripture" is fruitless. We are finite and sinful. Hence, our reading of the Bible, as you put it, "is not infallible or immune to correction." We do need each other, as I have written in my most recent letter. I would only add, however, that we need more than each other. We need the entire community of the saints, those present and those who have gone before. That is, if I discover that my interpretation of a text goes dead set against the church's reading of the text, particularly in the church's earliest years, I need to take a second and third look at my interpretation. I think you and I differ at this point. I'm more willing to accept the church's exegetical tradition as the framework for my own interpretation of Scripture, and you're more likely (as a good Protestant!) to hold on to your interpretation until you're proven

130

incorrect, even when your interpretation is quite new, novel, and provocative.

2. You're correct in noting that certain texts in Scripture do present God as changing and others as unchanging. As for Helm's interpretation, I resonate with his warning against a "theological reductionism" that distills God to "human proportions," a tendency that I've noted in the openness model. Yet, as you rightly observe, no openness theologian I know of desires to "make God into a very large human—creating God in the image of humans." The question remains, however, as to whether there are weaknesses or blind spots in the openness model and hermeneutic that seem to humanize God in a manner the church has been reluctant to advocate. When Clark Pinnock argues, for instance, that "God anticipates the future in a way analogous to our own experience," I think he's inverting or turning the dynamic of the *imago Dei* on its head. Too often the openness model makes human characteristics or qualities the measuring rod for understanding God, something we've already discussed quite a bit.

3. The question of God "risking" remains interesting and problematic for me. The possibility of divine risk certainly entails specific positions regarding the extent of God's knowledge and God's relationship to time. If God's knowledge of the future is exhaustive, as I will argue, it is difficult for me to understand how God can risk in the sense of taking chances.

4. I'm glad to have the opportunity to work with you through the issue of God's immutability. I'm not sure I will agree that God cannot change in any respect, at least when relational issues are involved, but you're probably going to call me incoherent! I'll try to argue that God is immutable and yet still grieves over human sin and responds to our prayers. We'll see how successful I am. I would affirm strongly with you that "God's nature cannot change." The conclusions we deduce from this proposition might well differ. By the way, your reference to Walter Kaiser interested me. I would agree with Kaiser that "God is not a frozen automaton who cannot respond to persons," but I'm not convinced that a strong view of immutability would turn God into such.

5. I think you're wrong in your insistence that texts in which God accommodates his revelation to human understanding and capabilities "do not depict God as he really is." As I mentioned in my last letter, if an openness theologian is going to consistently and coherently argue against any kind of accommodation in divine revelation, then God is going to end up as an embodied divinity.

Pinnock seems to me more consistent at this point than you in his movement toward advocating the embodiment of God.

6. Your proposal concerning set A texts and set B texts is quite interesting, but I doubt it will be convincing to theists who contend that God is eternal (outside of time). The idea of set A texts only works if certain aspects of the future are indefinite or open in the sense you describe, and of course that is part of the debate itself. Your advocacy of "presentism" is a possible way to bring set A and set B texts into congruence, but it in turn hits me as problematic. Think, for instance, of our debate on the testing of Abraham in Genesis 22. God seems to be ignorant of both Abraham's future action and of the present state of Abraham's heart. The fact that the testing of Abraham is a future action does not belie the fact that God is testing Abraham to find out what is in his heart, not what will be in his heart. Hence, I think you need to come up with a more convincing demonstration that God knows the present exhaustively, but not the future.

Indeed, I find the openness model's contention that God does not know the future exhaustively terribly difficult to swallow, but this is no surprise to you. God's purported ignorance of the future is surely one of the most troubling and provocative aspects of the openness model and clearly includes the possibility of divine error.

As you put it, God may give a forecast of what he thinks will occur "based on his exhaustive knowledge of the past and present." The limitation of God's complete or exhaustive knowledge to the past and present (your "presentism"), at least when the extent of God's knowledge includes the decisions of free persons, leaves open "the possibility that God might be 'mistaken' about some points." I find the possibility of divine error to be terribly problematic and its implications, theologically and pastorally, horrific. If so, it's only fair for me to offer an alternative explanation of what divine omniscience and foreknowledge entail. A few opening thoughts: Omniscience is clearly a watershed issue for the openness model. If I'm correct, all of the following propositions would be included in the openness understanding of omniscience:

1. God's knowledge is complete and perfect. God knows all things that are possible to know. As you write, "Omniscience may be defined as knowing all there is to know such that God's knowledge is coextensive with reality."

2. God knows completely all future acts and events that God has sovereignly ordained must come to pass. Question: Do these sovereignly ordained future acts/events include the choices and responses of

people? If so, is God in these specifically future cases willfully violating the freedom of humans? In *The God Who Risks* you describe "nonconsensual control" as "divine rape," precisely because "the will of one is forced on another." The specific context for this divine rape concerns salvation, but the principle can be extended. Further, you admit "the desire God forces on the elect is a beneficent one—for their own good—but it is rape nonetheless." If so, how can other sovereignly ordained, beneficial decisions and acts of God related to the future avoid the charge of divine rape? Only, I suppose, if these future choices and actions of God do not involve the choices and actions of human beings. God's future actions and knowledge then become severely limited. Is this what you mean to say? God ends up with a knowledge of the future that is quite limited indeed. Or else God occasionally rapes us, but only when absolutely necessary.

3. God does not know exhaustively all of the future, precisely because the future includes the decisions and actions of free human agents, defined in a libertarian sense. If God were to know the decisions and actions of free human agents before the agents themselves act, the decisions and actions of these agents would not be free. That is, if God knows beforehand what I am going to choose to do, I am no longer free to do otherwise. Hence, significant aspects of the future remain "open" to God. God is "open" to the decisions and actions of free human agents, genuinely "vulnerable" to what we choose to do, a divine risk taker of sorts. Indeed, as you put it in the title of your book on providence, God is "The God Who Risks."

I want to debate these ideas with you in this letter in two ways (it might take two letters!). First, I want to present what I think has been the church's understanding of omniscience for by far the greater part of its history. Second, I want to apply pressure to possible cracks in the openness model of omniscience itself. What almost all opponents of the openness model find fault with is its limiting of the extent of God's knowledge, i.e., there are some aspects of the future that God simply does not know. We need to explore together carefully the implications of this proposition. Of course, other propositions, both of the traditional model of omniscience and of the openness model, will have to be examined. Is it true, for example, that God's knowledge of the actions of free individuals, defined in a libertarian fashion, precludes the possibility of human agents acting freely? Is this a necessary conclusion? Or are there other possible models that preserve the traditional or classical understanding of omniscience and also preserve libertarian freedom?

I contend that God's knowledge of the future is perfect and exhaustive. In Oden's words, "God's incomparable way of knowing knows the end of things even from the beginning." Or as Isaiah states, "I reveal the end from the beginning, from ancient times I reveal what is to be; I say, 'My purpose shall take effect, I will accomplish all that I please'" (Isa. 46:9–10).

Patristic writers consistently affirm exhaustive divine omniscience. Clement of Alexandria writes, "For God knows all things—not those only which exist, but those also which shall be—and how each thing shall be." In fact, Clement contends that God's knowledge extends to the innermost secrets of the human heart. "And foreseeing the particular movements, 'He surveys all things, and hears all things,' seeing the soul naked within; and possesses from eternity the idea of each thing individually." For Clement at least, God sees all things, knows all things, with a single glance: "For in one glance He views all things together, and each thing by itself."

While God knows all things in a single glance, Clement does not believe that this knowledge eliminates human freedom and the benefits reason provides for human life. "Now, then," Clement writes, "many things in life take their rise in some exercise of human reason, having received the kindling spark from God. For instance, health by medicine, and soundness of body through gymnastics, and wealth by trade, have their origin and existence in consequence of Divine Providence indeed, but in consequence, too, of human reason."

Augustine argues that God's knowledge is immeasurable. God's knowledge cannot be bounded or comprehended. "Let human voices be hushed, human thoughts still: let them not stretch themselves out to incomprehensible things, as though they could comprehend them." Paul speaks in a similar fashion in Romans 11:33–34: "O the depth of the riches and wisdom and knowledge of God! How unsearchable are his judgments and how inscrutable his ways! 'For who has known the mind of the Lord? Or who has been his counselor?'" Nothing is hidden or unknown to God. "There is nothing in creation that can hide from him; everything lies naked and exposed to the eyes of the One with whom we have to reckon" (Heb. 4:13).

Oden speaks of divine omniscience as "the infinite consciousness of God in relation to all possible objects of knowledge." The question then becomes, as you oftentimes have mentioned, What are possible objects of knowledge? If God cannot know the actions of free agents before these actions take place without violating or erasing freedom, as you maintain, then God's knowledge of the future does not include the actions of free agents.

As I've mentioned earlier in this letter, you do argue that certain aspects of the future are settled and the subject of God's knowledge, i.e., those aspects that God has sovereignly ordained to take place. How God can avoid your charge of divine rape in these future ordained areas remains a mystery to me. Maybe you can help me here.

Still, the openness model does argue that God possesses complete knowledge, but this knowledge does not include certain aspects of the future. These aspects—entailing the choices of libertarian free agents—are simply not present in the future for God to know. I remain unconvinced that the openness model is the only alternative available to those who desire to maintain both libertarian freedom and exhaustive divine omniscience. And compatibilists might have other models they can use in making sense of omniscience and human freedom.

To begin to wrap things up for this letter, my position, and the majority position in the church's history of exegesis, is that God's knowledge is perfect and complete, encompassing all aspects of the past, present, and future, including the actions of free agents. John of Damascus, for instance, writes that God "knew all things before they were" and specifically includes in God's knowledge the future fall of humanity into sin. He "saw that in the future man would go forward in the strength of his own will, and would be subject to corruption."

I find Hilary's discussion of Christ's knowledge to be helpful in making sense of the extent of God's omniscience. In commenting on Christ's knowledge, Hilary directs his reader to "appeal to the judgment of common sense." "Is it credible," Hilary asks, "that He, Who stands to all things as the Author of their present and future, should not know all things?" Indeed, Hilary points to Paul's statement that in Christ are hidden "all the treasures of wisdom and knowledge" (Col. 2:2–3). Thus, "Jesus Christ knows the thoughts of the mind, as it is now, stirred by present motives, and as it will be tomorrow, aroused by the impulse of future desires."

Interestingly, Hilary comments that the apostle John specifically writes that "Jesus knew from the beginning who they were that believed not, and who it was that should betray Him" (John 6:64). The implication of John's teaching is that by Christ's "virtue His nature could perceive the unborn future, and foresee the awakening of passions yet dormant in the mind: do you believe that it [Christ's knowledge] did not know what is through itself, and within itself? He is Lord of all that belongs to others, is He not Lord of His own?" Human knowledge, founded on "human natures" with their inherent limitations, foresees "what they determine to do: knowledge of the end desired accompanies the desire to act." In like manner, divine nature and the extent of divine knowledge are inextricably linked. "Does not He Who is born God, know what is in, and through, Himself? The times are through Him, the day is in His hand, for the future is constituted through Him, and the Dispensation of His coming is in His power."

Well, I think I've hooted at you long enough for one letter. You're in my prayers and thoughts.

---

Chris

# 28 **John:** Views of Omniscience

Hey, Chris,

Regarding your last letter, I was disappointed that you did not respond to my main concern: What view of God do you bring to the biblical text such that you are able to differentiate the correct way of interpreting the passages of Scripture I raised? If there is a clear set of texts, how do we ascertain it? How do we determine when we are reducing God to human proportions and when we are not?

You say that open theism has a tendency to distill God to human proportions. What criterion are you using to make this judgment? You do not seem to accept all the divine attributes of classical theism. For instance, you don't seem to accept the classical definition of impassibility, and in your last letter you say that God may be able to change in some respects. Hmm. Do you know what Augustine, Aquinas, Calvin, and contemporary classical theists would say about you? They would say, "Chris Hall has a tendency to reduce God to human proportions." You see, it all depends on the view one holds as to whether someone is reducing God. I don't think I am but you think I am. You don't think you are but Aquinas would say you are. Aquinas did not think he was but Tillich would say even Thomas made God too human. So, I welcome you to the "club" of those who are accused of reducing God to human proportions.

Concerning your comments about my statement about "divine rape": you have me there and I cry "uncle." That statement was a mistake. I

137

don't know why the rest of the information on the note card did not make it into that paragraph in my book. The statement was supposed to cite some feminist theologians who refer to meticulous providence as divine rape. Most evangelical open theists believe that God can remove our free will if God sees the need to accomplish some specific action—which would most likely be related to the redemption of humanity. Some open theists believe God does this regularly. I think God does it rarely, if ever. John Polkinghorne and others say that God never overrides human freedom.

You say you are unconvinced that open theism is the "only alternative available to those who desire to maintain both libertarian freedom and exhaustive divine omniscience." You are quite correct. Let me try to clarify three different views on the subject (I will include another chart at the end of the letter that differentiates these views). The first view, classical theism, affirms that God is strongly impassible, immutable, unconditioned, and exercises meticulous providential control. God never responds to what we do, is never grieved, and the divine will is never influenced by our prayers or actions. God's omniscience includes knowledge of what is, for us, the future. God knows everything that we will do in the future because God is the one who has determined the future. Libertarian freedom for humans is rejected. Calvinist classical theists, for instance, argue that if humans had libertarian freedom, then God could not know what we would do in the future. Since God does know what we will do in the future, humans do not have libertarian freedom. So God knows the future because God ordains the future.

The next two views have much in common over against classical theism. They agree that God is omniscient, but they disagree as to the precise content of that omniscience. Specifically, does omniscience include exhaustive definite foreknowledge of future contingent events? Both of the following views agree that God is affected by our prayers and actions, and both views reject specific sovereignty where God knows what will happen in the future because God determines the future. Both views reject the classical theist definitions of impassibility and immutability because they affirm that God enters into genuine dynamic give-and-take relations of love with us. Both views believe that humans have libertarian freedom and that God takes the risk that we will not do what God would like us to do. I call these two views "freewill theism" because they have so much in common. They do, however, divide on a couple of issues.

The first version of freewill theism I call traditional freewill theism. This has been one of the most popular views among Jews and Christians. In Christian theology this was the view of most of the fathers prior to Augustine; today it is typically called "Arminianism." In this view God knows everything that creatures with free will are going to do in the future (though it is claimed that God's foreknowledge does not cause us to do what we do, so humans still have free will). This view of foreknowledge is typically called "simple foreknowledge" or "timeless knowledge." God simply "sees" all of history/time at once, since God is not subject to time—everything is an eternal present to God—no past or future. Hence, God has exhaustive definite knowledge of all future contingent events (there is nothing that will ever occur that God did not know prior to creation). But God does not determine everything that will occur. According to this view, when God says to Abraham "now I know that you fear me" (Gen. 22:12), or when God "changed his mind" after Moses prayed (Exod. 32:14), these texts are not to be taken at face value, since God always knew these things and it is logically impossible for God to change his mind.

The other version of freewill theism is open theism (sometimes it is called "neo-Arminianism"). This position agrees with traditional free-will theism (Arminianism) on the rejection of strong immutability and impassibility, as well as on soteriology, guidance, prayer, grace, sin, etc. However, it is a distinctive version of freewill theism in two respects: divine timelessness and exhaustive foreknowledge. In this view God knows all the past and all the present exhaustively, but it views the future as partly definite and partly indefinite. God knows that certain events will happen because certain causal factors have occurred (e.g., when an earthquake will occur) or God knows that God will bring about specific events because God determines them to be (e.g., the new heaven and new earth). God does not "know" precisely what creatures with free will will do in the future, though God may have very accurate "beliefs" about what we will do, since God knows our pasts and our characters exhaustively. God is involved in genuine give-and-take relations with us, inviting us to join him in carrying out the divine will on earth. According to this view, God tested Abraham to find out whether Abraham would trust God, and God was affected by the prayer of Moses. Of course, Arminians want to affirm that God is in genuine give-and-take relations with us and that our prayers make a difference even to God. However, we believe that our Arminian brethren are inconsistent when they affirm that God timelessly foresees all that we do and also that God responds to us and even "grieves" over our sin.

So, we have two different understandings of the divine nature and the type of sovereignty God exercises: classical theism and freewill theism. We also have two different understandings as to how God knows what humans will do in the future and whether humans have free will. For classical theists, God knows the future because God determines it. For traditional freewill theists, God knows the future without determining humans. Most of the early fathers said that God timelessly foresaw which individuals would place their faith in Jesus and so God elected them prior to creation. Classical theists reject this approach, since it means that God is affected (conditioned) by creatures.

This last point is very important, for it is the key to answering your question about how God can exhaustively know the future and yet be said to take risks. If God gets exactly everything he wants, then God takes no risks. For classical theists this is the case, since the divine will is never thwarted in the least detail. For classical theists, God exercises meticulous providential control and humans do not have libertarian freedom. Things are much different, however, in traditional freewill theism. For this view, God exercises general providential control, is conditioned by creatures in some things, and grants humans libertarian freedom. Hence, humans can sin, which thwarts God's will, for God does not want sin. So God takes the risk in creating humans with such freedom that they will rebel against him.

But how can it be a risk if God eternally foreknew that humans would sin? To understand this we need to break down the "logical order" of God's decisions. We are not speaking about a "temporal order" (in time) of God's decisions, so the words I will use will make use of verb tenses, but please remember that we are not speaking about these decisions taking any time for God—it is simply the logical order of thought. According to the simple foreknowledge view God decides to create a particular type of world. He decides that he will grant humans libertarian freedom and that God will not tightly control everything. "Next" God looks ahead in time and foresees what humans will do. What God foresees is that humans do sin. Technically, God's knowledge that humans would sin is subsequent to his decision to create us with free will. Consequently, God took a risk in making the decision to create, for it was only "after" this decision that God knew we would not do what he wanted us to do. So, even though God foreknew that humans would sin before God created anything, God still took a risk. Once God creates, God knows everything that will ever happen, but the fundamental risk has already been taken. Thus, the early fathers, Eastern Orthodoxy, Arminius, Wesley, C. S. Lewis, Philip Yancey, and many others believe that God has taken risks, even though they also affirm exhaustive definite foreknowledge of future contingent events.

Summarizing, the crucial issues for the question whether God takes risks are (1) the type of sovereignty God decided to practice and (2) the type of freedom God granted humans. Both traditional freewill theism and open theism agree on these points and thus agree that God takes risks (*contra* classical theism). But open theism goes beyond traditional freewill theism by denying divine timelessness and exhaustive definite foreknowledge. I will leave the arguments that open theists use for another letter. Here, I have simply tried to clarify the different views rather than argue for one.

Have a good weekend, Chris.

---

**Blessings,**
**John**

## Chart: Classical, Freewill, and Open Theism Compared

All three views agree that God is creator, savior, self-sufficient, personal, wholly good, omnipotent, omniscient, and omnipresent. They disagree on divine changeability, whether God can be influenced by us, the type of sovereignty God exercises, foreknowledge, whether God experiences time, and the nature of human freedom.

| | Classical Theism | Freewill Theism | Open Theism |
|---|---|---|---|
| **Operative Root Metaphors** | God as creator, judge, and king. | God as savior, lover, and friend. | Same as freewill theism. |
| **Nature of God** | Emphasis on divine control. God is unchangeable and unaffected by creatures. God has no emotions. | Emphasis on divine relationality. God is changeable in will and emotions and is affected by creatures. Divine nature is unchangeable. | Same as freewill theism. |
| **Type of Sovereignty** | God exercises unilateral power in creation, providence, and redemption. God takes no risks because he tightly controls every detail. | God exercises unilateral power in creation, but bilateral power with creatures in providence and redemption. God takes risks because he exercises general control. | Same as freewill theism. |
| **Creaturely Freedom** | Humans have compatibilistic freedom: we can act on our desires but our desires are determined. | Humans have libertarian freedom: we could have done otherwise than we did—not determined. | Same as freewill theism. |
| **Problem of Evil** | All evil is planned by God to display the divine glory. Every evil has a specific purpose and serves God's good plan—humans respond exactly as God wants. | Evil is permitted but not wanted by God in order to make possible relations of love with creatures. Humans do not necessarily respond as God wants them to. | Same as freewill theism. |
| **Salvation/ Election** | Solely of God's choosing—we respond to God's choice. Irresistible grace, unconditional election. | God's choosing is based on our choice—we cooperate with God. Enabling grace, conditional election. | Same as freewill theism. |
| **Petitionary Prayer** | Our prayers never influence God; they are God's means of bringing about what God has ordained. | May influence God; God makes some of his decisions dependent on whether we pray or not. | Same as freewill theism. |

| | | | |
|---|---|---|---|
| **God's Will** | God's will cannot be thwarted—it is always done. God has a blueprint for our lives regarding job, marriage, etc., and we always fulfill it. | God's will can be thwarted. Some believe God does not have a blueprint for our lives regarding job, marriage, etc. Together with God we determine our lives. | God's will can be thwarted. God does not have a blueprint for our lives regarding job, marriage, etc. We cooperate with God to decide what the future will be. |
| **The Relationship between God, Time, and Eternity** | God as "eternal." God is timeless. He experiences all time at once (the eternal "now"). | Most (not all) Arminians agree with classical theism here: God is timeless. Some Arminians agree with openness on this point. | God as "everlasting." God endures forever in "time" and interacts with us in give-and-take relationships. |
| **The Nature of the Future** | The future is completely definite because God determines it. | The future is completely definite because God timelessly sees all that will happen in history. God does not determine all of the future. | The future is partly definite and partly indefinite—God is working with us to bring about the future. God does not determine all of the future. |
| **Foreknowledge** | Eternally definite foreknowledge. God knows all that humans will do in the future because he controls what we do. Foreknowledge is based on foreordination of all things. | Eternally definite foreknowledge. God knows all that humans will do in the future because he "foresees" it—he does not control what we do. Foreknowledge is based on timelessness, not foreordination. | Presentism: God knows the past and present exhaustively as well as that part of the future that is determined or foreordained. God knows all the possibilities of what humans could do and what we are likely to do but lacks absolute certainty about what we will do. |

**Note:** Some people who claim to be "classical theists" affirm that God has changing emotions (e.g., grief) and that God is affected (passible) and influenced by humans. Some even reject divine timelessness. Those who make such changes are really not "classical" theists.

# 29 **Chris:** Further Thoughts on Some Divine Attributes

Dear John,

Thanks much for your recent letter. I don't mind you pressing me on my preconceptions of God and how they affect my perceptions of the biblical portrayal of God. I have discussed in past letters how I read the Bible and the key voices from both past and present that have played a role in shaping my thinking. It is very difficult to discern my preconceptions, though, largely because they are just that—preconceptions. Preconceptions only rise to the surface, I suppose, when someone such as a debate partner forces them to the surface in the context of discussion and argument. Even after our extended discussions, though, it is difficult for me to identify exactly my preconceptions of God, that is, what God must be like.

I do realize that my thinking is not entirely settled, however. To say that I've shifted my point of view would be to speak too strongly. Nevertheless, I'm less settled in my thinking, particularly regarding the nature of human freedom. My earliest teachers were firmly grounded in the Western theological tradition: Augustine, Luther, and Calvin come to mind. Almost all my seminary professors were grounded in the Reformed tradition and I'm thankful for each one.

Part of me still struggles with the idea of libertarian freedom, largely because of the effect of sin on the mind and will. Unless God acts pre-

144

veniently, how can a human's fallen, distorted, skewed mind and will respond to the gospel? The mind and will need to be brought to life through the regenerating work of the Holy Spirit, with the result that we love those things that are indeed worthy of love, God being at the top of the list. Yes, I'm sure you can hear the voice of Augustine in the background. But I'd also argue that behind Augustine one can discern the form of Paul.

Having said this, over the past few years I've been listening to voices other than Calvin, Luther, and Augustine. The Cappadocians come to mind, along with John Chrysostom. In addition, Tom Oden's writing has been rich food for thought. These voices are encouraging me to take another look at the issue of freedom, and I'm reexamining the question carefully.

J. I. Packer has also had a profound effect on my thinking. It was Packer, for instance, who taught me that antinomy was a feasible means of dealing with the problem posed by divine sovereignty and human responsibility. Packer came to mind as I read your ideas about "the logical order" of God's decisions. How so? Packer, who one would think is a supralapsarian, is actually an infralapsarian. I remember distinctly sitting in Packer's office one day and Jim speaking of God's response against evil and sin. That is, in the "logical order" of God's decree and decisions, Packer saw God as responding against evil and sin, rather than God decreeing sin and evil "before the Fall" (supralapsarian).

As a result of Packer's influence I've been willing to think two thoughts side by side as it were, affirming both meticulous providence and human freedom and responsibility. I don't know whether Packer affirms libertarian freedom or not. The more I think about this, though, if there is an antinomy here, as Packer argues, at least one pole of the antinomy must be libertarian freedom. Compatibilism wouldn't require the antinomy, as far as I can tell.

All this to say that I'm rethinking the issue of human freedom. On the one hand I continue to affirm that true freedom is found in the ability to love God, our neighbor, and the goodness inherent in the created order. On the other hand I'm thinking through the issue of libertarian freedom and whether the synergism (cooperating with God) advocated by the Eastern fathers and theologians such as Oden makes more sense than the monergism (only God works) of the Reformed tradition. William Craig's thoughts concerning middle knowledge and the Molinist tradition also have been thought provoking for me.

As I look at your different charts I find myself in agreement with the following propositions (some from your charts and some not):

1. I think that we need to affirm God as creator, judge, and king along with God as savior, lover, and friend. All are root metaphors that teach

us important truths about the nature of God. It's unclear to me why we would prioritize one set of metaphors over the other set. On what basis do we ascertain metaphorical priority? For example, a fallen human being such as myself is apt to flee from the metaphors that present God to me in an image or illustration that I do not like. While I might naturally like to prioritize God as lover and friend, the metaphor of God as judge or king might actually be what I need to hear loud and clear. Evangelical students are frequently comfortable and familiar with God as savior, lover, and friend, and not infrequently commit the sin of presumption. That is, they (and we) presume on God's friendship, imagining God to be the chum next door, and act accordingly. Lewis is helpful at this point. When Aslan appears in the tales of Narnia, the children delight in rubbing against him, jumping on him, kissing his face, and so on. Simultaneously, though, we can hear Aslan softly growling. His claws remain unsheathed. This is not a tame lion.

I'm reminded of a favorite passage in *The Lion, The Witch and the Wardrobe*. Susan comments on the prospect of meeting Aslan: "'I shall feel rather nervous about meeting a lion.' 'That you will, dearie, and no mistake,' said Mrs. Beaver, 'if there's anyone who can appear before Aslan without their knees knocking, they're either braver than most or else just silly.' 'Then he isn't safe?' said Lucy. 'Safe?' said Mr. Beaver. 'Don't you hear what Mrs. Beaver tells you? Who said anything about safe? Course he isn't safe. But he's good. He's the King, I tell you.'"

I think Lewis has got it just right. Nearness and distance. Transcendence and immanence. Intimacy and awe.

2. As I've mentioned in my discussion of impassibility, I don't believe that God is a stone pillar. God does respond to us, though how God does so remains a mystery to me. The issue of petitionary prayer comes to mind, and once again Lewis proves helpful. Lewis comments that "any petition is a kind of telling. If it does not strictly exclude the belief that God knows our need, it at least seems to solicit His attention." The formula "Hear us, O Lord" comes to mind. Does God really need to be reminded to listen to us? Does God need to be informed? Lewis replies, "But we cannot really believe that degrees of attention, and therefore of inattention, and therefore of something like forgetfulness, exist in the Absolute Mind. I presume that only God's attention keeps me (or anything else) in existence at all."

So if in petitionary prayer we are not trying to grab God's attention, what are we doing? Lewis believes that "our whole conception of, so to call it, the prayer-situation depends on the answer." So what is going on in prayer? In answering this question, Lewis writes that though God's knowledge of us "never varies, the quality of our being known can." How so? Well, in an "ordinary" sense, God knows lots of things as things:

"earthworms, cabbages, and nebulae," among others. Lewis believes that God's knowledge of us includes this kind of ordinary knowledge but can clearly go beyond this, depending on how we respond to God. When we become "aware of the fact" of God's knowledge of us and "assent with all our will to be so known, then we treat ourselves, in relation to God, not as things but as persons. We have unveiled. Not that any veil could have baffled this sight. The change is in us. The passive changes to the active. Instead of merely being known, we show, we tell, we offer ourselves to view."

It would be presumptuous on our part to "put ourselves thus on a personal footing with God," if it were not God "who gives us that footing." "For," as Lewis reminds us, "it is by the Holy Spirit that we cry 'Father.' By unveiling, by confessing our sins and 'making known' our requests, we assume the high rank of persons before Him. And He descending, becomes a Person to us. But I should not have said 'becomes.' In Him there is no becoming. He reveals Himself as a Person." Lewis's thoughts provide fertile ground for future discussion and lead to my next point.

3. God is, I would argue, intensely relational, as seen in the eternal love shared by Father, Son, and Holy Spirit. Both the Cappadocians and Augustine seem to be in agreement here (although I know that there is controversy today regarding Augustine's position). How divine relationality and human relationality are related, though, remains an area where much work needs to be done. How do we know God is a person? He has revealed himself to us as such. Hence, there is something in me as a person that corresponds to God as person, though I have no reason to believe that the congruence is exact. As Lewis says, "the Person in Him—He is more than a person—meets those who can welcome or at least face it. He speaks as 'I' when we truly call him 'Thou.' (How good Buber is!)"

Having said this, however, Lewis is quick to comment, I think rightly, that speech concerning an "I-Thou" relationship with God "is, no doubt, anthropomorphic; as if God and I could be face to face, like two fellow-creatures, when in reality He is above me and within me and below me and all about me. That is why it must be balanced by all manner of metaphysical and theological abstractions." Thus, the need for discussions and debates such as ours! Neither the abstractions nor the anthropomorphisms, however, are the literal truth. "Both are equally concessions; each singly misleading, and the two together mutually corrective. Unless you sit to it very tightly, continually 'Not thus, not thus, neither is this Thou,' the abstraction is fatal. It will make the life of lives inanimate and the love of loves impersonal."

4. I have affirmed compatibilistic freedom in the past. I'm less settled in this area in the present. Perhaps there is a way to combine the best

aspects of both understandings of human freedom. I need to read more deeply in the Eastern fathers and in the Orthodox theology that is rooted in the patristic tradition if I'm to make greater sense out of this issue.

5. God is eternal, i.e., timeless. This seems to me to be an essential aspect of what it means for God to be creator. That is, time, space, and matter are all aspects of the created order. I'm trying to stay on top of the current debate concerning God's relationship to time, and I am listening particularly to Alan Padgett and William Lane Craig.

6. If I choose to affirm middle knowledge or God's simple foreknowledge of the actions of libertarian free agents, can I not say that God's meticulous providence includes the actions freely chosen by human beings? Do I necessarily have to affirm "general" rather than "meticulous" providence?

7. The future is definite, either because God has determined the future or because God timelessly sees all that will happen in history. I'm still ruminating on this issue.

8. I am moving in the direction of foreknowledge based on God's timelessness, rather than foreknowledge based solely on God's foreordination of all things.

Having said all this, it remains unclear to me in what way the openness model is significantly improving on past models for understanding God's providence. There are two distinguishing marks of the openness model. First, a rejection of divine timelessness based on biblical texts that present God as changing his mind, growing in knowledge, grieving over the actions of human beings, reevaluating past decisions, etc. Second, a rejection of exhaustive divine foreknowledge based on one principal philosophical argument: timeless foreknowledge is useless for God since God cannot change what he foresees human beings doing. It is contradictory to say that God foresees what will actually happen and to also say that God changes it to make it not happen. This response would render God's foreknowledge incorrect.

Food for thought, but this letter is already long enough. I'll be in touch soon.

_____

With warm greetings,
Chris

# 30 **John:** Classical Theism

Dear Chris,

Thanks so much for your last letter. I appreciate the fact that you are a theological pilgrim still on the journey. I consider myself a pilgrim as well. Since I agree with most of what you said I will only add some remarks to see if I can further the discussion.

My earliest theological teachers held diverse theological positions, so I was not inculcated into one stream of thought. In seminary my teachers were, like yours, steeped in the Western tradition of Augustine and Calvin—they had little appreciation of the Eastern fathers, Arminius, or Wesley. Later I transferred to a Lutheran seminary where I was exposed to Luther, Bonhoeffer, Barth, Pannenberg, and the like. So I've had quite an eclectic mix of teachers.

However, I think I'd have to say that throughout my education I've always leaned towards the Eastern fathers, Arminius, and Wesley regarding free will. None of these people minimized our enslavement to sin or the effects of sin on our wills and minds. Without the gracious help of the Holy Spirit enabling us to understand the gospel and encouraging us toward faith, none of us would come to Christ. Though many of the people I draw from did not use the term "prevenient grace," they affirmed the concept. In my *The God Who Risks* I cite some studies by Eastern Orthodox theologians that say just this. Going in this direction is not semi-Pelagian, but it does affirm a form of synergism (but only after grace). For monergists such as Calvin, we do not cooperate with divine grace, for God gives us everything, including "our" faith.

149

You mention that J. I. Packer is an infralapsarian rather than a supralapsarian. That is, he rejects the notion that God first ordained some individuals to salvation and then ordained the fall into sin in order to bring about a state of affairs needing redemption. Instead, he affirms that God allowed the fall into sin and then ordained to elect some for salvation. You are correct in saying that this implies that God "responds" to sin rather than decreeing it. In his great work on predestination, Louis Berkhof rails against infralapsarians (e.g., such as Packer) for conceding too much and contradicting classical theism. The problem, he says, is that saying that God *responded* to human sin means that God is conditioned or affected by creatures. This flies in the face of strong impassibility and immutability—making God dependent on creatures, forcing God to react to them.

Berkhof maintains that Reformed theology denies any conditionality in God—God is not affected by us. Of course, other Reformed theologians disagree. James Daane, for instance, says, "classical, creedal Reformed theology is not an unconditional theology. . . . Election in Reformed thought is God's gracious *response* to a sinful world." Karl Barth wrote, "If ever there was a miserable anthropomorphism, it is the hallucination of a divine immutability which rules out the possibility that God can let himself be conditioned in this or that way by his creature." This kind of Reformed theology warms the Arminian heart. A point typically unnoticed by my critics is how many Reformed thinkers I draw on in *The God Who Risks*. I'm not against Reformed theology; rather I am in conflict with all forms of theological determinism, most of which are based on classical theism.

Classical theism affirms strong immutability, impassibility, simplicity, and meticulous providential control and rejects libertarian freedom in humans (please refer to the chart included in letter 25). The logical implications of this set of beliefs result in doctrines such as unconditional election, irresistible grace, that everything that happens (including sin) is exactly what God intends to happen, and that our prayers never affect God. Calvin and other classical theists understood this very well, so if Packer and others do not want all these implications, they will have to modify or reject some of the divine attributes affirmed by classical theism. I welcome such changes!

You are attracted to such changes especially as they impact our prayer life, but you worry about the nature of true human freedom. Let me comment first on prayer and then on freedom. There are various kinds of prayer that both classical and freewill theists can agree on. However, when it comes to *impetratory* prayer, only freewill theists can coherently affirm it. Impetratory prayer means that God does something because we asked, something that God would not have done had we not asked.

"You have not because you ask not" (James 4:2). This particular type of prayer entails that God responds to our requests—God is, in some things, influenced by us. Classical theists understand that this means that God would be dependent on humans for some things, and since they believe that God cannot be dependent on us for anything, this type of prayer does not happen. Instead, our prayers of request are simply God's means (tools) by which he brings about what he had previously ordained to accomplish. Our prayers are meaningful for classical theists, but they are not impetratory—they never affect God.

Does this mean that we are to "put ourselves on a personal footing with God?" Are we to give God advice? As one critic asked me: "Who do you think you are to advise God what to do?" In his book *The Divine Conspiracy*, Dallas Willard has a very good chapter on prayer in which he defends the same view I do. He admits that some views of petitionary prayer degrade God. For instance, those that think we can get whatever we want if we just use the correct words. However, against the critic who asks "Who do you think you are to speak to God that way?" Willard claims that this is not against God's honor. To suppose that "because of the interchange God does what he had not previously intended, or refrains from something he previously had intended to do, is nothing against God's dignity if it is *an arrangement that he himself has chosen*." I don't claim that God is obligated to listen to my prayers or take my wishes into account. However, God has adopted me in Christ and invited me to "make my requests known" and to ask what we will in Jesus' name (Phil. 4:6; 1 John 5:14–15; John 14:13–14). We cannot force God to do our bidding but, incredibly, God elevates us to dialogue with himself. Biblical characters such as Abraham, Moses, and Elijah reasoned with God—even argued—and God approved of this because God desires dialogue rather than a monologue. This is solely of God's choosing; we in no way force ourselves on God. If God wants to be flexible in his relations with us, that is his choice, and as Willard concludes, "It is not inherently 'greater' to be inflexible."

I think you agree with this but you worry that this synergism runs counter to true human freedom: we are truly free only when we are in proper relationship with God. Outside of being properly related to God we are in bondage. Let me suggest an old theological distinction that may be of service. We have "formal" freedom to choose many things, but as sinners we do not have "material" freedom—the freedom to properly love God. That is, we have libertarian freedom but we have misused it in sin and so find ourselves unable to be in proper relationship with God (materially unfree). In grace, the Holy Spirit enables us to begin the process of reconciliation. We are now given the opportunity to use our libertarian (formal) freedom to live out the material freedom of a new life in Christ. Because of the grace of God we are brought into the sacred dance of the

Holy Trinity and, after we learn to dance, we are to teach others the same (except on evangelical college campuses, of course. Ha!).

While I'm on the subject of libertarian freedom, let me answer one of your questions. You ask whether you can affirm both libertarian freedom and meticulous providence. Sorry, but you can't (unless you want to contradict yourself). Meticulous providence means that God guarantees that everything that occurs is precisely what God intends to occur. God's will is never thwarted in anything, no matter how minute. Libertarian freedom means that we have the ability to do things that God does not want us to do (such as sin). Thus, God's will can, for some things, be thwarted. Following C. S. Lewis we could say that God takes risks if he creates us with libertarian freedom. However, if God exercises meticulous providence then God does not take risks of any kind. You see, meticulous providential control and libertarian freedom are incompatible.

You are also worried whether this view of God makes us too "chummy" with God, rendering him a "tame lion." Like you, I love those lines from Lewis's *The Lion, The Witch and the Wardrobe*. Of course the Christian God is not "safe." He wants to redeem and transform every aspect of our lives, society, and the created order affected by sin. Such transformation is not safe, but it is for our well-being.

The opposite problem, as you point out, is turning God into such an abstraction that we lose both the concept of divine love and the personhood of God. I believe that this happens in a number of religions. In some forms of Hinduism, for instance, Brahman is considered neither to love nor not to love, for God is abstracted beyond the category of the personal. The same is true for certain Buddhist understandings of Nirvana, where the ultimate reality is totally beyond human language. The same problem arises in Plato's and Aristotle's conceptions of highest being. When you try to attain that which is beyond all human language and thought, you find the impersonal silence. Unfortunately, many of these detrimental ideas have entered into Christian theology, shaping our understanding of God. My thesis is that many classical theists come perilously close to losing the Christian God who loves. Even though all Christian classical theists have affirmed that God is personal and that God loves us, their formulations often leave us with impoverished understandings of God. I do not disagree with all aspects of classical theism, but I do want to correct certain points that I believe have had a negative impact on Christian thought and practice.

Well, that is all for now. I look forward to hearing from you again.

May God bless you in all that you seek to do for him,
John

# 31 **John:** Biblical Texts Supporting Open Theism

Hi, Chris,

I thought it would be helpful to provide an overview of the kinds of biblical texts proponents of openness use as evidence for our position.

*1. The Bible portrays God as authentically responding to his people's petitions.* When God called Moses to be the one to lead the Israelites out of Egypt, Moses gave God several reasons why he was inadequate for the task. In response, God attempted to satisfy Moses' felt needs. At one point God seems to switch to Plan B by allowing Aaron to do the public speaking instead of Moses. God is flexible. God had the prophet Isaiah announce to King Hezekiah that he would not recover from his illness. However, Hezekiah prayed and God responded by sending Isaiah back to announce that God had changed his mind, Hezekiah would recover and not die (2 Kings 20).

In the New Testament, Jesus is said to heal a paralyzed man because of the faith of his friends (Mark 2:5). He responded to the faith of this small community by granting their request. People's faith, or lack of it, deeply affected Jesus and his ministry. Mark says that Jesus could not perform many miracles in Nazareth due to the lack of faith on the part of the people in the community (6:5–6). It is not that their unbelief completely tied God's hands, but it did seriously alter what Jesus would have done had they been more receptive to his message. Not only did

153

the response of the community affect what Jesus did, it also disturbed him, for "he was amazed at their unbelief" (6:6). Oftentimes, what God decides to do is conditioned on the faith or unbelief of people. As James says, we have not because we ask not (4:2).

2. *The Bible portrays God as being affected by creatures and as sometimes being surprised by what they do.* Genesis 6:6 says that God was grieved because humans continually sinned. Why would God grieve if God always knew exactly what humans were going to do? It makes no sense to say that a timeless being experiences grief. The biblical writers, when describing God's speeches, use words such as "perhaps" and "maybe." God says "perhaps" the people will listen to my prophet, and "maybe" they will turn from their idols (e.g., Ezek. 12:1–3; Jer. 26:2–3). Furthermore, God makes utterances like, *"If* you repent then I will let you remain in the land" (Jer. 7:5). Such "if" language—the invitation to change—is not genuine if God already knew they would not repent. Classical theism has a very difficult time with this. Since God specifically ordains everything that happens, God is in total control as to how the people will respond. Why would God use conditional language since God is the one in control of whether the people repent or not? It seems then that such utterances were disingenuous on God's part.

Moreover, God says, "I thought Israel would return to me but she has not" (Jer. 3:7; cf. 32:35). God also planted cultivated vines and did not expect that they would produce "wild grapes" (Isa. 5:1–4). In these texts God is explicitly depicted as not knowing the specific future. God gave King Zedekiah two possible courses of action with the outcome of each (Jer. 38:17–23). It does not seem from the text that the future was as yet determined. If God knew it was determined, then why give Zedekiah options? Similarly, God repeatedly sent Elijah to call King Ahab to repentance, but the king refused to do so. Was God playing a cat-and-mouse game with Ahab? If God foreknows from the moment he gives the invitation that it will be pointless, then God is holding out a false hope. On the other hand, if God is genuinely inviting the people to change, then the future is not yet definite.

Scripture mentions occasions where God "consults" with certain people of faith in deciding the course of action God will take. God does this with Abraham concerning judgment on Sodom (Gen. 18), and with Amos regarding judgment on Israel (Amos 7). God, in freedom, decides not to decide without consulting these figures of faith or, in the case of Moses (Exod. 32), to decide to change his decision in response to Moses' intercession. Finally, God asks questions regarding an indefinite future. God agonizes over what to do with his sinful people (Hosea 6:4; Jer. 5:7). When God asks, "What am I going to do with you?" God is seeking a response from the people. God desires dialogue, for if the people will join in dialogue, reconciliation is yet possible. By asking such questions God puts a choice before the people and judgment is not yet inevitable.

*3. The Bible portrays God as testing people in order to discover what they will do.* In addition, God tests people to find out how they will respond. God puts Abraham to the test and says, "Now I know that you fear me" (Gen. 22:12). God puts the people of Israel to the test to find out what they will do (Exod. 15:25; Deut. 13:3). After the sin with the golden calf God told the people, "Put off your ornaments that I may know what to do with you" (Exod. 33:5). Why test them if God eternally knew with certainty exactly how the people would respond? One could say the testing was only for the benefit of the people, since it added nothing to God's knowledge, but that is not what the texts themselves say. Unless we have good reasons for overriding the texts why not go with what they teach?

*4. The Bible portrays God as changing his mind—altering his plans—as he relates to his creatures.* God announced his intention to destroy the people of Israel and start over again with Moses, but Moses said that he did not want that, and so God did not do what he had said he was going to do (Exod. 32). It is not that God had to do what Moses wanted. Rather, it is that Moses had become a "friend" of God such that God values what Moses desires. Sometimes God made promises that were stated in unconditional terms, yet God changed his mind due to human rebellion. For instance, God had promised Eli that his descendants would be priests forever in Israel. But after the horrible exploitation of the priestly office by his sons, God changes his mind and removes the line from the priesthood (1 Sam. 2:30). Another illustration of this occurs with King Saul. God's original plan was to have Saul and his descendants as kings forever in Israel (1 Sam. 13:13). In other words, there would have been no Davidic kingship. Later, however, due to Saul's sin, God changes his mind and rejects Saul and his line (1 Sam. 15:11, 35). Though Samuel and Saul plead with God to change his mind back to the original plan and go with Saul and his sons, God declares that he will not change his mind again on this matter (1 Sam. 15:29). If God always knew that he was never going to have Saul's line be kings, was God deceitful?

God changing his mind is an important theme in the Old Testament, for the expression is used of God around three dozen times. Moreover, the statement that God can change his mind is added to the great summary of the divine nature given to Moses (Exod. 34:5–7). God was said to be compassionate, gracious, longsuffering, and abounding in lovingkindness and truth. This is a sort of creedal formula about God. It is no small matter that this creedal statement is enlarged to include "and one who changes his mind" (Jonah 4:2; Joel 2:13). Change of mind is placed right alongside graciousness as a key descriptor of God.

One may try to explain all of these texts about divine change of mind in terms of law. That is, if the people sin then God threatens punishment. But if the people repent of their sin then God withdraws the threatened punishment. This would mean that God did not really change his mind at all, since it only amounts to God saying that his punishments are conditioned on what humans do, and since God knows what they will do, God was never going to punish the people in the first place. It only "looks to us" like God changed his mind, but God in fact did nothing of the sort. This is the way Calvin, for instance, understands these texts. Why does he think God cannot change his mind? Interestingly, Calvin does not provide a scriptural reason. Rather, he appeals to Plato's philosophical argument that any sort of change in God would only be a change for the worse. Change of mind is a change, so it would be a change for the worse and that would imply imperfection in God.

Reading Scripture in the light of philosophical argument is legitimate, but I do not find this argument convincing enough to reinterpret the three dozen texts that say that God changes his mind to mean that God does not change his mind. Moreover, not all passages about God changing his mind can be explained by their being conditioned on what humans do. Sometimes God changes his mind even though the Israelites do not change their sinful behavior (Judges 10; Hosea 11). God can change his mind if he wants to, whether we change or not.

It is no accident that brilliant classical theists such as Aquinas and Calvin said that God could not change his mind, was never affected by our prayers, never grieves, cannot suffer, does not test us in order to find out what we will do, and that terms such as "perhaps," "maybe," "if," and "expectation" do not apply to God. Such notions simply do not make sense if God is timeless, immutable in all respects, and has exhaustive definite foreknowledge. This is why Jonathan Edwards said that intercessory prayer has no effect on God. Rather, it is only "as if God were moved by the prayers of his people." Of course God cannot be moved by our prayers! Who would think such foolish thoughts? What kind of being do you think God is? Do you want to reduce God to human proportions by believing that God actually responds to our prayers?

If affirming that God can be grieved, respond to our prayers, test us, and interact with us in time is reducing God to human proportions, then so be it. I am guilty as charged. However, I really don't think I'm reducing God at all, for I believe this is the way God actually is and there simply is no greater God. The sorts of texts I've cited are just a sampling and are not intended to be an exhaustive list. I just wanted to summarize the types of Scripture passages that open theists use to arrive at our view. This certainly does not prove our case. It simply shows how we are reading Scripture. I'm trying to help you see the "method in our madness." Not that you will agree with me, but I hope that you can understand how this view makes sense to me.

In previous letters you have asserted that this understanding of God is out of harmony with the church fathers. I don't think it is—at least, not totally. I will write another letter on that.

Shalom,
John

# 32 **Chris:** Biblical Texts Supporting Open Theism

Dear John,

Thanks for the letter laying out in succinct form how openness theologians read key biblical texts. I found this letter to be quite helpful, though it should be no surprise that I disagree on a number of points. Indeed, it's probably fair to say that I think the weakest link in the openness argument is its exegesis. We've already discussed in some detail the story of Hezekiah, the question of whether Judas was destined to betray Jesus or not, and the testing of Abraham in Genesis 22. In this letter I hope to make a comment or two on other important texts on which the viability of the openness model seems to depend.

Undergirding the question of how we interpret specific texts, however, is a constellation of broader theological questions and issues that I think affects both how we read the Bible and the exegetical conclusions we reach. For instance, as you ponder Genesis 6:6 (God's grief over humanity's continuing sin) you ask, "Why would God grieve if God always knew exactly what humans were going to do? It makes no sense to say that a timeless being experiences grief."

I'm not so sure. Does exhaustive divine knowledge of past, present, and future events *logically* demand that God can't experience grief over these events? Why are God's timeless knowledge and the possibility of divine grief *necessarily* incoherent? It seems that your argument

158

assumes the impossibility of reconciling a divine response of grief on the one hand and God always knowing that evil and suffering would characterize human history on the other. But why can grief be coherently related only to events that surprise God when they happen? Even on a human level, it seems that our experience of grief is not restricted to events or occurrences that we did not know were going to occur.

Think, for example, of past events in human history. I know there is a difference between "past" events and timelessness itself, but there are some similarities between the two. Past events are irreversible, irrevocable, and unchangeable, a permanent aspect of human experience. Though my knowledge of the past is deficient, the past as an irreversible, unchanging reality can easily produce grief within me. For instance, the horror of the Holocaust is a permanent part of my intellectual landscape. I must have first learned about Hitler and the concentration camps when I was seven or eight, but for as long as I can recall, this information has been part of who I am. As a past event, the Holocaust is irreversible. Once I heard of its occurrence, I always knew it was "going to happen." This knowledge, however, still produces deep sadness within me.

Now if this is true on a human level, it also seems to be true of God. If God possesses exhaustive, timeless knowledge of the past, present, and future, there is no logical reason why he could not experience grief, particularly since God is a personal being who experiences love, joy, compassion, etc. For the emotion of grief seems no more dependent on being surprised than any other emotion. Indeed, the constancy and certainty that exhaustive knowledge entails would only accentuate the level and quality of divine sadness and divine love.

I stress this because you seem to be arguing that God's knowledge must be limited and time-bound if divine grief is to be genuine. I don't see why this must be the case. In other words, I disagree with the statement you make in *The God Who Risks* that grief is solely a temporal word. Time-bound creatures temporally experience *the object of grief*. But your argument that grief itself is therefore temporal transfers the temporal experience of creatures to the very nature of grief. Yet if timeless experience is possible at all, there is nothing intrinsically incoherent about timeless experiences including grief.

I like the way you use the verb "portrays" in your discussion of various biblical texts, i.e., "The Bible portrays God as being affected by creatures and as sometimes being surprised by what they do." You're right. The Bible does contain texts such as these. The question then becomes, "What do biblical writers mean to communicate by such a portrayal?" I think the openness model is forcing all of us to think through this question more carefully. This is a good thing. We must investigate carefully what biblical writers mean when they speak of God changing his mind. The openness model contends that divine repentance texts teach that God's omniscience is not exhaustive, at least regarding the future. God changes his mind as God's knowledge of the future changes, i.e., God's knowledge base increases as the future moves into the present and God responds accordingly.

The following propositions, based on your exegesis of key texts, seem to be included in the openness model:

1. God exists in time rather than outside of time.
2. God possesses perfect knowledge of the past, present, and those aspects of the future that God has ordained will come to pass. The rest of the future remains unknown for God, precisely because there is nothing for God to know. The boundaries of time are as binding on God as on other creatures.
3. God's omniscience must be defined as God's knowledge of those things that can actually be known. Hence your advocacy of "presentism." God's knowledge of the past and present is perfect. Yet God's knowledge is constantly increasing as the future moves into the present.

I hope I've represented your position fairly. If I haven't, I'm sure you'll let me know! My response to the openness model of omniscience is one of dissatisfaction. Here's why. Suppose God acts in the present on the basis of what God believes will happen in the future. However, God errs. What God thought was to occur in the future has not taken place. For instance, God thought free agent A was going to do X, but A actually does Y. Hence, God's act or response in the present to what he thought free agent A was going to do is incorrect. This divine action, unfortunately, is now written in cement. Thus, we end up in the unfortunate position of affirming God's present exhaustive knowledge of God's own mistakes, mistakes made on the basis of God's own decision to limit his knowledge of significant aspects of the future.

My thoughts turn to Isaiah. What distinguishes God from all human idols, Isaiah argues, is God's wondrous omniscience. "Remember this and consider, recall it to mind, you transgressors, remember the former things of old; for I am God, and there is no other; I am God, and there is no one like me, declaring the end from the beginning and from ancient times things not yet done, saying, 'My purpose shall stand, and I will fulfill my intention,' calling a bird of prey from the east, the man for my purpose from a far country. I have spoken, and I will bring it to pass; I have planned, and I will do it" (Isa. 46:8–11).

Your response to this text from Isaiah runs as follows: "God declares 'the end from the beginning' (Isa. 46:10) can be interpreted harmoniously with either divine foreknowledge or the present-knowledge model defended here. It all depends on the content the interpreter gives to the expression. I think God is declaring the 'end' (exile and restoration) before it happens. But this does not entail exhaustive foreknowledge, only the ability of God to bring it about."

Your explanation is reasonable but not, I think, terribly helpful for the openness model. How so? For God to bring about the exile and restoration, surely God is going to have to violate the freedom of at least some people. As you put it, "Sometimes God simply discloses what God is going to do irrespective of creaturely decision. God can bring some things about on his own if he decides to do so (Isa. 46:9–11). But this does not require foreknowledge, only the ability to do it. Many of the biblical predictions commonly cited as requiring foreknowledge actually only require foreordination. . . . God foreknows what he determines to do."

It seems to me that you are incorporating aspects of a different model of God's sovereignty and providence that don't align well with the openness model but are necessary if you are to account adequately for all the biblical data. For example, in *The God Who Risks* you describe the different types of relationships God can choose to have with "human personal agents" and employ Vincent Brümmer's two types of "games" for describing models of God's sovereignty.

In game one, "God, a personal agent, creates human personal agents and establishes rules whereby both parties in the game may say yes or no to each other. In this game God makes the initial move by saying yes to us, loving us, and desiring a relationship of mutual love. It is now our turn to respond to God's move, and we may respond with either a yes or a no." Game one, then, is based on what you argue is required for a "relationship of mutual love." That is, love cannot be coerced and can be rejected. In game two, "humans do exactly what God decrees they will do. God determines, directly or mediately, all that happens. In game 2, if God says yes to humanity, then humans still have to say yes or no to God, but our 'response' is caused by God." Hence, game two is based on what you describe as "causal relations."

The relationship between these two models is confusing to me. Game one appears to be the model that best represents the openness view. Yet you yourself allow for God to play game two at key junctures in the biblical narrative, such as the exile and restoration of Israel. If so, how is love also operative at these junctures, at least from an openness perspective? If, as you put it, "God . . . does not want to dance alone, dance with a mannequin, or hire someone who is obligated to dance with him," how can God ever play game two and still exercise relational love at the same time? Every time God foreordains something to occur involving human moral agents, love must be absent from God's action, at least from an openness perspective. Yet, I would argue, it is divine love that motivates every act of divine foreordination. I'd like to see openness theologians explain more clearly how both models coherently relate to one another. In addition, how does God's love manifest itself according to the rules of game two?

Perhaps causal relationships can also be relational. As I've stated in earlier letters, if I saw my child happily running in the direction of an oncoming train, my love would motivate me to intervene immediately, whether my child wanted me to or not. The openness model, with its heavy reliance on reciprocity for genuine love to be exercised, doesn't allow enough room for the various manifestations of divine love present in salvation history. I agree that reciprocity often manifests itself in relationships of love, but at certain specific points, especially when "rescue" is involved, love moves beyond reciprocity while still remaining deeply relational.

Further on in your letter you comment that the Bible "portrays God as testing people in order to discover what they will do." You then ask: "Why test them if God eternally knew with certainty exactly how the people would respond? One could say the testing was only for the benefit of the people, since it added nothing to God's knowledge, but that is not what the texts themselves say. Unless we have good reasons for overriding the texts, why not go with what they teach?" Good question.

I believe the following considerations weigh strongly in favor of considering the divine-repentance texts as instances of divine accommodation, God "lisping to us," to use Calvin's phrase.

First, and by far the most important consideration in favor of divine accommodation, is that the openness model's rejection of accommodation necessarily leads to the assertion that not only is it possible for God to err, but that God has erred in the past, errs in the present, and will continue to make mistakes in the future. God makes mistakes, as you have argued, because God is in time rather than timeless, and knows only the past and present exhaustively. As you put it, "Though God's knowledge is coextensive with reality in that God knows all that can be known, the future actions of free creatures are not yet reality, and so there is nothing to be known." God's temporality, God's choices, and the nature of libertarian freedom combine to necessarily limit the extent of God's knowledge. God can think I am going to act in a given fashion in the future but be dead wrong. Hence, God has made mistakes in the past, is continuing to make them in the present, and is bound to err in the future. The predication of divine error is the inevitable outcome of the openness model, or of biblical teaching if the openness model is correct.

You acknowledge in *The God Who Risks* that the "notion that God could be dismayed or wrong about anything may not sit well with some people" and attempt to ameliorate this difficulty by qualifying what you mean by error. "Using the term more loosely, we might say that God would be mistaken if he believed that X would happen (for example, Israel in Jeremiah's day would come to love him) and, in fact, X does not come about. In this sense the Bible does attribute some mistakes to God."

Your exegesis, particularly of the divine repentance texts, has led you to this conclusion. I contend that any theological model that predicates God erring in the past, present, and future because of limited knowledge is *ipso facto* fatally flawed. In a word, if the result of openness exegesis is the predication of error of God and a drastically revised understanding of God himself, then these are sufficient reasons for asking whether one has interpreted the biblical text well. I'm deeply troubled by the assertion that God has made mistakes in the past and will do so in the future, but underlying my aversion to divine error is significant biblical testimony that must be included in the construction of a viable model of God's omniscience and providence, including texts such as Isaiah 46. That is, I don't think I'm speaking out of a biblical and theological vacuum at this juncture.

God is "perfect in knowledge" (Job 36:4; 37:16). I realize that you might argue that God's knowledge possesses a kind of perfection. Perhaps God's omniscience is as perfect as time-bound knowledge can be. Yet key biblical texts unreservedly proclaim that God's plans and purposes, including Christ's cross and his role as the paschal lamb of God, have been formed "before the foundation of the world" (1 Peter 1:18–20; Eph. 1:4). Peter comments that his readers "were ransomed from the futile ways inherited from [their] ancestors . . . with the precious blood of Christ, like that of a lamb without defect or blemish. He was destined before the foundation of the world, but was revealed at the end of the ages for your sake." Paul writes that God "chose us in Christ before the foundation of the world to be holy and blameless before him in love" (Eph. 1:4). The writer of Revelation speaks of people whose names have "not been written from the foundation of the world in the book of life of the Lamb that was slaughtered" (Rev. 13:8). What is one to do with texts such as these, all of which speak of decisive acts of God taken before "the foundation of the world"? I believe the openness perspective produces fairly thin exegesis in response to these and other significant texts that appear to undermine the openness model. Let me provide some examples from *The God Who Risks*:

1. As we've already discussed, you don't believe Judas actually betrayed Jesus, a conclusion based on a questionable definition of *paradidomi* and heavily dependent on the idiosyncratic exegesis of William Klassen. You write "it is clear that Judas is not betraying Jesus and that Jesus is not issuing any prediction of such activity." As I've written before, I think the portrayal of Judas you provide is highly optimistic, particularly in light of John's comment that after Judas received the piece of bread at the Last Supper, "Satan entered into him" (John 13:27).

2. What are we to make of Jesus' request in the Garden of Gethsemane that the Father "remove this cup"? I believe Christ's request reflects his genuine humanity and the fear he deeply felt as his trial and crucifixion drew near. You, on the other hand, believe Jesus is seeking "to determine the will of God. Jesus wrestles with God's will because he does not believe that everything must happen according to a predetermined plan." I don't agree. From Caesarea Philippi on, Jesus had been insistent that he "must undergo great suffering, and be rejected by the elders, the chief priests, and by the scribes, and be killed, and after three days rise again. He said this quite openly" (Mark 8:31–32). Indeed, when Peter tries to modify Christ's prediction, Jesus brands the attempt as demonic. Why, then, would Jesus in the Garden of Gethsemane still be attempting to determine the Father's will? The Father's will had already been revealed to him and he knew that this would include the crucifixion.

Thus I'm less than convinced by your argument that the "incarnation was planned from the creation of the world," but not the cross. A fundamental aspect of the incarnation was the cross itself. Can we really say that in Gethsemane "Jesus is in the canoe heading for the falls. There is yet time to get over to shore and portage around the falls. Jesus seeks to determine if that option meets with his Father's favor. But the canyon narrows even for God." I don't think so. Where would we be left if Jesus had made it to shore or found portage from the falls of the crucifixion? We would be left in our sin, separated from God, lost for eternity.

You comment that the "notion that the cross was not planned prior to creation will seem scandalous to some readers." I think you're right. Yet your exegesis is plausible if God does not genuinely know the future or has not foreordained the cross. The level of plausibility is the question. You write: "Perhaps God knew the possible outcomes (what might happen if sin did come about or did not come about) and planned a different course of action in each case. Each one included the incarnation, but it took on a different rationale depending on which case came about."

I think you're underestimating the strong predictive element in the Old Testament concerning the cross. In *The God Who Risks*, for instance, you mention Isaiah 53 only once in passing. The New Testament writers, however, refer to this text directly or allude to it as they mine the riches of the cross and analyze its grounding in prophetic literature (cf. John 12:38; 1 Cor. 1:18; Mark 9:12; Heb. 4:15; John 1:10; Matt. 8:17; Matt. 26:66; Acts 8:32; 1 Peter 1:19; Matt. 27:57; 1 Peter 2:22; 2 Cor. 5:21; Gal. 3:13; Rom. 6:9; Eph. 1:5; John 17:3; 1 John 2:1; Rom. 5:18; Phil. 2:9; Col. 2:15; Mark 15:28; Luke 23:34). One of the most striking instances is Philip's interaction with the Ethiopian eunuch. The eunuch specifically asks Philip "about whom" Isaiah is writing in Isaiah 53. Philip's response? "Then Philip began to speak, and starting with this Scripture, he proclaimed to him the good news about Jesus" (Acts 8:35).

I'd like to add a final thought on the biblical portrayal of God testing people. If, as I've argued, God does not test people in order to find out how they will respond—with an accompanying change in his own mind—why does God allow such providential testing to occur? At least one reason for God's testing is to aid in the process of character formation. John Chrysostom believed that God desires to transform the human soul into "a serviceable condition for virtue" and does so in the present life through his providential ordering of each individual's life, with accompanying testing. For example, Chrysostom writes that the "present life is a wrestling school, a gymnasium, a battle, a smelting furnace, and a dyer's house of virtue." Through divine providence God "works" the soul, "melts it, and delivers it over to the testing of trials." Why? "In order to strengthen those who have lost heart and who have let themselves go, in order that those who have already been tested might be even more approved and unconquered by the plots of the demons and the snares of the devil," and thus "completely worthy for the reception of the good things to come."

Chrysostom illustrates this testing and cleansing process in his exegesis of the story of the paralytic let down through the roof and subsequently healed by Jesus. God allowed the man to suffer for an extended period, not out of negligence, cruelty, or ignorance, but rather as "a sign of the greatest care for his welfare." "For as a gold refiner having cast a piece of gold into the furnace suffers it to be proved by the fire until such time as he sees it has become purer: even so God permits the souls of [human beings] to be tested by troubles until they become pure and transparent and have reaped much profit from this process of sifting: wherefore this is the greatest species of benefit."

Chrysostom is confident that God knows how long the metal must remain in the fire to be thoroughly cleansed. God will not allow it to remain in the fire "until it is destroyed and burnt up." Thus, we can know in the midst of our trials and testings that "when God sees that we have become more pure, he releases us from our trials so that we may not be overthrown and cast down by the multiplication of our evils." This cleansing is only one of the reasons Chrysostom posits for God's testing, but I think it is a helpful one. Got to run.

With warm greetings,
Chris

# 33 **John:** Openness and Tradition

Hi, Chris,

I have some brief remarks about your last letter, and then I want to discuss a topic we've touched on several times: the role of tradition in theology. First, you are correct that one can experience grief again and again based on the memory of an event. The issue is whether a timeless being can experience changing emotions. You say, "If timeless experience is possible at all." A timeless consciousness has an unchanging experience, not changing experiences based on responses to humans, for that implies that God experiences time. A timeless deity does not have different experiences at different times.

Second, you raise the issue whether presentism implies that God "errs." God errs, according to you, if "what God thought was to occur in the future has not taken place." What if God thought Saul or Israel would obey him in specific instances but they disobeyed? The Scripture, of course, says exactly that. Even proponents of divine timelessness have a problem here because God sent a famine expecting Israel to put away her idols but she did not. How could God timelessly know they would not repent and still intend for them to repent? I don't believe God is making an "error" when he wants something to happen but it does not. The only way to avoid this issue is to say that God sent the famine and never intended for the people to repent. In other words, you have to affirm meticulous providence and reject all forms of freewill theism. This is precisely why scholastic Calvinists have hammered on Arminians, because freewill theism implies that God sometimes fails to get specifically what he wants. If you think that traditional Arminianism overcomes this problem because it affirms God's timeless knowledge of all future actions, you are wrong. The reason is this: God cannot use knowledge of what he knows will occur to make it not occur. For instance, God cannot use his knowledge of Israel's not repenting at a specific time as a basis for doing things for them in previous times so that they will, in fact, repent. That would imply that what God foreknew would not happen so he really didn't foreknow it.

According to the open view, God's decisions and actions will be the wisest decisions and actions that are possible under the circumstances—that is what perfect wisdom means. This does not mean, however, that God's actions always have their intended results. If we believe the Bible we will have to say that sometimes people failed to respond as God wanted them to. God wanted Saul to be obedient but he was not—that is the *risk* God took in giving us freedom, but it is certainly not an *error* on God's part. At the end of your letter you say that God knows just how much to test us to produce what God wants in us. If this means that God does not give us more than we can handle, then fine. But if it means that everything God intends to produce in us comes about, then you are affirming meticulous providence. In this case, God then tested Saul but never intended for Saul to be obedient, since whatever happens is what God wanted produced. God never intended to produce obedience in Saul. Clearly, I reject the notion that God never wanted Saul to be obedient. Rather, God wanted Saul's obedience but God did not receive it. However, this does not constitute an error on God's part.

Also, I said that for God to be mistaken or hold a false belief it would have to be the case that God "declared infallibly that something would come to pass and it did not. God would never be mistaken so long as he never said that X (for example, Adam will not sin) would infallibly come to pass and it did not." God will not *definitely believe* that something will occur unless it is *certain* to occur. If an event is not certain to occur, then God knows the degree of probability that it will happen. But God will not hold probabilities as absolutely certain and in order for God to be in error, God's knowledge of the probability of the event would have to be wrong. However, I deny that God's knowledge of probabilities is ever wrong, so I deny that God errs.

Let me move on to the role of tradition in doing theology. On several occasions you have suggested that openness theology significantly modifies the traditional view. I would like to make some comments about traditions and the nature of heresy. It is claimed that we do not agree with "the" tradition. Well, what might "the" tradition refer to? Is there a single tradition in church history regarding creation, anthropology, original sin and its transmission, Christology, atonement, salvation, ecclesiology, eschatology, and the nature of Scripture? Clearly, there is not. Just think of all the ink—and, unfortunately, blood—that has been spilled over these topics. However, one might say, "Hold on, Sanders, you know very well what we mean—the traditional doctrine of God and providence." But I contend that there never has been a single doctrine of God or view of providence in the church. To speak of "the traditional" view of sovereignty as meticulous providence is to ignore the actual tradition! The understanding of providence put forth by Augustine and others has always been contested by others in the church. Millard Erickson says that the history of Christian thought on the doctrine of God is not uniform. From early on issues such as divine immutability, impassibility, the content of divine omniscience, and the nature of sovereignty were debated. There is no single old model of God.

One of the claims made against open theists is that we are "revisionist" theologians. It is true that we are attempting to revisit some (not all) commonly accepted attributes of God and correct them in light of Scripture. Now, we may be incorrect in our conclusions, but the attempt to improve what has gone before us is certainly part of our Protestant heritage from the Reformation—a period of incredible revisions made in doctrines and practices. The Reformers thought that the process of reformation is never complete (*semper reformanda*). The history of theology is filled with people who made attempts to revise and improve what had been said before them. Augustine, Aquinas, Luther, Calvin, Arminius, and Wesley were "revisionists" in this sense. James Oliver Buswell Jr., former president of Wheaton College, proposed major revisions in classical theism when he rejected the doctrines of divine timelessness, immutability, impassibility, and pure actuality. "We should," he says, "shake off the static ideology which has come into Christian theology from non-Biblical sources." I am trying to follow Buswell's advice.

Many of the most vociferous evangelical critics of open theism claim they are defending "the traditional view of God." Yet, at the same time, they make significant modifications to the traditional view! The following Calvinist critics of openness make some rather shocking revisions to the divine nature. Ronald Nash says that the traditional understandings of pure actuality, divine simplicity, and impassibility must be rejected, immutability must be modified so that "human beings can make a difference to God," and he has serious doubts about divine timelessness as well. Bruce Ware revises the traditional doctrine of immutability and says that God enters into reciprocal relations with us (yet, he also holds that God exercises meticulous control over all we do). Wayne Grudem criticizes the Westminster Confession for accepting the "unbiblical" notion that God is "without passions." Millard Erickson surveys recent evangelical theologians and claims that "the traditional doctrine of impassibility is not the current one" among contemporary evangelicals. Erickson himself sees the problems with many of the traditional attributes and attempts to make some needed revisions. Few evangelicals today, even conservative Calvinists, are genuine classical theists.

These thinkers are to be commended for the courage to revise aspects of conventional theism in light of Scripture and philosophical argument. They are definitely revising classical theism, since Aquinas and Calvin certainly would not agree with these revisions. The great classical theists read their Bibles and concluded that God did not have changing emotions, or suffer, or respond to creatures. Nonetheless, it is really wonderful to see these sorts of reforms being pursued by conservative Calvinists. It does an Arminian heart good. Frequently in this debate, open theists are made to look like they are the only ones doing the revising. Our critics posture as defenders of the tradition affirming Vincent's Monitor: "what has been believed always, everywhere, and by everyone." They want people to think that they simply believe what everybody has always believed—and all the while they are revising the tradition in ways that would be unrecognizable to the great classical theists! Moreover, they make these revisions while condemning open theists for flaunting tradition!

The issue is not whether we should revise conventional theism. Rather, the question is what specific revisions we should make and whether these revisions are faithful to Scripture and logically coherent. Open theists argue that it is logically incoherent to affirm both that God is timeless and also say that God responds, suffers, and grieves, since these are temporal terms. It is incoherent to say that God is a God of meticulous providence who ensures that everything happens exactly as he intends and that God is saddened by what we do. The great classical theists of yesterday and today understand these logical problems, which is why they would not make the revisions that these evangelical Calvinists today are making. It is my belief that they make these revisions in spite of logic, because they know that the majority of evangelicals believe that God responds to us, may be influenced by our prayers, and is saddened when things go badly. One of my former pastors believed that our prayers of petition never affected what God decides to do. However, he would never clearly say that to the congregation! Small wonder, since they would have been aghast. Many of these theologians know that their old views of God just won't sell in the evangelical marketplace and so they try to infuse divine responsiveness and openness to creatures into their old views. Though I applaud these theologians for making needed revisions, I believe they will either have to return to a more robust classical theism or make even more revisions in the direction of open theism if they wish to be logically consistent.

Proponents of openness theology do revise certain aspects of the traditions but certainly not all. We have no desire to keelhaul the tradition. In fact, all of us, including open theists, are shaped by various traditions that inform our reading of Scripture, how we pray, as well as our worship. Traditions are helpful but not necessarily perfect, and this raises the question of the extent to which any of us are allowed to disagree with those who have gone before us. Of course, none of us can accept all of the tradition, since it is too diverse. We do take sides on issues such as infant baptism, whether clergy have to be male, and the form of church government. Hence, in some respects all of us have to sift through the history of Christendom, selecting those doctrines and practices we want to hand on as well as those we either reject or modify.

That is precisely what open theists are doing. We are simply trying to make the ancient relational model of God and his creatures more coherent. Just as Reformed theology has sought to make the Augustinian tradition more logical, so we are trying to modify the freewill tradition. Hence we see ourselves in continuity with previous theologies. Even on the issue of divine omniscience we see continuity. In the freewill tradition, divine foreknowledge was used to explain how God could eternally elect individuals to salvation without removing their libertarian freedom. God simply foresaw that they would exercise faith in Jesus and elected them on the basis of that knowledge. Open theism is in this freewill (Arminian) tradition but wants to reform it so that it is more biblically faithful and rationally coherent.

It is true that until the twentieth century there have not been many who could be labeled open theists. Although there have been many in the freewill tradition who have modified the divine attributes of impassibility and immutability, not many have taken up our understanding of foreknowledge (presentism). However, even this is not without precedent. Calcidius, a late-fourth- to early-fifth-century Christian writer, wrote an influential commentary on Plato's *Timaeus* and a lengthy treatment against fatalism in which he affirms the theory of presentism. In the Middle Ages Jewish writers discussed how the kinds of biblical texts open theists appeal to should be interpreted. Two very respected thinkers, Ibn Ezra and Gersonides, disagreed with the majority and held the open view of the future. Andrew Ramsay, one of Wesley's contemporaries, held that God chooses not to know what we will do in the future. Adam Clarke, a famous eighteenth-century biblical commentator, utilized presentism. It has been defended in various forms by the Methodist circuit rider Billy Hibbard; W. T. Brents, a giant of the Restoration movement; the Roman Catholic Jules Lequyer; and L. D. McCabe, who wrote two lengthy volumes on presentism in the nineteenth century, supporting it from Scripture.

In the twentieth century this trickle of support has turned into a rather substantial flow. Biblical scholar Terence Fretheim has published numerous studies detailing that this understanding of omniscience is taught in the Old Testament. Among theologians one finds it in the works of Greg Boyd, Clark Pinnock, John Polkinghorne, and Jürgen Moltmann. Among Christian philosophers there are so many that reject divine timelessness and affirm presentism that I will only list a few: Richard Swinburne, J. R. Lucas, Keith Ward, Peter Geach, and William Hasker. Respected spiritual writers such as Dallas Willard and Richard Foster affirm presentism. Willard believes that for God to have personal relationships with us, he cannot know what creatures with libertarian freedom will do. He writes: "I too was raised in a theology that presents God as a great unblinking cosmic stare, who must know everything whether he wants to or not." From this brief list it is clear that presentism is affirmed by a wide array of thinkers who are considered orthodox.

Some, however, claim that the idea that God does not know with absolute certainty all that we will do in the future is not orthodox—it is "heretical." The evangelical critics of open theism are fond of quoting Tom Oden's remark that presentism is a heresy. What Oden seems to mean is only that it was not the predominant view in the first eight centuries of the church. He does not mean by "heresy" that open theists should be expelled from Christian fellowship. When asked about this Tom said, "When I use the word 'heresy' I mean that the discussion now begins, not that it is finished." Well, that is certainly not what the Calvinists cited above mean by the term! They mean a teaching for which a person who affirms it is damnable. Heretics are those who should be cast out of all Christian communities. Though they can't remove us from all Christian communities, they are certainly trying very hard to kick us out of evangelicalism; using unseemly tactics to do so.

On what basis is openness classified as heresy? One possible ground for condemning openness is to claim that it conflicts with the teachings of some of the seven ecumenical councils. However, none of the Councils discussed the issue of omniscience and foreknowledge. If open theism is going to be condemned on the basis of the Councils it will have to be done on the basis of immutability and impassibility. The definition of the first Council of Nicea says, "The holy catholic and apostolic church anathematizes those who say: 'There was when he was not' . . . and those who assert that . . . he is mutable or liable to change." That is, the Son of God cannot experience change because he is fully God. The definition of the Council of Chalcedon reads: "[The Synod] expels from the priesthood those who dare to say that the Godhead of the Only-Begotten is passible/capable of suffering." Anyone who says the divine Son can suffer or who mixes the two natures is heretical. Openness asserts that the divinity of the Son is capable of suffering, so openness seems to conflict with these two councils. However, we need to tread carefully here. There are questions as to precisely what these writers meant by "mutable" and "passible." Did they mean change in any respect or only change in the being of God? Did they mean that God could not experience changing emotions and could not be affected by creatures? If they meant that the being of God does not change, then open theists are not anathematized and are not heretics. If, however, they meant that God does not change in any respect and thus can have no emotions and is incapable of being grieved, then open theists are indeed heretics. But then, so are Wayne Grudem, Ronald Nash, and Bruce Ware among others.

Moreover, if we must affirm all that the seven ecumenical councils said, then what are we to do with, for instance, this assertion from Second Nicea: "Following the royal pathway and the *divinely inspired authority of our holy fathers* [emphasis mine] and the traditions of the Catholic Church, we define with all certitude and accuracy that . . . the venerable and holy images are to be set up in the holy churches of God . . . in houses and by the roadside . . . images of . . . Jesus Christ, our undefiled Lady, the *theotokos*, of the honorable angels and of all saints and holy men. . . . In accordance with ancient pious custom, incense and lights may be offered to images, as they are to the figure of the precious and life-giving cross, to the book of the Gospels and to other holy objects." There is so much in these admonitions for Protestants in general and Baptists in particular to choke on as to warrant a theological Heimlich maneuver (Ha!). The Council declares that we are to perform these practices, but it is clear that most of us do not. On what grounds do we reject the authority of this Council? It claims that the holy fathers were "divinely inspired"! Were they divinely inspired about divine immutability, impassibility, and the veneration of icons? Most Protestants don't think so.

David Wells, professor of theology at Gordon-Conwell Seminary, asserts that the Creeds are often wrong. He says, for instance, that the Nicene Creed contains Origenist concepts and that Chalcedon conferred on Mary the title "Mother of God." The council said that this teaching was to be held inviolable, so Wells is rejecting the inviolable teaching of the seventh ecumenical council. Is Wells a heretic? Must we follow the canons of the seven councils? If so, then the following apply to us: we are to stand, not kneel when praying on the Lord's day; a woman under the age of forty cannot become a deaconess and if, after becoming one, she "despises the grace of God" and marries, she shall be anathematized; if you do not salute the icons you are anathematized; if you do not accept the gospels and the holy relics of the martyrs you are anathematized; Jews who convert must put away all Jewish customs including the Sabbath or they must not be allowed to take communion. Are those who do not follow all the teachings of these seven councils heretics? If one claims that open theists are heretics for conflicting with certain elements in the seven ecumenical councils—and it is not certain that we are in conflict—then we are in good company with Luther, Calvin, and many others.

In the history of the church, the word *heresy* has been used for a very large number of views. What Protestant belief was *not* labeled heretical when it was first proposed? John Eck, the theologian selected to champion the Catholic cause against Luther, repeatedly calls Luther and other Protestants "heretics." Eck asserts that the "Church as the pillar of truth, with Christ as leader and the Holy Spirit as teacher, does not err." Eck drips with sarcasm when he says how fortunate the Church is to have Luther to correctly interpret the Scriptures to us, since the Church has been in error for more than a thousand years. In response to open theism, Gerald Bray reproduces the arguments of John Eck: "It is hard to believe that in the late-twentieth century a few radicals have arrived at a truth which has escaped generations of sincere searchers." I find it discomfiting that evangelicals would use such anti-Protestant arguments to label other evangelicals "heretics." Remember, people died for "heresies" such as believers' baptism, separation of church and state, refusal to take oaths, and the priesthood of all believers.

Though not all branches of evangelicalism like to use the H-bomb on those with whom they disagree, that branch of evangelicalism that gave rise to neo-evangelicalism frequently threw heresy bombs at one another. B. B. Warfield called the holiness and pietistic understanding of providence heretical because they led to faith-healing movements. Machen called premillennialism "a very serious heresy." Van Til called Gordon Clark a heretic, and Clark was tried for heresy at Wheaton College. E. J. Carnell called fundamentalists "cultic," "sectarian," and "heretics." Evangelicals have demonized other evangelicals over evolution, charismata, megachurches, worship styles, women in ministry, inerrancy, and different views of the millennium. J. I. Packer and Charles Colson have been accused of giving up the gospel because they signed a statement written by evangelicals and Catholics.

Today's enemy that must be destroyed is open theism. It is as though some believe that if you confess with your mouth the Lord Jesus and believe in your heart that God has exhaustive definite foreknowledge of all future events, then you will be saved. Must we believe divine timelessness, immutability, and impassibility as well? To make this move is to confuse biblical Christianity with our developed theories about specific aspects of the faith. A theory of omniscience has never been the touchstone of orthodoxy. It does not appear in any of the ecumenical councils. We are saved by the grace of God manifested in the atonement and resurrection of Jesus Christ, not by theories about divine foreknowledge or eternality. We must never confuse what C. S. Lewis called "mere Christianity" with our theologies. Certainly, our doctrines make a difference in the ways we practice our Christianity—they are important. But a doctrine of foreknowledge is not part of the core of the Christian faith.

Presently, there is a strong call by evangelicals to "return to the tradition." Personally, I believe this is sorely needed. Evangelicals are far too ignorant of the Christian heritage. There is much we can retrieve from the traditions that will enrich our worship and our theology. However, this "return" to "the" tradition must not assume that there is a single tradition. The Christian theological heritage is and has been multiform. We should be careful of any naïve return that fails to scrutinize the traditions. As I demonstrated above, evangelicals simply cannot accept what some consider essential aspects of the tradition. Finally, labeling open theists heretics because they don't line up with the majority view regarding omniscience does not settle this issue, because all Protestants are heretics by that criterion. Nobody likes to be called a heretic, for it places you in some unsavory company. On the other hand, being labeled a heretic places you in some excellent company as well!

Sincerely,
John

# 34 **Chris:** Tradition and Theology

Dear John,

I'm eager to discuss the issue of tradition with you and where the openness model might fit or not fit into the church's history of biblical and theological reflection. But before I deal directly with the issue of the openness model and tradition, I want to present my own understanding of what tradition is and how it functions within the church. In a recent essay, Stan Grenz and John Franke provide a helpful definition of the Christian tradition. They write that the Christian tradition is "the history of the interpretation and application of canonical Scripture by the Christian community, the church, as it listens to the voice of the Spirit speaking through the text." Hence, the Christian tradition is surely related to the church, Scripture, and the Spirit.

Grenz and Franke continue, "More specifically, we might define the Christian tradition as the ongoing historical attempts by the Christian community to explicate and translate faithfully the first-order language, symbols and practices of the Christian faith—by means of the interaction among community, text and culture—into the various social and cultural contexts in which the community has been situated." Thus, tradition is not "static" but grows and develops. Key issues in understanding tradition include:

1. The issue of authority.
2. The authenticity of development, i.e., how does the church determine whether a theological model is a valid, authentic development of the tradition or a distortion?

176

Both authenticity and authority are key issues for understanding and identifying the Christian tradition, precisely because the concept of tradition "denotes," as D. H. Williams puts it, "the acceptance and handing over of God's Word, Jesus Christ (*tradere Christum*), and how this took concrete forms in the apostles' preaching (*kerygma*), in the Christ-centered reading of the Old Testament, in the celebration of baptism and the Lord's Supper, and in the doxological, doctrinal, hymnological and creedal forms by which the declaration of the mystery of God Incarnate was revealed for our salvation."

Tradition, then, includes the faithful passing on or handing over of the gospel from generation to generation in a form that speaks faithfully and relevantly to each new generation of the Christian community. Inherent in the concept of tradition is the confidence that the gospel of God's saving act in Christ can be appropriated, understood, and communicated clearly, faithfully, and correctly across the years. Included here, Grenz and Franke note, would be "the narrative of God's redemptive activity," "the basic teachings," and the "practices" of the early Christian community, a body of teaching and practice the church is called to faithfully pass on from generation to generation.

More particularly, how is tradition related to theology itself? I like Grenz and Franke's description of tradition as the "hermeneutical context for theology." That is, tradition offers a "hermeneutical trajectory" for theological reflection and construction, a trajectory composed of "the history of worship," "the history of theology," and "classic theological formulations and symbols."

Among other things, the history of theology demonstrates that some theological models have failed in their attempts to represent the gospel well. That is, in Grenz and Franke's words, the history of theology provides the Christian community "with a record of some of the failures of past efforts that have emerged over the course of time." Indeed, these failed models have played a vital role in helping the church to understand more clearly what teaching *is* in line with the gospel and what teaching doesn't fit. As you point out, this sifting process of discerning truth from error generally takes a long period of testing, although I would expect the time involved in analyzing a theological model to be shorter in our age than in past eras, simply because we have more help available to us from the past.

Theological models have been judged as heresy in the past, and there is no reason to believe that heresy cannot erupt in the present. But we must be quite careful in understanding what heresy is and how the church judges a model to be heretical. Grenz and Franke are quite helpful at this point: "The Christian community did not simply receive orthodox belief and pass it on in a static fashion. Rather, throughout its history the community has struggled to determine the content and application of orthodoxy in ways that are faithful to the canonical narratives. This process grew through the challenges presented by those whose teachings were eventually deemed heretical."

Perhaps a closer look at the early church would help at this juncture. Exactly what is heresy? Tertullian (a third-century African church father later identified as a heretic by some!) argued that heresy could be identified by its divergence from apostolic teaching and doctrine. He describes a distinct paradigm of revelation and authority.

First, Jesus in his earthly ministry "declared what he was, what he had been, what was the Father's will which he was carrying out, what was the conduct he laid down for humankind: all this he declared either openly to the people or privately to the disciples."

Second, Tertullian explains that Jesus "chose twelve leading ones to be his close companions, appointed as leaders of the nations." These men proceeded to plant churches throughout the Mediterranean Basin and in doing so "published the same doctrine of the same faith." These churches, founded by apostles who had in turn been selected by Jesus as his authoritative representatives and interpreters, were all part of one connected plant or vine. Indeed, Tertullian contends, newer churches "borrowed the shoot of faith and the seeds of doctrine" from those previously planted. It is this shared seed, a dissemination of common apostolic life and doctrine, that identifies a church as "apostolic, as being the off-spring of apostolic churches. Every kind of thing must needs be classed with its origin. And so the churches, many and great as they are, are identical with that one primitive Church issuing from the Apostles, for thence they are all derived. So all are primitive and apostolic, while all are one."

I think Tertullian's metaphor of apostolic teaching as seed sown by the church is an important one. The Christian tradition surely has grown and developed over the centuries, and a reforming of the tradition has occasionally occurred. The crucial question for any proposed theological model, though, is whether the model contains the biblical "DNA" contained in the apostolic interpretation of Christ's person and work and other key theological loci. Thus, we can have a theological model such as the Trinity accepted by the church as orthodox, though we never run across the word "Trinity" in the Bible. The church recognized the "DNA" for a Trinitarian model as present in the Scripture, though the precise model of the Trinity took years to develop and test. To expand the metaphor, heresy is a theological model that the church determines to contain defective or mutant "DNA." Orthodox theological models are like oak trees that have sprouted from acorns. The mature tree is a natural, healthy development of the biological blueprint contained within the acorn. Heretical models, on the other hand, resemble weeds that have erupted in a field where one expected lush grass. There will usually be enough "DNA" in a faulty model to warrant its testing by the church to determine its authenticity. If the model is finally determined to be heretical, however, it is because the church determines it to be a distortion of the truth rather than a genuine representation. The genetic pattern of the gospel has somehow been distorted or mutated.

What specifically characterizes heresy? For Tertullian at least, heresy is teaching that can be identified by its diversity and contrariety. That is, as Tertullian puts it, "it originates neither from an apostle nor from an apostolic man; for the Apostles would not have diverged from one another in doctrine; no more would the apostolic man have put out teaching at variance with that of the Apostles."

Irenaeus (a second-century bishop) also emphasized the importance of apostolic teaching and tradition in the propagation of the gospel and particularly stressed the important role bishops played in preserving and protecting apostolic truth. "By 'knowledge of the truth,'" Irenaeus writes, "we mean the teaching of the Apostles; the order of the Church as established from the earliest times throughout the world." Irenaeus contends that the "distinctive stamp of the Body of Christ" is "preserved through the Episcopal succession: for to the bishops the Apostles committed the care of the church which is in each place, which has come down to our own time." Heresy can be identified, Irenaeus believes, by the willingness of the heretic to proclaim a message "that he himself has discovered by himself—or rather invented." When the heretic is presented with the tradition derived "from the Apostles, and which is preserved in the churches by the successions of presbyters, then they oppose tradition, claiming to be wiser not only than the presbyters but even than the Apostles, and to have discovered the truth undefiled." Irenaeus explains that in distinction from the heretic—a theological maverick of sorts—the genuinely "talented theologian . . . will not say anything different from these beliefs (for 'no one is above his teacher'): nor will the feeble diminish the tradition."

Heresy, then, is the propagation of a position or perspective that runs against the grain of apostolic teaching and tradition. It is frequently linked to specific personalities, precisely because at the core of heresy is often an individual's choice to advocate and promote a teaching that the church cannot discover in or reconcile with the teaching of the apostles and hence does not accept as orthodox or "lining up" with the pattern of the gospel. Athanasius (a fourth-century bishop) comments that heresy is often marked by the name of its teacher, specifically because it is that teacher's unique doctrine that sets a group apart from the church at large.

I think that evangelicals face a significant problem when it comes to identifying "heresy." It would be nice to think that all we have to do is turn to the pages of Scripture and all will become clear regarding the viability of a theological model, but things are not so easy. Why? How are evangelicals to determine *communally* the meaning of Scripture itself? For instance, I ran across a comment of Richard John Neuhaus in *First Things* regarding the most recent meeting of the Evangelical Theological Society and the debate that occurred there concerning the openness model. Neuhaus observed that "evangelicals are inclined to launch questions from scratch and demand knock-down proofs from explicit biblical passages. In the absence of a Magisterium, or authoritative teaching office, this makes for lively arguments." Where does authority ultimately reside in the evangelical world?

Thomas Howard explores the question of authority in a recent article in which he discusses the distinguishing marks of the church. While many evangelicals might feel uncomfortable with the need for creeds and councils, Howard highlights the difficulty of adjudicating theological questions and issues on the basis of the Bible alone. "The great difficulty here," Howard writes, "is that Eutychius and Sabellius and Arius got their notions straight out of the Bible as well. Who will arbitrate these things for us? Who will speak with authority to us faithful, all of us rushing about flapping the pages of our well-thumbed New Testaments, locked in shrill contests over the two natures of Christ or baptism or the Lord's Supper or the mystery of predestination?" One could just as well add "or the nature of God or God's relationship to the future!"

The issues of authenticity and authority, I think, will continue to pressure the evangelical consciousness, and rightfully so. That is, what process and methodology possess the inherent authority within evangelicalism to judge whether a theological model such as openness is an authentic development of the Christian tradition or an aberrant mutation? Of course, all evangelicals would argue the Bible is a fundamental resource for determining the viability and trustworthiness of a theological model, but the Bible as understood by whom? Reformed theologians and churches? Freewill Baptists? Independent Bible churches? Chris Hall? John Sanders?

Howard writes, "When a crucial issue arises—say, what we should teach about sexuality—who will speak to us with a finally authoritative voice? The best we can do is to get *Christianity Today* to run a symposium, with one article by J. I. Packer plumping for traditional morality, and one article by one of our lesbian feminist evangelicals (there are some), showing that we have all been wrong for the entire 3,500 years since Sinai, and that what the Bible really teaches is that indeed homosexuals may enjoy a fully expressed sexual life. The trouble here is that J. I. Packer has no more authority than our lesbian friend, so the message to the faithful is 'Take your pick.'"

The thoughts of Tertullian, Irenaeus, and Athanasius I have drawn on in this letter indicate how differently early Christians appear to approach the issue of authority. Howard comments that "the faithful in those early centuries were certainly aware of a great Babel of voices among the Christians, teaching this and teaching that on every conceivable point of revelation. But the faithful were also aware that there was a body that could speak into the chaos and declare, with serene and final authority, what the faith that had been taught by the apostles was."

Is it true that evangelicals have only one authority, the Bible, for adjudicating theological truth and error? I think Clark Pinnock is correct in observing that Protestants and evangelicals have their own interpretive traditions that aid them in making sense of the Bible and in distinguishing truth from error. Both the Catholic and Protestant traditions, Pinnock argues, have a threefold understanding of authority:

1. The primary authority is the Bible itself.
2. The second level of authority addresses "the problems of interpretation and misinterpretation." Here operate, in the Catholic tradition, for instance, the "'rule of faith' and other official documents that could stand as the key to the interpretation of the Bible." The Apostles' Creed and the Nicene Creed would be included here. I would also add at least the first four ecumenical councils. In the Protestant world we have authoritative traditions such as the Formula of Concord, the Belgic Confession, and the Thirty Nine Articles. Even within seemingly autonomous bodies such as independent Bible churches, interpretive traditions such as dispensationalism have played a prominent role in how Christians interpreted the Bible.
3. The third level of authority encompasses "church office and institution." In the Roman Catholic Church the papacy and the Magisterium possess the authority "to stand guard over the Scripture and the tradition." Pinnock helpfully reminds us that Protestants have their own institutions and offices, and although they do not view these as infallible, they clearly see God's hand in their organizations, churches, and denominational histories.

How might my thoughts on tradition and authority inform my responses to the openness model? For one thing, I'm not as skeptical as you seem to be regarding the existence of a "tradition" that we can look to for guidance and direction in our theological work. I think we can discern a consensus in the tradition regarding a number of central core themes and issues: the deity of Christ, the Trinity, the genuine humanity of Christ, the deity of the Holy Spirit, the universal character of human sinfulness, and so on. Yes, it did take the church a number of years to think through and formulate these doctrines, but we can discern a central, solid core to the tradition.

The openness model offers two significant challenges to the tradition's understanding of God's nature and providence. First, the openness model argues that God knows only the past, present, and those aspects of future events that God has foreordained will occur. Second, the openness model contends that God can make mistakes on the basis of God's limited knowledge of the future actions of human free agents. Neither of these propositions finds significant, weighty support in the history of Christian exegesis nor in the communal dogmatic decisions of the church. The figures you mention as supporting the openness model—Calcidius, Andrew Ramsay, Adam Clarke, Billy Hibbard, W. T. Brents, Jules Lequyer, and L. D. McCabe—are worth listening to but are not major, authoritative figures in the history of Christian exegesis. They represent a minority opinion that the church has never accepted as authoritative. You are right in observing that a wide range of perspectives on providence have been debated in the history of the church, but very few Christian exegetes and theologians have supported the openness perspective. Why? The limitations the openness model places on God's omniscience and its predication of divine error weigh too heavily against the acceptance of the model. Even Eastern fathers such as John Chrysostom (fourth century), fathers who support strongly the concept of libertarian freedom, refuse to accept the idea that God's knowledge is potential rather than actual, or that God can make mistakes. I believe Chrysostom would argue that God does know what free human beings are going to do before their free will is exercised, though he also believed that God's knowledge and providence itself would in many ways remain incomprehensible to us. The fathers as a whole were willing to live with the incomprehensibility of God's providence in a manner that openness theologians dispute.

For instance, in your letter certain phrases repeatedly show up: "logically coherent," "logically incoherent," "logically consistent," "more coherent," "more logical," "more biblically faithful and rationally coherent." It's fair for you to accentuate the need for logical consistency in theological reflection, but I believe that the attempt to encompass providence within a consistently coherent, rational framework necessarily leads openness advocates down a blind alley: "presentism" and the predication of divine mistakes.

God's providential ordering of human history is incomprehensible. Incomprehensible in what sense? Providence is beyond our present capability to comprehend and explain coherently. Both the complexity of human affairs and the limited revelation God has provided to help us understand providence clearly place boundaries on our attempts to explicate rationally God's governance and ordering of human life. At times, as I have argued in earlier letters, we will have to affirm logically contradictory truths as we think about providence, thinking thoughts side by side in a sense, much like biblical writers do. If the revelation God had given us about providence and time was complete rather than limited, I would argue differently. For the present, however, we must rest content with limited knowledge and occasional incoherence. The alternative provided by the openness model is logically consistent but results in such a radical reshaping of the doctrine of God, particularly in its insistence that God makes mistakes, that it must be seriously questioned.

This is not to say that the openness model is heretical. That is an issue the church has yet to adjudicate, and much more discussion and debate are necessary. I would like to see Eastern Orthodox and Roman Catholic scholars more fully involved in the discussion. Their insights would add much to the mix, especially on issues of ecclesiology and authority and the relationship of these two concepts to the construction of theological models.

As I've already stated in this letter, the evangelical understanding of authority makes it quite difficult for evangelicals as a community to identify heretical ideas. As you have pointed out in your letter, evangelical scholars are pretty much free to advocate a wide variety of opinions, as long as their ideas can be shown to have a biblical basis. Whether it is a James Oliver Buswell Jr., Ronald Nash, David Wells, or John Sanders, each has room in the evangelical tent to advocate his ideas, a situation that is both positive and negative. This freedom of expression is positive because it continually forces evangelicals back to Scripture and should result in fruitful exegetical insights. It is negative in that it encourages the individualism that has plagued evangelical exegesis and theology for years. The result is a reading of Scripture that can be highly idiosyncratic and frequently divorced from the insights that historically informed, consensual exegesis has to offer.

When evangelicals do attempt to identify heresy, they often do so with the use of second- or third-level authorities, rather than by simply relying on Scripture itself. This should not surprise us. I've already commented in this letter that second- and third-level authorities are necessary for effectively adjudicating theological issues. Evangelicals, though, tend to be blind to their use of second- and third-level authorities, while simultaneously employing these very authorities in attempts to distinguish orthodoxy from heresy. As you've noted, B. B. Warfield, Machen, and Carnell have all had their own ideas about what was orthodox and what was heretical—perspectives informed by both their reading of the Bible and the second- and third-level authorities that composed their interpretative grid. As far as I can tell, you have just as much right to call your theological opponents heretics as they you, on the basis of an evangelical understanding of authority alone.

Indeed, the lack of a communally recognized authority within evangelicalism beyond the Bible itself fuels the insecurity, shortsightedness, intolerance, and mean-spiritedness that often marks evangelical theological discussion and debate. Hence the pressing need for evangelicals to immerse themselves more broadly and deeply in the Christian tradition as a whole, particularly in its consensual core. At present I am hopeful that evangelicals are increasingly aware of the need for a much more thorough grounding in the consensual tradition of Christian exegesis and theology. Apart from grounding in this authoritative core, the evangelical love of Scripture and insistence on its fundamental authority will increasingly be undermined. As David Lyle Jeffrey has observed in a recent *Books and Culture* essay, "Loss of authority of the Church, *de jure,* has led inexorably, on these lines, to the *de facto* loss of authority of Scripture. . . . When an insistence on absolute interpretative independence is coupled, as increasingly it is, with an almost staggering loss of biblical literacy among its champions, then the actual authority of Scripture can become so negligible as to make any claim to a biblical foundation either comic or tragic, depending on your point of view." Amen.

With warm regards,
Chris

# 35 **John:** Can We Question Theology?

Dear Chris,

Writing back and forth with you has been a great learning experience. You have sharpened my thoughts, to say the least. I want to say that I appreciated your remark that you are not completely "settled" in all your views. Neither am I. Regarding the authority of traditions you are much closer than I to the Roman Catholic approach. I remember you telling one of my classes that you were "Catholic light" (Episcopalian). Ha! As an aside, I agree that the traditions teach that God does not make mistakes and open theism affirms that God does not make mistakes (you are not reading me correctly here). You and I hold a great many traditional teachings in common and neither of us is challenging the core of the gospel. Yet, both of us are thinking through subsidiary issues. Both of us believe it is all right to challenge some accepted beliefs. Doing this, however, makes some people nervous. My experience in church life is that many people feel guilty if they question what they have been taught. We don't typically model theological reflection in congregational life. Instead, we teach people the "correct" doctrines and give anyone who asks questions a hard time.

When I was in college my pastor at the time was teaching our Sunday school class. One day I asked him how he knew that God knew everything we would do in the future. He replied, "That is a stupid question and should

185

not be asked!" Instead of being put off by his response, I realized that my pastor was afraid of the question. Unfortunately, he had not been taught how to think theologically. He had been taught to memorize the correct beliefs rather than how to work through theological issues. Hence, he had to try to intimidate me into submission. Though most pastors are not so blunt, I feel that the attitude embodied in his response is fairly typical—we don't need to rethink anything because we already have it all figured out.

Sometimes I've been told that we must simply have the "faith of a child" and not try to think about our beliefs. However, when children are being illogical do we consider that a good thing? Does God ask us to be closed minded in order to be spiritual? I don't mean to imply that we will understand everything or have it all figured out. But I don't believe it is wrong to try to understand our faith. As Saint Anselm (eleventh century) put it: "Faith seeks understanding."

Theology is and always has been a reforming enterprise. Augustine (fourth century), for instance, was rather radical in changing some long-established views. Aquinas's (thirteenth century) theology was vehemently denounced in his day for being innovative. Today, we tend to forget that such stalwarts of the faith were indeed reforming what went before them and were innovative in a number of ways. We forget this because many of their views are now taken for granted. The same pattern is true for Luther, Calvin, and the Anabaptists. They were considered "radicals" in their day for calling into question certain beliefs that were simply taken for granted. Many people today feel that we are questioning God if we challenge beliefs about impassibility, immutability, and foreknowledge. But we are not. Rather, we are questioning the theologies developed by fallible human beings.

This does not mean that we take their views lightly. We must have good reasons for going against them, and open theism seeks to provide such reasons. Our critics may respond that it seems too unlikely that, for instance, the understanding of omniscience held by so many people would need modification. I don't deny that it is unlikely. But other doctrinal changes that have occurred in church history were also unlikely. Who could have predicted that a significant doctrine that had stood in the Western church for about thirteen hundred years would be overturned in just a few decades? I'm speaking about the long-established belief that young children that died unbaptized were damned. This was Augustine's view and it became the predominant view in the West. The only modification it received for quite some time was the notion that such children did not suffer pain in hell. Yet in the early eighteenth century this view was so thoroughly repudiated that nearly all Western Christians today believe that such children are saved, not damned. How unlikely was that? Today, my students find it hard to understand how anyone could have believed that children who died unbaptized were damned. I have to show my students that the theologians who held this position had reasons to support their view. Of course, we no longer find their reasons persuasive.

My point in bringing this up is just to observe that theology always has been a reforming activity. It is not wrong to attempt to improve our beliefs— though this does not guarantee that our reforms will be correct. The fact that we cannot guarantee correctness produces anxiety in many Christians. This is especially so among evangelicals, for much of their theological "method" is hitched to the philosophical wagon known as "strong foundationalism." I was taught this approach in seminary. It lay behind what we did in hermeneutics and apologetics courses as well as in many of the courses in biblical studies. The main idea of strong foundationalism is that you must have an absolutely certain starting point (foundation) in order to construct your theology (the building) or else you fall into relativism.

Think of a ten-story building. If you are on the tenth floor and somebody comes along and begins undermining your foundation or even tampering with any of the floors beneath you, it makes you nervous. One of the problems with the approach of strong foundationalism is that any weakness under you threatens the security of everything above it. My professors at a highly respected evangelical seminary worried incessantly about relativism and liberalism and they wanted their students to be immune from such views. Hence they sought to provide us with absolutely certain interpretations of Scripture and theological formulations.

Let me illustrate this from an experience in one of my seminary courses. My advisor, whom I greatly admired, taught hermeneutics. He proposed a detailed method based on supposedly objective criteria by which to interpret the Bible in order to arrive at unquestionable interpretations of the text. One day I asked, "If I use your method will I arrive at the meaning, the whole meaning, and nothing but the meaning so help my grammatical-syntactical analysis?" After some hesitation he replied, "Yes." I then asked why two professors, in the same department at this seminary, using the same method, arrived at different interpretations of some key biblical passages. My professor, who was both smart and witty replied, "Oh, John, that's easy—depravity!" The house came down with laughter. It was a great retort. Afterwards, however, I asked him why both professors could not be depraved and that even if only one was depraved, how he determined which one. Because sin affects our supposedly objective criteria, we do not arrive at an absolutely certain method for interpreting the text.

Again, this makes many evangelicals extremely anxious, since they believe there are only two options—absolute certainty or relativism. Though I don't believe that strong foundationalism and relativism are the only options on the epistemological market, many evangelicals do.

Hence they simply have to have certainty of the correctness of their views—they have to be right. This, in my opinion, leads some of them to develop a "demon of rightness." They act as though it is impossible for them to be wrong on theological matters, for they tend to conflate their own understanding with God's. They are deeply threatened when anyone questions their beliefs and they tend, like my former pastor, to strike out at the one asking the questions.

As you know, some extremely vicious remarks have been made about open theists. In fact, you are the one who pointed out to me that in a book written against open theism one of the authors said he was praying that God would "destroy" both the "iniquity" of open theism as well as the open theists themselves. In such an environment, constructive dialogue is impossible. Your approach is so different. Yes, we disagree strongly on some matters but it does not keep us from loving one another and trying to learn from each other.

You also know that some of these same folks have put in thousands of hours of work trying to get open theists fired from their colleges or kicked out of their denominations. Sometimes they have resorted to power politics and distorting our views. You were present at one such power play and it was an ugly affair. You may wonder what keeps me going in the face of unceasing opposition. It is not because I desire controversy. Rather, it is because I am trying to serve the church of our Lord Jesus. Here is what a pastor wrote me recently after reading my book, *The God Who Risks*. "I don't think I've been so excited about walking with God in a VERY LONG TIME. The notion that God cared what people of faith THOUGHT and FELT (and could possibly care what I THINK) has kind of, well, blown me away. I've prayed more in the last few days than I have in a while. Suddenly I'm thinking—what if God DOES care what I think? What if it DOES make a difference whether or not I pray for these people or that situation." Another person, who was drifting into "something like Gnostic mysticism," said that *The God Who Risks* "brought me back into a closer relationship with God. I just wanted to let you know how much God used that book to do battle with various other 'idols of the theatre' that were keeping me from embracing the idea of a personal God." I receive several such letters every week, so I am convinced that God is using my work. It is encouraging to know that what we are doing helps God's people. I know, Chris, that people all over the world are helped by your speaking and writing and I pray that God will continue to work through you.

Blessings,
John

# 36 **John:** Dialogical Virtues

Dear Chris,

I've been thinking about what I call "dialogical virtues." That is, ethical issues in the way we handle our intellectual inquiries and how we discuss our disagreements. You and I have witnessed what are, unfortunately, rather typical tactics used by conservative evangelicals engaged in the openness debate in an attempt to silence their opponents. Name-calling and guilt by association are two of the favorite tactics. For instance, openness theology has been labeled Socinianism and Pelagianism by some of evangelicalism's most esteemed scholars. Perhaps this is not so bad, however, since the very same accusations were made against Arminius himself by proponents of the same brand of Calvinism. A letter written in Arminius's day says that with incredible zeal "some persons accuse this man of schism and others of heresy, some charge him with the crime of Pelagianism and others brand him with the black mark of Socinianism." Socinus denied the Calvinistic understanding of predestination, the resurrection of the body, the Trinity, the full deity of Jesus, and the atonement of Jesus. Hence, it is easy to see why Arminius was Socinian—both rejected Calvinistic predestination! Ha! It seems that if you have one point in common with another view, then your view can be labeled as that other view. Socinus rejected exhaustive definite foreknowledge, so some believe it is fair to label openness Socinianism. Bernard Ramm called these tactics "bad-mouthing" and said that,

189

unfortunately, evangelicals practice them all too often instead of doing solid scholarly work.

This same guilt-by-association move is made when openness is claimed to be process theology because both views have a couple of points in common. A former professor of mine quotes a remark in one of our books that openness and process agree on a particular point. He then says that this remark proves that open theism derives from process theism! Of course, having a point in common does not prove dependency, so I wrote my former professor about this error in logic. He responded that he was right and that was that! Those who claim openness is simply process theology need to read what process theologians are saying about openness. David Ray Griffin, a prominent process theologian, says that he cannot stomach open theism any more than he can classical theism because openness is just too similar to the classical view and thus not worthy of God. Open theism is a hot potato being tossed back and forth between classical and process theists. Nobody wants us. The sons of openness have nowhere to lay our heads.

Those who play with these rhetorical weapons typically do not notice that those weapons can be turned back on themselves. What if we were to say that both Islam and Calvinism affirmed meticulous providence, so Calvinism is really Islam? Again, since astrologers and classical theists both believe the future to be exhaustively definite, classical theism is dependent on astrology! Of course Calvinists would rightfully cry "foul."

It is said that we are "making God in our own image." We could turn this around, however, and claim that the God of meticulous providence is really in our image, since that God typifies the ideal Western male—in control and not relying on anyone else. This God exemplifies the Platonic, Aristotelian, and Stoic understandings of human perfection.

It has even been suggested that the reason I became an open theist is due to a psychological imbalance—I did not deal properly with personal tragedy. Again, I can just as easily turn this attempted psychoanalysis back on my critic by suggesting that a deep-seated insecurity leads him to fashion an all-controlling God. What is sauce for the goose is sauce for the gander.

At this point I want to highlight some contrasts I see between the work of members of two academic societies: the Society of Christian Philosophers (SCP) and the Evangelical Theological Society (ETS). Members of the SCP typically build up their opponents' position until they arrive at what they consider to be the strongest case for the other view before they criticize it. Evangelical theologians, on the other hand, tend to highlight the weakest arguments of their opponents or make a big deal about statements that are tangential to the main point.

Another problem is a serious lack of imagination in our critics in that they fail to think of ways in which we might answer their criticisms. My Arminian students are unimaginative when they fail to see how Calvinists might answer the objection "Why bother to evangelize if it is already determined who will be saved?" The job of the professor is to make them aware of possible answers. At ETS, critics of open theism make it seem as though we are just plain stupid. In contrast, members of the SCP commonly try to come up with helpful suggestions for how their opponents could handle their objections.

Another point of concern is that at times our critics state as fact what is clearly a falsehood. For example, it is distressing when critics state that we say that the being of God changes. No texts of ours are cited to support this and no argument is given that we really believe this. It is simply stated as fact. In our writings we have repeatedly said that God can change in will, emotions, and thoughts, but *not* in his essential nature. On several occasions I have written the authors as well as the publishers concerning this error. To date I have received no replies, and one of the authors—a very respected evangelical theologian—has made the same accusation in print again. I am not suggesting that members of the SCP are perfect, but these tendencies are one of the reasons their journal is held in incredibly high regard. If you attend an SCP conference you will hear spirited debate, but you will see that they care about their opponent and the integrity with which they pursue their debates. Unfortunately, I believe evangelical theological debate falls seriously short here. A couple of years ago a friend of Tom Oden's attended ETS for the first time and after several sessions asked, "Why is there so much anger among the members of this society? They don't just disagree with one another, they hate each other" (by the way, the issue was not openness).

Bruce Ware and Thomas Schreiner warn, "Our hearts are in danger of being captivated by a negative spirit if we find ourselves drawn toward attacking the views of others." We need to learn how to carry on a debate without knee-jerk reactions that demonize the other. Terrance Tiessen's work demonstrates that a Calvinist can state the open view without caricature and criticize it without using caustic rhetoric. On several occasions Reformed evangelicals have engaged me in public discourse, exemplifying civility and a willingness to wrestle with the issues. Unfortunately, I find this all too rare regarding any controversial topic in evangelical theology.

If we are to improve we need to practice the intellectual virtues. A very helpful study of them is found in *Epistemology: Becoming Intellectually Virtuous* by Jay Wood of Wheaton College. When dialoging on various issues there are virtues we can cultivate in the pursuit of truth. Honesty, integrity, empathy, teachableness, persistence, precision, articulateness, and foresight are some of the virtues discussed by Wood. The following questions highlight some of these virtues. Am I willing to learn from others without being an intellectual pushover? Have I come to the point where I can understand why someone would take a different position from my own? Do I, as a theological educator, talk too much and listen too little? Do I reflect before I speak or am I more interested in making my next point? Am I on a power trip—do I simply want to control what others are allowed to think? When we discuss issues around the table, is it the most aggressive person who "wins"? What are we modeling to our students and the church? Are we really equipping people for the process of theological reflection or are we only teaching them how to eviscerate fellow Christians?

One very important dialogical virtue is the ability to state the other person's view in such a way that the other person would say, "Yes, that is my position." Nicholas Wolterstorff recites the following to his students once a week:

> Thou must not take cheap shots. Thou must not sit in judgment until thou hast done thy best to understand. Thou must earn thy right to disagree. Thou must conduct thyself as if Plato or Augustine, Clement or Tertullian, were sitting across the table—the point being that it is much more difficult (I don't say impossible) to dishonor someone to his face.

You and Terry Tiessen have argued with me about divine providence in respectful ways. Moreover, we have prayed for one another's family situations. It is tough to demonize someone when you are praying for them. Yes, we disagree on some important theological matters but more importantly, we share a common life in Jesus Christ. Bruce Ware says, "Calvinists and Arminians have more points of agreement than disagreement in their respective soteriologies." I agree but find it disappointing that Ware does not show this same attitude when criticizing open theism. Someone looking in on the openness debate from outside evangelicalism would see a lot more agreement between the respective positions than disagreement.

Another virtue to inculcate is humility. None of us has the truth, the whole truth, and nothing but the truth. This side of the eschaton we only "know in part" (1 Cor. 13:12). Calvin said that no theologian is more than 70 percent correct. That may be generous. All of us are finite and we must never forget the noetic effects of sin on our research, reasoning, and theological formulations. We need epistemic humility and we need one another, for the wisdom of God is shared in the body of Christ. I admit that open theism may turn out to be a footnote in historical theology. We may be wrong, but it takes time to investigate and debate theological proposals. Look how long it took the early church to work through the issue as to whether Jesus had two wills or only one. Committed Christians held various positions. Some wanted to short-circuit the debate and simply exile their opponents by political control. However, in its better moments the church allowed debate to work its slow way forward over decades and even centuries before the church came to official positions, and the church was stronger, not weaker, for the debate.

At the SCP I have observed spirited debate on important matters and then watched the debaters go have coffee together. They recognize that their common heritage in Jesus Christ is greater than our differences. The other option is to politicize the discussion and claim that our particular version of evangelical Christianity is the only way to protect the gospel. Mark Noll and Alister McGrath call on evangelical theologians to explore new areas and to develop responses to the many issues raised today. However, at least a part of the scandal of the evangelical mind is the fear many evangelical theologians have of investigating certain topics because they are afraid of losing their jobs. Many evangelical institutions only allow professors to teach doctrine, not to do theology. One prominent evangelical historian has told me that most of the brightest evangelical minds of the past thirty years have gone into philosophy instead of theology because they see what the gatekeepers of evangelical orthodoxy do to those who question the status quo. Presently, evangelicalism is witnessing the resurgence of a fundamentalist spirit—a meanness of heart and a drawing of narrow doctrinal boundaries. This saddens me greatly, for I do not find such messengers bearers of "good news." If we are going to overcome the scandal of the evangelical mind, we are going to have to stand up to these individuals, point out their unseemly tactics, and practice the dialogical virtues.

Your friend,
John

# 37 **Chris:** Learning and Virtue

Dear John,

I think this is going to be my last letter, at least for this book. I want to respond briefly to your thoughts both on the role of questioning and reforming the tradition and on the dialogical virtues. As I read through your last two letters it became clearer to me that you have experienced an aspect of the evangelical world that I am less familiar with. I'm referring specifically to the lack of freedom you have encountered in asking questions and receiving viable and convincing answers. I did experience some of this resistance when I was a young believer attending the Light and Power House, a Jesus People Bible school in West Los Angeles. One of the main teachers at the school was an individual who has since become well known as an author and TV teacher. I soon realized that there were some questions this man did not welcome, particularly questions regarding biblical prophecy. He didn't like questions that seriously threatened his detailed interpretation of the end times. Questions that appeared to undercut a dispensational perspective on biblical prophecy were likely to meet steep resistance. I think that this resistance to deep probing of his views was related to the foundationalist perspective you mentioned. If theological or biblical probing effectively pulled one or two blocks out of his prophetic system, the entire structure was liable to fall.

I have not met this kind of resistance to questions from other key mentors in my life. For example, Ward Gasque, J. I. Packer, and Tom

194

Oden have all welcomed questions and occasional disagreement and debate in my interactions with them. None of them felt the need to handle me with kid gloves, and I'm sure I emerged bruised from some discussions! The bruises came, though, not from ignoring or deflecting my questions, but from debating and answering them robustly. Just knowing that I could ask the questions I needed to ask was more than worth the bruises I received. In fact, I remember times in my doctoral work at Drew when Tom would ask the questions I was dying to pose, and by doing so he let me know it was fine to ask whatever I needed to ask. The freedom to explore and ponder was invaluable to me.

I'm not sure I'd describe theology as "a reforming enterprise." Theology occasionally performs this function, but I think its normative role is more one of passing on the tradition faithfully and exploring carefully and creatively how the Christian tradition is applicable and relevant for new cultural contexts. Doesn't Roger Olson see the history of theology as the interaction between the traditionalists and the reformers in his recent historical theology? Perhaps our correspondence reflects this kind of paradigm. In addition, if we do attempt to reform the tradition it is essential that we understand what the tradition actually is teaching.

I'm in full agreement that all theologians and the church at large need to continue to cultivate and nurture the dialogical virtues that Jay Wood discusses. Name-calling, guilt by association, and bad-mouthing accomplish very little in the long run. What we all struggle with is learning to listen well to another person's position. I love the maxim of Nicholas Wolterstorff you related in your last letter. It's too easy to take cheap shots. We too quickly criticize before understanding our opponent's position well. We must earn the right to disagree by immersing ourselves in the position we find problematic. It is much more difficult to dishonor someone to his face. I, like you, am attracted to forums where ideas can be discussed openly, vigorously, fairly, honestly, and empathetically.

Well, I suppose we need to draw our correspondence to a close, at least for now. Know that you remain in my thoughts and prayers.

With warm greetings,
Chris

# Chris and John: Postscript

Does God have a future? We take different views on this issue. Chris tends to side with the more traditional outlook that God does not experience time and so words such as past and future cannot be applied to God. John, on the other hand, believes that God does have a future, since God experiences time with us. Throughout our letters we have tried to bring out some of the implications of these different views, since this topic intersects with a wide array of subjects. We have discussed specific biblical passages as well as how we go about interpreting them. Theological topics such as the attributes of God, God's relation to the world, and the nature of human understanding of God have been addressed. We have also covered how these issues relate to the Christian life—especially prayer. Also, the role of tradition in theology has been discussed along with the question of reforming theology. Some of these topics were brought up in several letters, while other topics that perhaps should have been covered were not. Writing letters back and forth has made for some uneven coverage and we have in no way finished, but for us the conversation has been both helpful and enjoyable.

While some of the topics we have discussed are easy to comprehend, others are extremely difficult. We hope that, at the least, our readers now understand that this issue is not a simple one with an open-and-shut case for one side. Anyone who believes this matter is simple and easily settled has not understood the problems. Putting forth a few biblical proof texts does not end the discussion, for people on different sides of this debate are seriously engaged with Scripture. It is fine to come to a conclusion on this matter and take a position, but please do not think those people stupid who take a different view.

We have carried on a theological discussion attempting to think the issue through together. That last word is very important, for we have done it together, as a joint effort, rather than as a contest between us. We wrote these letters into a book for several reasons. First, the debate over openness theology is a hot topic among contemporary North American Christians and it needs to be discussed and reflected on. Questions must be asked, answers given, and follow-up questions asked. The editors of *Christianity Today* have stated that it is their desire that this discussion continue, and they chastise those attempting to cut off the conversation. The discussion can be carried forward in books, magazines, academic journals, scholarly societies, as well as in local congregations and colleges. This book is simply one part of this larger process.

In our search for truth we definitely need one another. The two of us have benefited greatly from the dialogue. We feel that we have learned a lot through the process. Both of us have had to rethink some of our statements as well as try out some new thoughts. In fact, both of us have been "experimental" at times, trying out different ideas or explanations. We have sought to allow each other the freedom to think out loud, knowing that we may be expressing something that just won't wash—but we don't know it won't wash until we try it. Both of us are searching for the truth and view the other as an aid in this endeavor. We wrote this book in order to serve God and the Christian community as theologians. We have tried to provide some insight and clarity in this debate. Our hope in allowing others to read our letters is that other Christians will be helped to live more meaningful and devout lives.

Aside from the content of the debate we see a great need for modeling how to carry on theological debate in irenic and loving ways with those who hold positions different from our own. This is especially needed in evangelicalism, where congregations split over minuscule points of difference. Though evangelicalism is, and always has been, a phenomenon of diverse theological perspectives, there has been a repeated tendency to attempt to narrow the movement theologically. Attempts have been made to demarcate the boundary over premillennialism, the Rapture, and the like. Discussing issues is fine, but all too often evangelicals have resorted to power politics, name-calling, threats of exclusion, and other unseemly tactics in order to "win." Insecure people tend to want to short-circuit debate and get their way by other means. It is a sad testimony when a friend of ours, who is frequently asked to debate atheists and proponents of other religions on university campuses, says he would rather debate these folks because he finds much more honest wrestling with issues and even love among them than among fellow evangelicals.

We desire to model a more excellent way. Last November we held a series of discussions on this topic at John's college. At times we disagreed sharply with one another, yet we did not let that get in the way of our love for one another nor of the shared commitment that we have in Christ. Afterwards, many students and pastors who attended said that they had never seen two evangelicals disagree on significant matters while displaying love and humility. In April, John was invited to discuss openness at another college with some professors who disagreed with him. Several hundred students as well as many pastors attended. Again, the most frequent comment made by people in the audience was not about the content but about the atmosphere of the discussion. They were deeply impressed that the presenters could speak to one another civilly while disagreeing theologically. Evidently, the reason these two discussions stand out in the minds of the listeners is that this sort of exchange happens so seldom in evangelical circles. We desire to see the process of theological debate within evangelicalism improve and have sought to model how to do it (though we don't profess to carry this out perfectly).

In part, we are able to carry on our discussion this way because we share a number of commitments. We believe that any theological proposal must fit well with Scripture and assist the church in its worship and service to our Lord Jesus Christ. Both of us believe that we should seek to preserve the insights produced by the Christian communion over the centuries while at the same time recognizing that theology is produced by humans and so should be open to reform. We need not fear examining issues from various perspectives. If our position is true it will hold up. If it is only partially true or even false, we want to know that so we can make the necessary changes. Also, we affirm that the process of debating proposed reforms takes time, decades or more, and so we should be wary of those who want to cut off discussion. Moreover, we see constructive theological debate as a sign of vitality, not decline, in evangelicalism. In fact, it is absolutely essential if we are to overcome what Mark Noll has called "the scandal of the evangelical mind."

Nevertheless, in the midst of discussing our differences we both want to highlight our common Christian identity. Too often we forget the incredible amount of faith and practice we have in common. If we think of Christian beliefs as a set of concentric circles, the smallest circle at the center represents the core beliefs and values of the Christian faith. The next largest circle symbolizes very important, but not core doctrines. As the circles expand we come to lesser issues and greater theological diversity among Christian communities. Of course, various Christian communities disagree over exactly which doctrines should be placed in what circles. That is, we don't all agree as to the content of each circle.

However, both of us affirm that some doctrines are much more important than others. Both of us affirm the center or core of the Christian faith expressed, for example, in the Apostles' Creed. Moreover, both of us share a great many other beliefs in the outer circles. Clearly, we disagree on some important matters. However, we believe that Christians can hold different theological beliefs and still work together to fulfill God's purposes. We desire to live out the motto "In essentials unity, in nonessentials liberty, in all things charity."

Though we both affirm the Lordship of Christ neither of us has a corner on the truth. We see the need for a *generous orthodoxy* that allows—even calls for—serious theological debate. We are saddened by those who establish themselves as the defenders of God, manifesting a visceral reaction toward anyone who disagrees with them. Such evangelicals tend to turn every theological issue into "the battle for" this and "the battle for" that. Not surprisingly, the title of a new book against openness is *The Battle for God*. In our letters we have disagreed sharply at times but we have not viewed our endeavor through the metaphor of "battle." We do not see the need to conquer or even slay one another intellectually.

Rather, we see ourselves as having a conversation among believers. During our conversation we have tried to practice "dialogical virtues." We have attempted to treat each other fairly, honestly, charitably, and forthrightly. We have tried to accurately state what the other person believes. We have tried to enter into each other's perspective with empathy to discern why the other thinks this particular point important. That is, when we objected to something the other had said, we sought to discover what matter of importance it is that the other person believes we are sacrificing. Are we giving something up that simply should not be given up?

The rhetoric against open theism is often mean-spirited and filled with caricatures. We have tried to avoid this. The issues raised are important and they affect some of the ways in which we live out the Christian life—how we think of prayer, for example. While some see open theism as a movement of the Holy Spirit, others view it as a scourge that will destroy churches. Given such polar perspectives, the discussion needs to continue. But let it continue in the framework of the dialogical virtues. Let us be virtuous in dealing with one another's ideas—treating them with respect even while asking significant questions. In essence, in our letters we have tried to embody in our dialogue the prophet Micah's admonition that the Lord requires us to treat each other justly, to love mercy, and to walk humbly with our God (6:8).

# Appendix: Summary Definitions

Note: Cross-references to the glossary are indicated by small caps (e.g., AUGUSTINE).

## Classical Theism

Classical theism is an influential school of thought that interprets the divine attributes in a particular way that differs from the interpretation given them by OPEN THEISM. These differences lead to disagreements on a range of theological issues as well as to divergent readings of scriptural texts. According to classical theism DIVINE PERFECTION means that God is absolutely independent of creation, not needing it in any respect. The motivation for this view arises out of a particular conception of perfection as applied to God. That is, if it is good to have qualities such as knowledge, will, power, and love, then what must a being that is perfect in these qualities be like? It is argued that God is perfect in the sense that there can be no possible improvement or POTENTIAL for change since any change in God could only be a change for the worse. From this conception of God a family of attributes arise: God is SIMPLE, IMMUTABLE, IMPASSIBLE, TIMELESS, necessary, PURE ACT, omnipresent, OMNISCIENT, omnipotent, and wholly good. Together, these combine to affirm that there is no change of any kind in God nor is God dependent upon anything other than God. SIMPLICITY means that there is no genuine differentiation in God. God is identical with God's properties such that God does not have, for instance, omnipotence and OMNISCIENCE as distinct parts. As PURE ACT, God has no potential for change of any kind, as this would mean God was less than complete. As IMMUTABLE, God cannot change in any respect including thoughts, intentions, or emotions. Being IMPASSIBLE, nothing external to God, such as creatures, can affect God in any way. God is TIMELESS in that there is no before or after for God, only an eternal present.

It is clear then that a TIMELESS and wholly IMMUTABLE being cannot change whatsoever, including changes in thoughts, will, or emotions. AUGUSTINE said: "Only what does not only not change but also cannot at all change falls most truly . . . under the category of being" (*On the Trinity* 5.2–3). If God were PASSIBLE (affected by creatures) then God would be changeable and less than self-sufficient. So God cannot be affected or influenced in any way by creatures. God has no emotions. Moreover, our prayers serve as instruments by which God brings about what God has ordained, but our prayers never affect what God has eternally willed to bring about. It is impossible that our prayers have any influence on God's decisions. Many classical theists, however, do claim that God responds to our prayers and thus are at pains to explain how a completely changeless God can respond to a temporal event.

Since the divine plan is unchanging, God exercises METICULOUS PROVIDENCE by specifically ordaining each and every event to occur. God tightly controls everything so that whatever happens is exactly what God wanted to happen. God has a meticulous blueprint for everything that happens in history, so evil and suffering are ordained by God for good reasons that remain hidden from us. The divine will cannot fail or be thwarted in any detail. God never takes risks. In salvation, this leads to the doctrines of unconditional ELECTION and irresistible grace. God's decision to save an individual cannot be dependent in any way upon humans, as that would deny the doctrines of IMMUTABILITY, IMPASSIBILITY, and self-sufficiency.

There can be no change in God's knowledge from before to after. Consequently, OMNISCIENCE must include exhaustive definite FOREKNOWLEDGE of future contingent events (human actions). The entire future is completely definite or certain for God. God knows the future as what will actually happen, not as what possibly might happen. God knows the future as certain, because God determines what the future will be. God's knowledge of what we will do in the future cannot be causally dependent upon us, since that would mean God was not IMPASSIBLE or self-sufficient.

Finally, many classical theists affirm COMPATIBILISTIC FREEDOM for humans in that you are free so long as you act on your desires, but your desires are determined. In this conception of freedom God can perfectly guarantee that humans do exactly what God desires in each and every situation.

### Open Theism

Open theism is a view of God that defines the divine attributes in ways significantly different from CLASSICAL THEISM. According to open theism, in the act of creating, God freely opened up to a wide array of future possibilities based on how the free creatures God made would react to the divine love. The motivation for this view arises out of the notion that the triune God created humans with the ability to experience divine love and to love in return. The members of the Trinity have always shared a dynamic love and desire to share that love with creatures. Open theists believe that God experiences rich reciprocal relations with creatures. Numerous consequences follow from this conception.

It is thought that a God who experiences our love, or lack of it, in dynamic relationships cannot be TIMELESS or completely unchangeable. Hence, God is EVERLASTING in that God experiences duration in ongoing relationships with creatures. God is not TIMELESS, for there is a reciprocal give-and-take between God and creatures in history. Also, though open theists believe that God is PERFECT, IMMUTABLE, and OMNISCIENT, they do not define these in the same way as classical theists do. God is perfect in that the divine character (love, wisdom, and holiness) is complete and incapable of improvement. But unlike classical theists, open theists believe that God has the POTENTIAL for change in some respects. For instance, God perfectly relates to creatures in ongoing dynamic interaction. For God to fail to change in relation to us as the relationship changes would be less than perfect. Thus, though the divine nature is IMMUTABLE, God can change in thoughts, will, and emotions. Unlike us, God cannot be forced to react or suffer. God can, however, voluntarily choose to enter into such relationships and be PASSIBLE. Consequently, God can be influenced and affected by what we do as well as by our prayers.

Along with ARMINIANS, open theists believe that God has given humans LIBERTARIAN FREEDOM and elicits our free cooperation with God's plans. This means that humans can accept or reject God's initiatives. God takes the risk that God's desires may be thwarted in some cases—we may not do what God desires. Hence, evil is allowed but not desired by God, and ELECTION to salvation is dependent upon human response to divine grace. This does not undermine God's self-sufficiency, since God has chosen to be dependent upon humans for some things. Though God's existence is independent of creation, God's decisions and actions do not have to be unaffected by creatures. It cannot be said that everything that happens is intended by God, for God has chosen to exercise GENERAL PROVIDENCE rather than METICULOUS PROVIDENCE. God has chosen not to tightly control everything that happens and so, at times, God's will for us may be thwarted. Sometimes God alone decides what shall be, but most often, with regard to human action, God initiates and solicits our cooperation.

The future is not a blueprint but a journey whose course is set by both God and humans as we travel together in history. Consequently, for both God and creatures, the future is partly open rather than completely settled or definite. On this point open theism departs significantly from traditional ARMINIANISM and its belief in SIMPLE FOREKNOWLEDGE. According to simple foreknowledge, God previsions all future contingent events and so knows what definitely will happen, not merely what might happen. Open theists believe that God is open to the future, a view sometimes called PRESENTISM. In the open-future view, divine OMNISCIENCE means that God knows infallibly all the past and present and those aspects of the future that are determined to occur (such as those that God has unilaterally ordained to come to pass). This means that God knows future human free choices as possibilities rather than as certainties. God knows the range of possible choices available to us and the likelihood of each possible choice. God knows, for instance, that at a future time Susan will face three options and God knows which option she is likely to choose. God does not, however, know with absolute certainty (as actual) which option she will choose until she selects it. This means that the future is partly open or indefinite and partly closed or definite and God knows the future as it really is, as both definite and indefinite. Though open theists affirm that God is OMNISCIENT (i.e., knows all that can be known) and has complete FOREKNOWLEDGE of all fixed truths, they disagree with classical theists concerning what is knowable (future human free choices) and whether the future is totally definite, containing no possibilities or alternatives. Clearly, this is the most controversial aspect of the openness model.

In addition to having different understandings of PERFECTION, IMMUTABILITY, and OMNISCIENCE from classical theists, open theists reject the doctrines of divine SIMPLICITY, IMPASSIBILITY, and PURE ACTUALITY.

# Notes

ANF — Ante-Nicene Fathers
$NPNF^1$ — Nicene and Post-Nicene Fathers, first series
$NPNF^2$ — Nicene and Post-Nicene Fathers, second series

### Letter 2  Chris: My Pilgrimage

15 **What is perhaps**  Stanley Grenz, *Renewing the Center: Evangelical Theology in a Post-Theological Era* (Grand Rapids: Baker, 2000), 162.

16 **the intruding of rationalistic**  J. I. Packer, *Evangelism and the Sovereignty of God* (Downers Grove, Ill.: InterVarsity, 1961), 16.

16 **God's incomparable way**  Thomas Oden, *The Living God* (Systematic Theology 1; San Francisco: Harper & Row, 1987), 69.

### Letter 4  Chris: Abraham and the Sacrifice of Isaac

21 **God genuinely does not know**  Walter Brueggemann, *Genesis* (Atlanta: John Knox, 1982), 187.

22 **The answer is to be found**  John Sanders, *The God Who Risks: A Theology of Providence* (Downers Grove, Ill.: InterVarsity, 1998), 52–53.

22 **three fundamental problems**  Bruce Ware, *God's Lesser Glory: The Diminished God of Open Theism* (Wheaton, Ill.: Crossway, 2000), 68–73.

22 **present knowledge of Abraham's**  Ware, *God's Lesser Glory*, 67.

23 **What open theists claim**  Ware, *God's Lesser Glory*, 73.

24 **thrown out against us**  Origen, *Genesis Homily* 8; quotation from Origen, *Homilies on Genesis and Exodus* (trans. Ronald E. Heine; Fathers of the Church 71; Washington, D.C.: Catholic University of America Press, 1982), 143.

24 **when the true Isaac**  Caesarius of Arles, *Sermon 84: On Abraham and His Son Isaac*; quotation from Caesarius of Arles, *Sermons*, vol. 2 (trans. Mary M. Mueller; Fathers of the Church 47; Washington, D.C.: Catholic University of America Press, 1964), 17.

### Letter 6 Chris: Judas's Betrayal and Peter's Denial

28 **your interpretation of the Judas narrative** Sanders, *God Who Risks*, 98–99.

29 **secular Greek sources** Henry George Liddell and Robert Scott, *A Greek-English Lexicon*, revised by Henry Stuart Jones (9th ed. with supplement; Oxford: Clarendon, 1968), 1308.

### Letter 7 John: Judas's Betrayal and Peter's Denial

30 **Methodist proponent of openness** Lorenzo McCabe, *Divine Nescience of Future Contingencies a Necessity* (New York: Phillips & Hunt, 1862); idem, *The Foreknowledge of God* (Cincinnati: Cranston & Stowe, 1887).

### Letter 8 Chris: Implications of Open Theism

32 **thread dangling from a sweater** Cf. Nicholas Wolterstorff, "Does God Suffer?" *Modern Reformation* 8.5 (Sept. 1999): 47.

### Letter 10 Chris: Openness and the Problem of Good and Evil

38 **perfect knowledge of what** David Hunt, "The Simple-Foreknowledge View," in *Divine Foreknowledge: Four Views* (ed. James K. Beilby and Paul R. Eddy; Downers Grove, Ill.: InterVarsity, 2001), 53.

### Letter 12 Chris: Antinomies and Logic

43 **a colleague of mine** Material for this chapter was supplied by Phil Cary via private e-mail correspondence.

45 **the use of antinomy** William Lane Craig, "The Middle-Knowledge View," in *Divine Foreknowledge: Four Views* (ed. James K. Beilby and Paul R. Eddy; Downers Grove, Ill.: InterVarsity, 2001), 119–43.

### Letter 13 John: Antinomies and Logic

47 **Though I discussed** Sanders, *God Who Risks*, 34–37.

47 **criticizes his fellow Calvinist** Paul Helm, *The Providence of God* (Downers Grove, Ill.: InterVarsity, 1994), 61–66.

48 **God determines everything** Packer, *Evangelism and the Sovereignty of God*.

### Letter 14 Chris: Logic and Metaphor

51 **the words are Wilson's** Douglas Wilson, "Metaphor in Exile," in *Bound Only Once: The Failure of Open Theism* (ed. Douglas Wilson; Moscow, Idaho: Canon, 2001), 31–51.

51 **many people will be shocked** Sanders, *God Who Risks*, 11.

52 **metaphors have the peculiar** Sanders, *God Who Risks*, 15.

52 **if a concept is contradictory** Sanders, *God Who Risks*, 17.

52 **we are concerned** David Kelley, *The Art of Reasoning* (2d ed.; New York: Norton, 1994), 72; quoted in Wilson, "Metaphor in Exile," 35.

53 **Metaphor calls up many** Wilson, "Metaphor in Exile," 36.

53 **to escape the rules** Sanders, *God Who Risks*, 36–37.

53 **The limits of my language** Wittgenstein quotation from Wilson, "Metaphor in Exile," 41.

53 **It is only if** Ayer quotation from Wilson, "Metaphor in Exile," 41.

53 **the use of metaphors** Sanders, *God Who Risks*, 38.
54 **If God decides** Sanders, *God Who Risks*, 38.

## Letter 15 John: Metaphor and Interpretation

57 **Among these is the work** George Lakoff and Mark Johnson, *Metaphors We Live By* (Chicago: University of Chicago Press, 1980).
57 **The metaphorical and anthropomorphic** Sanders, *God Who Risks*, 15.
58 **hard literal core** Sanders, *God Who Risks*, 25.

## Letter 16 Chris: Impassibility, Immutability, and the Incarnation

61 **impassibility is the most dubious** Clark Pinnock, Richard Rice, John Sanders, William Hasker, and David Basinger, *The Openness of God* (Downers Grove, Ill.: InterVarsity, 1994), 118.
62 **The mystery of Christ** Cyril quotation from Christopher A. Hall, *Learning Theology with the Church Fathers* (Downers Grove, Ill.: InterVarsity, 2002), 82.

## Letter 17 John: Impassibility, Immutability, and the Incarnation

65 **Wayne Grudem, for instance** Wayne Grudem, *Systematic Theology* (Grand Rapids: Zondervan, 1994), 165–66.
65 **the traditional doctrine of impassibility** Millard Erickson, *God the Father Almighty: A Contemporary Exploration of the Divine Attributes* (Grand Rapids: Baker, 1998), 155.
65 **But God is not a stone** For references and further discussion, see Sanders, *God Who Risks*, 142–47; and idem, "Historical Considerations," in Sanders, *The Openness of God* (Downers Grove, Ill.: InterVarsity, 1994), 72–76.
65 **God cannot be forced** See Sanders, *Openness of God*, 76.
68 **So the God who becomes** William Placher, *Jesus the Savior: The Meaning of Jesus Christ for Christian Faith* (Louisville: Westminster John Knox, 2001), 37.

## Letter 18 Chris: Impassibility and Prayer

71 **What do such texts** Sanders, *God Who Risks*, 69.
72 **comes from Paul Helm** Paul Helm, "Divine Timeless Eternity," in *God and Time: Four Views* (ed. Gregory E. Ganssle; Downers Grove, Ill.: InterVarsity, 2001), 80–84. Quotations from this article appear throughout this letter.

## Letter 19 John: Impassibility and Prayer

79 **real change** Helm, "Divine Timeless Eternity," 82.
79 **should appear to act** Helm, "Divine Timeless Eternity," 82.

## Letter 20 Chris: Impassibility and Ontology

82 **Clark understands the Greek** Clark Pinnock, *Most Moved Mover: A Theology of God's Openness* (Didsbury Lectures 2000; Carlisle, Cumbria: Paternoster/Grand Rapids: Baker, 2001), 7.
82 **openness model will help** Pinnock, *Most Moved Mover*, 9.
83 **must be criticized** Pinnock, *Most Moved Mover*, 8.

83 **borrowed from Weinandy's** The Weinandy quotations throughout the rest of this letter are from Thomas G. Weinandy, "Does God Suffer?" *First Things* 117 (Nov. 2001): 35–41.

## Letter 21 John: Thomism

87 **Aristotle's interest lies** See Sanders, *Openness of God*, 65–66.

91 ***To be God*** Robert Jenson, *The Triune Identity: God according to the Gospel* (Philadelphia: Fortress, 1982), 85.

## Letter 22 Chris: The Revelation of God in Jesus

96 **Now he does not want** Luther quotation from Thomas Oden, *The Word of Life* (Systematic Theology 2; San Francisco: Harper & Row, 1989), 184.

96 **honest money changer** Athanasius's illustration is found in Oden, *Word of Life*, 178.

96 **expressions used about His** Athanasius quotation from Oden, *Word of Life*, 178.

96 **The honest money changer** Oden, *Word of Life*, 178.

96 **As for the words** Cyril of Alexandria quotation from Oden, *Word of Life*, 178.

97 **teaching about the supreme nature** John IV quotation from Oden, *Word of Life*, 179.

97 **model of *perichoresis*** Quotation about *perichoresis* from Oden, *Word of Life*, 182.

97 **examples do not have** John of Damascus quotation from Oden, *Word of Life*, 183.

97 **If I believe** Luther quotation from Oden, *Word of Life*, 184.

98 **It was in one nature** John of Damascus quotation from Oden, *Word of Life*, 185.

98 **Wherefore, the Lord of Glory** John of Damascus quotation from Oden, *Word of Life*, 185.

98 **He hungered** Gregory of Nazianzus quotation from Oden, *Word of Life*, 185.

99 **As what is fitting** Leo quotation from Oden, *Word of Life*, 341.

99 **What is God in Christ** Novatian quotation from Oden, *Word of Life*, 340.

99 **died according to the assumption** Ambrose quotation from Oden, *Word of Life*, 340.

99 **He it was who suffered** Athanasius quotation from Oden, *Word of Life*, 340.

99 **Christ, while being two natures** John of Damascus quotation from Oden, *Word of Life*, 340.

100 **For God in his own nature** Luther quotation from Oden, *Word of Life*, 341.

## Letter 23 John: How Do We Know What God Is Like?

104 **a book on divine impassibility** See Sanders, *Openness of God*, 76.

104 **a treatise on God's anger** See Sanders, *Openness of God*, 76.

## Letter 24 Chris: The Church Fathers on Impassibility

107 **cold, as it were** Harold O. J. Brown quotation from Christopher A. Hall, *Reading Scripture with the Church Fathers* (Downers Grove, Ill.: InterVarsity, 1998), 178.

108 **It is the *church*** Robert Jenson quotation from Hall, *Reading Scripture with the Church Fathers*, 194.

109 **For he does not** Chrysostom quotation from Hall, *Learning Theology with the Church Fathers*, 184.

109 **the forces and passions** Prestige quotation from Hall, *Learning Theology with the Church Fathers*, 184.

110 **has as its chief characteristics** Roberta Bondi, *To Love as God Loves: Conversations with the Early Church* (Philadelphia: Fortress, 1987), 58.

110 **passions blind us** Bondi, *To Love as God Loves*, 65.

110 **For if the wrath of God** Chrysostom, *An Exhortation to Theodore after His Fall* 1.4; quotation from NPNF[1] 9.93.

111 **The prophet says this** Chrysostom, *On the Providence of God* 6.3; quotation from Christopher Alan Hall, *John Chrysostom's "On Providence": A Translation and Theological Interpretation* (Ann Arbor, Mich.: UMI, 1991).

111 **I have given these examples** Chrysostom, *On the Providence of God* 6.8.

111 **Do you see how** Chrysostom, *On the Providence of God* 6.5–6.

113 **There is an issue** Pinnock, *Most Moved Mover*, 33.

113 **Human beings are said** Pinnock, *Most Moved Mover*, 33–34.

113 **God loves to draw near** Pinnock, *Most Moved Mover*, 34.

113 **It is possible that God** Pinnock, *Most Moved Mover*, 34.

114 **The only persons we encounter** Pinnock, *Most Moved Mover*, 34.

114 **As human subjectivity** Pinnock, *Most Moved Mover*, 35.

## Letter 25  John: The Western Fathers and Impassibility

119 **But our God is not a stone** Justin Martyr, *First Apology* 28.

119 **Why do contemporary evangelical theologians** See, for instance, Ronald Nash, *The Concept of God* (Grand Rapids: Zondervan, 1983), 105, 114.

119 **this is the most questionable aspect** H. P. Owen, *Concepts of Deity* (New York: Herder & Herder, 1971), 150.

119 ***The doctrine that God*** Gordon Lewis, "Impassibility of God," in *Evangelical Dictionary of Theology* (ed. Walter Elwell; Grand Rapids: Baker, 1984), 553.

120 **But how art thou compassionate** Anselm, *Proslogium* 8.

120 **Why did the ancients** Nicholas Wolterstorff, "Suffering Love," in *Philosophy and the Christian Faith* (ed. Thomas Morris; Notre Dame: University of Notre Dame Press, 1988), 209–20.

121 **Once you pull on the thread** Wolterstorff, "Does God Suffer?" 47.

## Letter 26  John: Scripture on Immutability and Foreknowledge

125 **Scripture does not contradict itself** Helm, *Providence of God*, 51–52.

126 **theological reductionism** Helm, *Providence of God*, 52.

127 **God is not a frozen automaton** Walter Kaiser, "Our Incomparably Great God," *Contact* 32 (2002): 13.

128 **They claim that we** Greg Boyd, *God of the Possible: A Biblical Introduction to the Open View of God* (Grand Rapids: Baker, 2000), 13–15, discusses this.

## Letter 27  Chris: Omniscience and Foreknowledge

132 **based on his exhaustive knowledge** Sanders, *God Who Risks*, 131.

132 **the possibility that God** Sanders, *God Who Risks*, 132.

132 **Omniscience may be defined** Sanders, *God Who Risks*, 194.

133 **nonconsensual control** Sanders, *God Who Risks*, 240.

134 **God's incomparable way of knowing** Oden, *Living God*, 69.

134 **For God knows all things** Clement of Alexandria, *Stromata* 6.17; quotation from ANF 2.517.

134 **And foreseeing the particular** Clement of Alexandria, *Stromata* 6.17; quotation from ANF 2.517.

134 **For in one glance** Clement of Alexandria, *Stromata* 6.17; quotation from ANF 2.517.

134 **many things in life** Clement of Alexandria, *Stromata* 6.17; quotation from ANF 2.517.

134 **Let human voices** Augustine, *On the Psalms* 147.9; quotation from NPNF[1] 8.667.

134 **the infinite consciousness of God** Oden, *Living God*, 70.

135 **knew all things before** John of Damascus, *Exposition of the Orthodox Faith* 2.10; quotation from NPNF[2] 9.28.

135 **appeal to the judgment** Hilary, *On the Trinity* 9.59; quotation from NPNF[2] 9.175.

135 **Jesus Christ knows** Hilary, *On the Trinity* 9.59; quotation from NPNF[2] 9.176.

135 **Jesus knew from the beginning** Hilary, *On the Trinity* 9.59; quotation from NPNF[2] 9.176. The rest of the Hilary quotations in this paragraph are from the same work.

## Letter 29 Chris: Further Thoughts on Some Divine Attributes

146 **I shall feel rather nervous** C. S. Lewis, *The Lion, the Witch and the Wardrobe* (New York: Macmillan, 1950), chap. 8.

146 **any petition is a kind** C. S. Lewis, *Letters to Malcolm: Chiefly on Prayer* (New York: Harcourt Brace Jovanovich, 1963), 20. All of the Lewis quotations throughout the rest of this letter can be found on pages 20–22 of this same work.

## Letter 30 John: Classical Theism

149 **I cite some studies** Sanders, *God Who Risks*, 312 n. 120.

150 **Louis Berkhof rails** Louis Berkhof, *Systematic Theology* (3d ed.; Grand Rapids: Eerdmans, 1946), 118–25.

150 **classical, creedal Reformed theology** James Daane, "Can a Man Bless God?" in *God and the Good* (ed. Clifton Orlebeke and Lewis Smedes; Grand Rapids: Eerdmans, 1975), 166.

150 **If ever there was a miserable anthropomorphism** Karl Barth, *Church Dogmatics* (trans. and ed. Geoffrey W. Bromiley and Thomas F. Torrance; Edinburgh: Clark, 1961), 3/4.108–9.

151 **good chapter on prayer** Dallas Willard, *The Divine Conspiracy: Rediscovering Our Hidden Life in God* (San Francisco: Harper San Francisco, 1998), 253.

## Letter 31 John: Biblical Texts Supporting Open Theism

156 **intercessory prayer has no effect** Jonathan Edwards, "The Most High a Prayer-Hearing God," in *The Works of Jonathan Edwards* (2 vols.; Edinburgh: Banner of Truth, 1974), 2:115–16 (emphasis mine).

## Letter 32 Chris: Biblical Texts Supporting Open Theism

161 **God declares** Sanders, *God Who Risks*, 130.

161 **Sometimes God simply discloses** Sanders, *God Who Risks*, 130–31.

161 **God, a personal agent** Sanders, *God Who Risks*, 209.

161 **does not want to dance** Sanders, *God Who Risks*, 210–11.

162 **Though God's knowledge is** Sanders, *God Who Risks*, 198.

163 **notion that God could be dismayed** Sanders, *God Who Risks*, 133.

164 **it is clear that Judas** Sanders, *God Who Risks*, 99.

164 **to determine the will of God** Sanders, *God Who Risks*, 100.

164 **incarnation was planned** Sanders, *God Who Risks*, 100.

164 **Jesus is in the canoe** Sanders, *God Who Risks*, 100–101.

164 **notion that the cross was not planned** Sanders, *God Who Risks*, 101.

164 **Perhaps God knew** Sanders, *God Who Risks*, 102.

165 **present life is a wrestling school** Chrysostom, *On the Providence of God* 21.1.

165 **Through divine providence God** Chrysostom, *On the Providence of God* 21.3.

165 **For as a gold refiner** Chrysostom, *On the Paralytic Let Down through the Roof* 1; quotation from NPNF[1] 9.212.

165 **until it is destroyed** Chrysostom, *On the Paralytic Let Down through the Roof* 2; quotation from NPNF[1] 9.212.

## Letter 33 John: Openness and Tradition

168 **That would imply** I've explained this in depth in my *God Who Risks*, 200–206.

169 **shake off the static ideology** James Oliver Buswell Jr., *A Systematic Theology of the Christian Religion* (Grand Rapids: Zondervan, 1962), 1.56.

169 **human beings can make a difference** Nash, *Concept of God*, 105, 114.

169 **Ware revises the traditional doctrine** Ware, *God's Lesser Glory*, 164.

169 **Grudem criticizes the Westminster Confession** Grudem, *Systematic Theology*, 165–66.

170 **the traditional doctrine of impassibility** Millard Erickson, *God the Father Almighty: A Contemporary Exploration of the Divine Attributes* (Grand Rapids: Baker, 1998), 155.

172 **I too was raised** Willard, *Divine Conspiracy*, 244–45.

173 **the Creeds are often wrong** David Wells, "Reflections about Catholic Renewal in Evangelicalism," in *The Orthodox Evangelicals: Who They Are and What They Are Saying* (ed. Robert Webber and Donald Bloesch; Nashville: Thomas Nelson, 1978), 214.

174 **Church as the pillar of truth** John Eck, *Enchiridion of Commonplaces: Against Luther and Other Enemies of the Church*, Ford Lewis Battles trans., (Grand Rapids: Baker, 1979), 10.

174 **It is hard to believe** Gerald Bray, *The Personal God: Is the Classical Understanding of God Tenable?* (Carlisle, U.K.: Paternoster, 1998), 4.

## Letter 34 Chris: Tradition and Theology

176 **the history of the interpretation** Stanley Grenz and John Franke, "Theological Heritage as Hermeneutical Trajectory: Toward a Nonfoundationalist Understanding of the Role of Tradition in Theology," in *Ancient and Postmodern Christianity: Paleo-Orthodoxy in the Twenty-first Century: Essays in Honor of Thomas C. Oden* (ed. Kenneth Tanner and Christopher A. Hall; Downers Grove, Ill.: InterVarsity, 2002), 228.

176 **More specifically** Grenz and Franke, "Theological Heritage as Hermeneutical Trajectory," 228.

177 **the acceptance and handing** D. H. Williams quotation from Grenz and Franke, "Theological Heritage as Hermeneutical Trajectory," 228.

177 **the narrative of God's redemptive activity** Grenz and Franke, "Theological Heritage as Hermeneutical Trajectory," 229.

177 **hermeneutical context for theology** Grenz and Franke, "Theological Heritage as Hermeneutical Trajectory," 230, 233.

177 **with a record** Grenz and Franke, "Theological Heritage as Hermeneutical Trajectory," 232.

177 **The Christian community** Grenz and Franke, "Theological Heritage as Hermeneutical Trajectory," 232.

178 **declared what he was** Tertullian quotation from Hall, *Learning Theology with the Church Fathers*, 28–29.

178 **chose twelve leading** Tertullian quotation from Hall, *Learning Theology with the Church Fathers*, 28–29.

179 **it originates neither from** Tertullian quotation from Hall, *Learning Theology with the Church Fathers*, 29.

179 **knowledge of the truth** Irenaeus quotation from Hall, *Learning Theology with the Church Fathers*, 29.

179 **heresy is often marked** Athanasius quotation from Hall, *Learning Theology with the Church Fathers*, 30.

180 **evangelicals are inclined** Richard John Neuhaus, "While We're At It," *First Things* 123 (May 2002): 77.

180 **The great difficulty here** Thomas Howard, "Recognizing the Church: A Personal Pilgrimage and the Discovery of Five Marks of the Church," in *Ancient and Postmodern Christianity: Paleo-Orthodoxy in the Twenty-first Century: Essays in Honor of Thomas C. Oden* (ed. Kenneth Tanner and Christopher A. Hall; Downers Grove, Ill.: InterVarsity, 2002), 133.

180 **When a crucial issue** Howard, "Recognizing the Church," 133–34.

181 **the faithful in those early centuries** Howard, "Recognizing the Church," 134.

181 **threefold understanding of authority** Clark Pinnock, *Tracking the Maze: Finding Our Way through Modern Theology from an Evangelical Perspective* (San Francisco: Harper & Row, 1990), 35–43.

184 **Loss of authority** David Lyle Jeffrey, "Houses of the Interpreter: Spiritual Exegesis and the Retrieval of Authority," *Books and Culture* 8 (May/June 2002): 30.

## Letter 36 John: Dialogical Virtues

191 **Our hearts are in danger** Thomas Schreiner and Bruce Ware (eds.), *Still Sovereign: Contemporary Perspectives on Election, Foreknowledge, and Grace* (abridged ed.; Grand Rapids: Baker, 2000), 16.

191 **a Calvinist can state the open view** Terrance Tiessen, *Providence and Prayer: How Does God Work in the World?* (Downers Grove, Ill.: InterVarsity, 2000), chaps. 4–5.

191 **A very helpful study** Jay Wood, *Epistemology: Becoming Intellectually Virtuous* (Downers Grove, Ill.: InterVarsity, 1998).

192 **Thou must not take cheap shots** Quoted by John Wilson, "Thou Shalt Not Take Cheap Shots," *Books and Culture* 5.5 (Sept.–Oct. 1999): 3.

192 **Calvinists and Arminians** Ware, "Effectual Calling and Grace," in *Still Sovereign*, 204.

193 **call on evangelical theologians** Mark Noll, *The Scandal of the Evangelical Mind* (Grand Rapids: Eerdmans, 1994); Alister McGrath, *Evangelicalism and the Future of Christianity* (Downers Grove, Ill.: InterVarsity, 1995).

## Chris and John: Postscript

198 **that this discussion continue** See "Do Good Fences Make Good Baptists?" *Christianity Today* 44 (Aug. 7, 2000): 36.

200 **title of a new book** Norman Geisler and Wayne House, *The Battle for God* (Grand Rapids: Kregel, 2001).

# Glossary

**Ambrose (339–397)**  Bishop of Milan frequently described as one of the seven great doctors or teachers of the church. A significant source for early Christian views on the Trinity, incarnation, and sacraments of the church.

**anthropomorphism**  Applying a human characteristic to God (e.g., the arm of the Lord or God changed God's mind).

**antinomy**  Affirming that two different truths that appear contradictory are, nonetheless, both true. For example, METICULOUS PROVIDENCE and LIBERTARIAN FREEDOM.

**Arianism**  Teaching related to the Alexandrian presbyter Arius. Arius appears to have taught that while the Son was the highest, most exalted creation of God, the Son was still a creature. To use a phrase frequently attributed to Arius, "There was a time when he [the Son] was not."

**Arminianism**  School of theology based on the teaching of James Arminius. Against strong CALVINISM, it affirms that God's ELECTION to salvation is based upon God's FOREKNOWLEDGE of who will freely believe. Hence, at least some of God's decisions are dependent upon human choices. See also SYNERGISM and GENERAL PROVIDENCE.

**Athanasius (300–373)**  Bishop of Alexandria and ardent opponent of ARIANISM. Under the leadership of Athanasius, the COUNCIL OF NICEA declared the Son to be *homoousios* (of one substance) with the Father.

**Augustine (354–430)**  The greatest theologian among the Western church fathers. Augustine's ideas have deeply influenced the

Western Christian tradition in both its Catholic and Protestant streams. Augustine was deeply rooted in the Platonic tradition, and the question remains whether Augustine's Platonic background too deeply influenced his understanding of God's PROVIDENCE and God's relationship to TIME.

**Basil the Great (330–379)**   One of the three great Cappadocian theologians, along with GREGORY OF NAZIANZUS and Gregory of Nyssa. Basil's work on the Holy Spirit and on the six days of creation (*Hexaemeron*) are to be particularly noted. All Eastern fathers (Basil the Great, Gregory of Nazianzus, JOHN CHRYSOSTOM) advocated what would later be known as LIBERTARIAN FREEDOM.

**Caesarius of Arles (470–542)**   Bishop, monastic leader, and writer.

**Calvinism**   School of theology based on the teaching of John Calvin. Commonly used of those who believe, contrary to ARMINIANISM, that God unconditionally chooses certain persons for salvation. It affirms METICULOUS PROVIDENCE in that none of God's decisions are dependent upon creatures. See also MONERGISM and UNCONDITIONED.

**classical theism**   See Appendix.

**Clement of Alexandria (150–215)**   Alexandrian Christian leader particularly known for his *Paidagogos* (Instructor) and *Stromateis* (Miscellanies).

***communicatio idiomatum***   Latin for "communication" or "sharing" of attributes. That is, whatever we say about Christ's human nature or divine nature is to be attributed to the person of the Son. It is in the hypostasis of the Son that the union with human nature takes place. Hence, we can speak of the Son suffering in the human nature that the Son has assumed and redeemed.

**compatibilism**   Also known as soft-determinism. Belief that human freedom and divine determination of all things are compatible. Human decisions are considered to be free if they are chosen without any external force or coercion. The person is free if she does what she desired to do; and since God determines the human desires, divine determinism and human freedom are compatible.

**Council of Chalcedon (451)**   The fourth ecumenical council after NICEA (325), Constantinople (381), and Ephesus (431) at which the relationship between Christ's human and divine natures was debated. The council ended by presenting the theological model of Christ as one person with two natures, divine and human.

**Council of Nicea (325)** The first great ecumenical council at which the Son was declared to be *homoousios* (of one substance) with the Father.

**Cyril of Alexandria (375–444)** Bishop of Alexandria and one of the key theologians involved in the formulation of christological doctrine in the late fourth and early fifth centuries. Particularly known for his extended debate with Nestorius over the expression *theotokos* (Mary as the "God-bearer" or "Mother of God").

*dignum Deo* Latin for what is "dignified" to ascribe to "God." It is not fitting to ascribe human limitations to God.

**divine perfection** See PERFECTION, DIVINE.

**docetic** A heresy that denies that Christ was fully human. It emphasizes the divinity over the creaturely nature of Christ.

*economia* See OIKONOMIA.

**election** God's choosing or predestining people for salvation. The dispute between ARMINIANISM and CALVINISM is whether God's election is dependent upon human choices (MONERGISM and SYNERGISM). Another issue is whether God's election is of individuals or is "corporate" (Israel and the church).

**Enlightenment** Period during the seventeenth and eighteenth centuries among Western intellectuals. Generally, they believed truth should be settled on the basis of human reason rather than by appeals to authorities such as the Bible or the church.

**everlasting** The view that God exists forever through time rather than in a TIMELESS state. God experiences succession or duration and works with us through time.

**exegesis** Deriving meaning out of a text or understanding what the author meant.

**foreknowledge** The belief, generally understood, that God knows everything that shall occur, including everything that humans will do in the future. The debate in this book is whether divine foreknowledge is exhaustively definite (i.e., settled) or whether some of God's foreknowledge is definite while some of it includes what may possibly happen (i.e., maybes). Both views agree that God knows all that can be known about the future. The dispute is over what can be known. See also SIMPLE FOREKNOWLEDGE.

**foundationalism** A theory of knowledge that demands an absolutely certain starting point or foundation on which to build knowledge. If the foundation is questionable, then all the rest of our knowledge is questionable as well.

**freewill theism**   An interpretive tradition that affirms LIBERTARIAN FREEDOM, such as ARMINIANISM and OPEN THEISM.

**general providence**   View that God established the overarching rules by which creation would operate and allows them a good deal of autonomy. God does not meticulously control every detail of our lives, so God takes risks that we might not do what God desires.

**Gregory of Nazianzus (329–390)**   Also known as Gregory the Theologian. One of the three great Cappadocian theologians, along with BASIL THE GREAT and Gregory of Nyssa. Particularly known for his five theological orations, in which Gregory responds in detail to ARIAN christological positions.

**Gregory Thaumaturgus (210–270)**   Bishop of Neocaesarea. Perhaps best known for his eulogy for ORIGEN, the great Alexandrian exegete.

**Hellenistic**   Of or relating to the ancient Greek culture and language.

**hermeneutics**   The study of how texts should be interpreted.

**Hilary of Poitiers (315–367)**   Bishop chiefly known for his great work *On the Trinity*.

**immutability**   The inability to change or develop. When applied to God, theologians disagree whether God is unchangeable in all respects (CLASSICAL THEISM) or whether, though God's character is unchanging, God can change in emotions, thoughts, and will (OPEN THEISM).

**impassibility**   The notion that God is unaffected by what happens in creation. God does not experience sorrow, suffering, or other changing emotional states, for the blessedness of God's life is wholly independent of creatures. Moreover, our prayers never influence God. See also PASSIBLE.

**impetratory**   Receiving something because one asked for it.

**indeterministic freedom**   See LIBERTARIAN FREEDOM.

***in se***   Latin for "in itself." For instance, what God is like apart from any relation to God's creatures?

**Irenaeus (115–202)**   Bishop of Lyons and lifelong opponent of gnosticism. Best known for his work *Against Heresies*.

**John Chrysostom (347–407)**   Bishop of Constantinople from 398. Two of Chrysostom's works are particularly relevant to the current debate over the nature of divine PROVIDENCE: *On the Incomprehensibility of God* and *On the Providence of God*.

**John of Damascus (died 749)**   Eastern monk and theologian. John's best known work, *Fount of Knowledge*, contains his well-known *An Exact Exposition of the Orthodox Faith*.

**Justin Martyr (died ca. 165)** Early Christian apologist and martyr.

**Lactantius (250–325)** Latin Christian apologist.

**Leo (400–461)** Bishop of Rome from 440 to 461. Also known as Leo the Great. A particularly influential figure in the formulation of christological doctrine. Insisted, against Eutyches, that Christ had two natures, one divine and one human.

**libertarian freedom** Also called indeterministic freedom since it is not compatible with the idea that God determines all things. Humans are free if they have the ability to do otherwise than they did in a particular situation despite the influences of upbringing and culture. Contrary to COMPATIBILISTIC FREEDOM, humans are not free if they simply do what they desire in a specific situation. Rather, they must have been able to desire something else.

**metaphysics** The study of reality. It addresses issues such as freedom and determinism, space and time, and what is necessary.

**meticulous providence** Also called specific sovereignty. The view that God tightly controls everything that happens such that nothing happens except what God specifically intends to happen. Contrary to GENERAL PROVIDENCE, God takes no risks because humans do precisely what God wants them to do in every situation.

**middle knowledge** Also known as Molinism, after the sixteenth-century Jesuit who developed this view. God not only knows what will actually occur in the future, God knows what humans would do under any hypothetical situation. For instance, God knows exactly what you would be like and all the decisions you would make if, say, you had been raised in a different culture.

**Molinism** See MIDDLE KNOWLEDGE.

**monergism** Greek for "one worker." The belief that salvation is exclusively the work of God without the human will adding anything. See SYNERGISM.

**Novatian (mid-third century)** Latin presbyter best known for his work *On the Trinity*.

*oikonomia* Greek for "economy." God's relationship to all created reality and particularly God's redemptive act in the sending of the Son to redeem humanity.

**omniscience** Literally, "all-knowing," indicating that God knows everything that is knowable or all truths. The dispute is over what is knowable. Does God know all things as definite certainties (CLASSICAL THEISM) or does God know some things as definite and some things as indefinite possibilities (OPEN THEISM)? See also FOREKNOWLEDGE.

**ontological difference**   The idea that God, as creator, is significantly different from creatures. The issue is exactly how different God is from humans, given that we are created in the image of God.

**open future**   See PRESENTISM.

**open theism**   See Appendix.

**Origen (181–251)**   The most prolific and perhaps most controversial early Christian exegete. Best known for his advocacy of allegory as a legitimate interpretive tool.

**passible**   The ability to be affected by someone else. See also IMPASSIBILITY.

**Pelagianism**   The teaching of a fourth-century monk who supposedly taught that humans could live free from sin without the aid of divine grace and thus merit salvation.

**perfection, divine**   The idea that there can be no possible improvement in the divine nature. CLASSICAL THEISM adds that there cannot be any POTENTIAL for change, for any change in God could only be a change for the worse. OPEN THEISM rejects this addition, holding that God changes perfectly in relating to us.

*perichoresis*   Greek for "mutual indwelling" or interpenetration of the persons of the Trinity. That is, the Son is always in the Father, the Father in the Son, the Son in the Spirit, and so on. One person of the Trinity, as Barth puts it, is always in the other two.

**potentiality**   Used by Aristotle and Thomas Aquinas to refer to the ability to change. For instance, an acorn is potentially a tree or a baseball bat. According to these thinkers, creatures have potentiality but God does not. See also PURE ACTUALITY.

**presentism**   Sometimes applied to the view of OMNISCIENCE held by OPEN THEISM. Perhaps a better term would be "open future." It is the belief that God knows all the past and present and that part of the future that is determined as definite certainties, but God does not know all that creatures with LIBERTARIAN FREEDOM will do in the future as definite. Rather, God knows these actions as possibilities and probabilities. See also FOREKNOWLEDGE.

**process theology**   A twentieth-century school of thought that holds that God and the universe are coeternal and necessarily dependent upon one another. God cannot exist without a world. Process theology denies omnipotence, creation out of nothing, God's ability to act unilaterally in creation, and a final consummation of history.

**providence** See GENERAL PROVIDENCE and METICULOUS PROVIDENCE.

**pure actuality** Used by Aristotle and Aquinas to refer to the inability to change in any respect. A being that is purely actual is one that is completely fulfilled, having no potential for becoming any different than it now is. God has no POTENTIALITY.

**Reformed** A theological tradition deriving from John CALVIN and Ulrich Zwingli emphasizing the glory of God. The Reformed tradition is quite broad and not limited to those who affirm METICULOUS PROVIDENCE. A number of Reformed theologians are, for instance, OPEN THEISTS.

**semi-Pelagian** The attempt to find a middle ground between PELAGIANISM and AUGUSTINE'S MONERGISTIC understanding of salvation. The human will, though weak in sin, can respond to God. Sometimes applied to ARMINIANISM.

**simple foreknowledge** The view that God simply previsions all of human history at once but that this knowledge does not determine what will happen. Rather, God foresees what we will freely do. This is the traditional ARMINIAN view as opposed to CALVINISM, where God knows the future because God determines all the future.

**simplicity** God's essence is an indivisible unity. Though we speak as though God has various characteristics such as omnipotence and IMMUTABILITY, God actually has none of them, for God, unlike us, is not composed of parts.

**Socinianism** Heretical teaching that denied Jesus' divinity and atoning work.

**soft-determinism** See COMPATIBILISM.

**specific sovereignty** See METICULOUS PROVIDENCE.

**synergism** Greek for "working together." The idea that God and the human will cooperate in conversion. The human will can accept or reject divine grace for, contrary to MONERGISM, grace is not irresistible.

**Tertullian (born ca. 160)** Early Christian apologist and controversialist.

*theologia* Greek for "true knowledge of God."

**theophany** A visible or audible appearance of God.

**Thomism** School of thought based on the teaching of Thomas Aquinas. Thomas said God is the first cause, unchangeable in all respects, PURE ACTUALITY, IMPASSIBLE, and TIMELESS.

**timelessness** Used synonymously with eternity, eternalist, and atemporality. Contrary to the view that God is EVERLASTING, timelessness asserts that God does not experience time, succession, or duration. Rather, God exists in an eternal present or now without change or any before and after. All of God's knowledge and decisions are eternal.

**transcendence**   God is "above" and independent of creation. Though God is involved in the creation, God is not a creature.

**unconditioned**   The idea that God is not influenced or affected by creatures. All of God's decisions and actions are based solely on God's will and independent of what we do. See also IMPASSIBILITY and METICULOUS PROVIDENCE.